Penguin Handbook

The Penguin Book of
Home Brewing
and Wine-Making

W. H. T. Tayleur was born in Worcestershire
and educated at Malvern and Oxford. He
learned about brewing by writing the
histories of many of the great pre-war
breweries. In 1963 he and his wife started the
firm of Brew It Yourself Ltd, of which their
younger son is now Managing Director. Ten
years of running an advisory service for home
brewers and wine-makers, as well as teaching
them in adult classes, have at least shown
him what kind of information they need. He
lives in Highgate, London, and the friendly
island of Alderney, and his hobbies are
brewing, wine-making and the restoring of
old clocks and automata.

THE PENGUIN BOOK OF

HOME BREWING AND WINE-MAKING

W. H. T. TAYLEUR

DRAWINGS BY
MICHAEL SPINK

PENGUIN BOOKS

Penguin Books Ltd, Harmondsworth,
Middlesex, England
Penguin Books Inc., 7110 Ambassador Road,
Baltimore, Maryland 21207, U.S.A.
Penguin Books Australia Ltd, Ringwood,
Victoria, Australia

First published 1973

Made and printed in Great Britain by
Hazell Watson & Viney Ltd, Aylesbury, Bucks
Set in Monotype Baskerville

for Margot and William

my wife and son (co-directors of Brew It Yourself Ltd), who did most of my work while this book was being written. My thanks also to William for his expert advice on biochemistry and to Joan for her immaculate typescript.

CONTENTS

Section I: General

Section II: Home Brewing

Section III: Home Wine-making

Section I

GENERAL

1

INTRODUCTION

Nunc est bibendum
(Now let's have a Drink!)
— Horace: *Ode on Cleopatra*

The origins of beer, wine, mead and cider are extremely remote, and it will be seen from the brief histories in their respective sections that in Great Britain at least their production remained exclusively domestic until the coming of ale-houses and imported wines in medieval times and of commercial breweries later on, and that home brewing and wine-making continued to flourish until the industrial revolution, repressive legislation, war shortages and other factors almost put an end to them.

They began to revive in this country in the 1950s and both the freeing of home-brewed beer from taxation and excise control in 1963 and the publicity that this measure received gave a tremendous impetus to the movement. Home brewing and wine-making have now become so popular that from being regarded as eccentric hobbies these pleasant and rewarding crafts have regained their rightful places in our national way of life; simpler and more fun (for men at least) than cooking, but almost equally a part of the ordinary domestic scene.

It has now become so easy to make really good beer or wine at home that anyone who enjoys a drink and has sufficient time, space, skill and kitchen facilities to heat up a can of beans can confidently start right away with one of the many excellent concentrates now on the market. These are preformulated to produce most popular types of wines and beers in batches of 1 gallon (6 bottles) of wine or 2 or 5 gallons (16 or 40 pints) of beer, and require only the most basic and inexpensive equipment. All that is necessary is to open the pack and follow the very simple instructions; additional ingredients are usually only water, sugar and yeast.

The next step is to use extracts or concentrates to produce not merely beer or wine as formulated in the can but drinks designed to please an individual palate. At this stage the home brewer can choose from a wide selection of malt extracts and concentrated brewer's worts designed to make any kind of beer from lager to stout, and there are named hop extracts, hop essence, wheat syrup, caramel and other ingredients with which to experiment. For the wine-maker there are many types of concentrated grape and other juices and scores of different yeast cultures from many of the world's famous vineyards.

At the third and final stage the home brewer parallels all the processes of the professional from the crushing and mashing of the malt onwards, while the home wine-maker uses the juices of fresh, dried or preserved fruit, berries and vegetables and the scent and flavour of flowers, often in conjunction with grape or other concentrates.

An endearing feature of home brewing and wine-making is that the cost, negligible to start with, becomes even less as skill increases and larger batches are made. Remembering the ladies of Mrs Beeton's era who used to recommend the lacing of home-made wine with 'French brandy which can be obtained for the sum of two shillings and eightpence per bottle', one is reluctant to quote comparative costs at any moment of time, but if taxes and prices continue to soar the already dramatic difference between the prices of the homemade and the commercial products is bound to increase. The beer cost ratio is now about 6 to 1 if it is brewed in small quantities from preformulated canned worts and the most expensive additives and methods are used, and better than 8 to 1 if top-grade materials are used but bigger batches are brewed. A gallon of the best home brew containing, say, 6 per cent alcohol by volume costs about the same as a pint of 3 to 3½ per cent beer over the bar at a modest pub. Lager costs no more than other beers to make and much more to buy, so the difference is even greater.

Using ordinary care the home brewer regularly produces better and certainly stronger beer than he can normally buy. Although truly great wines can be made only by professional vignerons from grapes grown on the spot and then only in favoured years, our own can be consistently better than many of the beverage wines drunk in the wine-producing countries or those that they export in bulk. Comparative costs are more difficult to assess than those of beer, but the most expensive wine that can be made at home from grape concentrates will cost about one fifth as much as the cheapest imported plonk, and equally good wine from one's own garden produce costs only the price of the yeast, sugar and any nutrient or other additives; maybe one fifteenth as much as the plonk.

Men are inclined to brew beer and women to make wine, possibly because men are less patient and thirstier than women and beer gives quicker results and more of them. Men, too, are apt to value the comfort of the inner man more highly than the shape of the outer one whereas in women this trend is usually reversed: they are well aware that while beer tends to round out the curves light, dry wine is included in many slimming diets. Most people try their hands at both.

A very pleasant aspect of the craft is its friendliness. Wine and brewing circles are to be found almost everywhere; they are purely social groups whose members live in the same neighbourhood, share the same hobby and meet regularly at each other's homes or a local hall to sample and discuss their latest brews. Clubs are formed by enthusiasts at their places of employment and are usually associated with the social or sports clubs sponsored by most large businesses or other organizations. Both give the beginner a hospitable welcome and the benefit of their members' skill and experience. However good a home-made wine or beer may be it tastes all the better when drunk in knowledgeable and appreciative company, and for the really dedicated there are local, regional and national competitions, exhibitions, festivals and study sessions throughout the year as well as organized tours of the great continental wine-making districts.

It is no exaggeration to say that in these days of high taxation only home brewing and wine-making make it possible for hospitable people of moderate means to keep open house for their friends.

2

LEGALITY

Home wine-making has always been free from taxation or excise control as long as none of the wine was sold, but the Inland Revenue Act of 1880 required the home brewer to pay up to £1 for a licence and to keep a record of all the malt, sugar and cereals used. These records were periodically scrutinized by the excise inspectors, who then levied duty on the amount of beer that they calculated could be produced from the ingredients declared, even though none of it could legally be sold.

This legislation remained in force for eighty-three years, but although at first many thousands of private brewing licences were taken out the number of home brewers steadily declined over the years until by the middle of this century, and after shortages of the necessary ingredients caused by two world wars, hardly any of the few that were left bothered to take out licences. In April 1963 Mr Reginald Maudling, Conservative Chancellor of the Exchequer, sensibly freed home brewing from these controls and put it on the same footing as home wine-making. Today there is no restriction on the strength, nature or quantity of the beer or wine that can be made at home, but it is still illegal to sell either of them. The position is therefore very simple, and while there may well be technical queries still unanswered concerning the legality of exchanges, the offering of samples and exactly who is permitted to drink wine or beer made for someone else's 'own consumption' the honest amateur need not concern himself with them, for they come under the general heading of *de minimis non curat lex*.* As long as we do not abuse the freedom we now enjoy it is devoutly to be hoped that they will remain there.

Any attempt to distil spirits from wine or beer, whether home-brewed or not, is both illegal and dangerous: it involves the risk of severe injury to health or even blindness and of a heavy fine or imprisonment if detected.

* The law does not concern itself with trifles.

3

FERMENTATION

> My Uncle George . . . discovered that
> alcohol was a food well in advance of
> modern medical thought.
> – P. G. Wodehouse: *The Inimitable Jeeves*

Fermentations are of many different kinds, but all involve the decomposition of organic matter by micro-organisms and many evolve quantities of gas with the boiling effect which gives the process its name, derived from the Latin *fervere*, to boil.

Broadly speaking, fermentation is part of a biological cycle whose purpose is to reduce inert organic material to a state in which it can nourish living animals and plants. Alcoholic fermentation takes place when a suitable yeast is introduced to starchy or sugary solutions, such as sweet fruit juices, of an acceptable specific gravity and temperature. The yeast converts the starches or sugars to ethyl alcohol, carbon dioxide and energy in the form of heat, and this process ends only when all the starches or sugars have been converted or when the alcoholic content of the wort or must, as the unfermented beer and wine are respectively called, becomes high enough to kill the yeast or inhibit its working. At this point in the natural cycle air-borne bacteria, moulds and yeasts such as *mycoderma candida* take over the unprotected wort or must and reduce it to water and carbon dioxide. The art of the brewer or wine-maker lies in initiating suitable ferments and in halting them so that their alcoholic contents are preserved. The cycle is then completed by man, who drinks the beer or wine and converts it to water and carbon dioxide.

The yeast converts the starches or sugars to alcohol by producing enzymes. These are organic catalysts, that is to say substances produced by living organisms which cause changes in other substances while remaining unchanged themselves. We produce many of them internally to change our food into forms that we can digest.

In brewing, the wort contains *maltose*, or malt sugar, which is converted to *glucose* by the yeast enzyme *maltase*. Another yeast enzyme, *zymase*, converts the glucose to alcohol and carbon dioxide.

In making wine from fruits yet another yeast enzyme, *invertase*, converts *sucrose*, present in the juice or added as household sugar, into *glucose* and *fructose*, both of which the zymase can turn into alcohol and carbon dioxide as above. In wines made from grain or starchy vegetables and sugar, both processes of conversion take place.

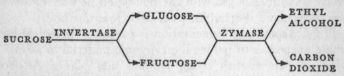

Wine-making fermentation sequence.
The enzyme invertase converts the sugar sucrose to the sugars glucose and fructose, both directly convertible to ethyl alcohol by the enzyme zymase.

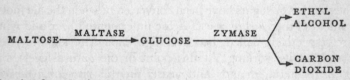

Brewing fermentation sequence.
The enzyme maltase converts the sugar maltose to the sugar glucose, which is directly convertible to ethyl alcohol by the enzyme zymase.

The essentials for making any fermented drink are therefore yeast and a solution of fermentable sugars. The solution must however be of the right specific gravity or strength, be within the range of temperatures at which yeast will work, and be based upon one of an innumerable range of substances embracing all the wholesome and pleasant fruits, besides many flowers, herbs and even vegetables, which will endow the wine with their flavour, colour and scent. Grain is also used in wine-making but more usually in brewing, in the form of malted barley. Whatever the basic ingredient, and whether wine or beer is being made, the process of fermentation is essentially the same.

In the case of the grape no additives are needed, for ripe grapes alone of soft fruits have exactly the right amounts of sugars, acids, vitamins and nutrient salts in their juice, pulp and skins to give the yeast everything it needs for both breeding and fermentation. When using other bases it is necessary to correct their sweetness and acidity and to add nutrient salts and vitamins, processes that modern equipment and ready-formulated additives have rendered extremely simple.

In a natural grape fermentation, when the ripe grapes are picked, trodden or pressed and allowed to ferment without any other additive, the yeast that causes the ferment occurs naturally in the bloom on the grape skin, and it is from this that all wine yeasts have been cultivated. The skins also harbour a great variety of moulds, yeasts of the wrong kind and bacilli, and to make quite sure that these do not get the upper hand the modern vigneron usually introduces a pure culture of the yeast from his own grapes. This allows a colony of the right type of yeast to start up with such vigour that it will inhibit the growth of moulds, wild yeasts or other spoilage organisms. All such sweet juices are ideal breeding grounds for deleterious organisms, but by keeping containers and equipment sterile and by adding substances to the must which kill or inhibit them but which the true wine yeast has been trained over the centuries to tolerate, all risk of infection can be avoided.

Though the grape is the only berry or soft fruit whose juice can be fermented by its own yeast to create a perfect drink, apples and pears also carry their own yeasts, hence the very great antiquity of cider and its variant from pears, perry.

Brewer's wort is another almost perfect host for yeast, but after boiling it is free of live wild yeast cells and cultured beer yeast must be added before it can ferment.

When yeast is introduced to a suitable medium there first occurs what is known as the 'lag phase' of fermentation, lasting hours, days or sometimes even weeks, during which the yeast acclimatizes itself to the wort or must and starts to breed. The second phase is a lively and sometimes violent fermentation, during which the liquid foams and generates heat. This is the breeding phase, during which little alcohol is produced while the small colony of yeast originally introduced builds itself up to the millions of cells per fluid ounce necessary for the production of a satisfactory amount of alcohol. Brewers call this the 'log', or logarithmic phase, during which the number of yeast cells doubles itself every four hours or so.

This phase can take place only in the presence of oxygen and is therefore known as aerobic fermentation. If fruit is being fermented 'on the pulp' – i.e. the juice, pulp and skins – or beer is being brewed, the containers used, though carefully protected from air taint (infection by air-borne spoilage organisms), must contain or give access to sufficient air to provide the necessary oxygen.

When a sufficiently strong colony of yeast has built up it is necessary to exclude the air. In professional wine-making this is effected naturally by the thick mat or cap of skins, stalks and pips that is carried to the top of the must by the gas given off during fermentation, while in brewing the yeast itself usually forms a thick layer over the wort. The amateur transfers his wine from the bin or bucket to fermentation jars and fits them with fermentation locks which allow the gas to escape but let no air in.

This initiates the anaerobic phase during which, having no oxygen available, the yeast is forced to use up the fermentable sugars in the must or wort and convert them into alcohol and carbon dioxide. Previous generations did not have the advantage of the fermentation lock, and while this did not affect their brewing (today only lagers are fermented by amateurs under lock) the fact that the air could not be excluded satisfactorily from their fermenting wines meant that these were not only liable to air taints which produced off-flavours but were also frequently sickly sweet from the failure of the yeast to attenuate (convert into alcohol) all the fermentable sugars present.

This final anaerobic phase can continue quietly for months or can be over in a matter of weeks, according to the type of yeast, the amount of sugar to be attenuated, the temperature and the nutrient salts and vitamins added.

When no more bubbles rise and the hydrometer reads at or near zero, the fermentation has stopped. Beer is racked (siphoned) into bottles or barrels and wine siphoned off any deposit and allowed to clear before it is bottled. The last stage of a wine fermentation is usually the stabilizing of the bulk by the addition of various preparations which inhibit further fermentation and help to preserve the wine in bottle.

In beer and sparkling wines and ciders a secondary fermentation takes place in the bottles, which are specially strong to withstand internal pressure and are fitted with screw tops, crown caps or wired-on corks. This produces both carbon dioxide under pressure and extra yeast, which is usually left in home-brewed beer but has to be carefully removed from champagne and most other sparkling wines. Commercial bottled beers and sparkling ciders are now usually chilled and force-filtered to kill and remove all yeast cells and then carbonized artificially during the bottling stage.

4

YEAST

A low form of life with a high destiny, yeast is a microscopic, single-celled, sugar-eating fungus to which scientists, notably Pasteur, have devoted a tremendous amount of research.

For centuries before Pasteur alchemists sought the secret of life in fermentation, and yeast and its mysterious workings were regarded with some awe. Until the invention of powerful microscopes yeast cells could not be seen and their presence could only be guessed at, but the importance of yeast in medieval times cannot be overestimated. Life for most people was 'poor, nasty, brutish and short'; there were no surplus meat or vegetables to preserve even could they have done so, and bread and ale, both dependent on yeast, were the only year-round staffs of life.

Ale was not only a necessary part of the meagre, under-vitaminized diet of the poor but also their only cheer, and the miraculous increase of the yeast in their brews was a perennial benison. They called it goddesgoode, or God's gift, and for centuries brewsters were legally required to sell their surplus 'yests, berme or goddesgoode' at a nominal price for brewing or baking. 'Berme' was of course barm, a word for yeast still used in the north.

Right up to a decade or so after the Second World War we in Britain were still using baker's yeast for what little home-made wine was produced, but encouraged by the scarcity and (as we liked to think then) the dearness of imported wine the almost lost arts of home wine-making began to be revived, and it was not long before a few yeast cultures from continental vineyards became available.

Today both dried and liquid cultures of beer and wine yeasts can be bought everywhere quite cheaply, including granulated, powdered and tablet forms and liquid yeasts suspended in various solutions in sealed sachets or bottles. The beginner will be well advised to select a liquid culture or a packet of reliable all-purpose wine yeast for wine and a sealed packet of good granulated beer yeast for brewing. The reasons for these selections are that, owing to the difficulty of ensuring absolute sterility during the processes of drying and packing, dried yeasts are more likely (though the risk is admittedly very slight) to be contaminated by unwanted air-borne organisms. In the long fermentation and maturing processes of wine-making such organisms may produce off-flavours, though in the rapid progress of brewing this remote possibility is outweighed by the fact that a good granulated beer yeast starts to work much more quickly. Of the dried yeasts the granulated usually start more quickly than powdered yeast or the tablets made from it. Tablet yeasts are usually the slowest to start.

There are many thousands of different types of yeasts, but of all these only the variants of one of the *saccharomyces* (sugar fungi) are used in brewing and wine-making. These are *saccharomyces cerevisiae* (from *cerevisia*, Latin for beer), of which brewer's and baker's yeasts are strains, and its variant *s. cerevisiae var. ellipsoideus*, the true wine yeast, so called because of its elliptical shape.

These yeasts are very adaptable and many variations can be derived from identical cultures by a process of selection. Baker's and brewer's yeasts have been bred from the same stock to carry out quite dissimilar tasks; brewer's yeast has been yet again subdivided into top- and bottom-fermenting strains, and originally identical wine yeasts cultivated for centuries in different environments produce widely differing results.

All these yeasts breed at a tremendous rate in the right media and at their favourite temperatures, converting the sugar of the wort or must into approximately equal weights of ethyl alcohol (the drinkable type) and carbon dioxide gas.

The amount of alcohol produced depends upon a number of factors, including the type of yeast used, the sugar content, acidity and temperature of the wort or must, and of course the alcohol tolerance of the yeast. If this is exceeded, the yeast cells either die or pass into a coma from which they can be reactivated only if the wort or must is diluted to a tolerable alcohol level. The average brewer's yeast will tolerate 10 per cent alcohol by volume, baker's yeast 12 to 14 per cent, and true wine yeast 16 per cent or over in normal circumstances. With laboratory coddling the record is over 20 per cent or half as strong as a good Scotch.

The beginner should never waste time and materials trying to follow one of the 'no yeast' recipes to be found in old books, which are still being reprinted to the confusion of the tyro and the ill repute of the craft. The fermentation of wine or beer is normally impossible without the use of live, active yeast, and those 'no yeast' recipes relied on exposing the must to the open air and hoping that a suitable wild yeast colony would take up residence before vinegar bacteria or other air-borne spoilage organisms got at it. Even if this happened the best that could normally be hoped for would be the advent of a wild yeast, known as *apiculatus* from its pointed shape, which could produce only 4 per cent alcohol, or about one third the strength of a light table wine. The result was a preponderance of sickly sweet, faintly alcoholic cordials that would not keep and gave country wines a bad name.

Wine Yeasts

Reliable cultures of many different wine yeasts can be bought from any good retailer in liquid, powdered or tablet form.

Some liquid cultures are date-stamped, which helps to ensure that they are not old stock, and some tablets, usually the slowest starters, have built-in nutrients to help them along.

Any wine yeast may be slow to start if it has been too long on the shelf but once it gets going the resulting wine will almost certainly be perfectly good. If you pick a slow starter, try a different brand next time.

Each proprietory range of wine yeasts is offered in up to fifteen varieties, for strains have been cultured from every well-known continental wine, but it should not be taken for granted that to ferment a Cyprus or Spanish red grape-juice concentrate with, say, a Pommard yeast will automatically produce a true Pommard wine. It will certainly help, but, as any sensible person will realize, the authentic grapes from the specified area or vineyard are even more important than the yeast. The right strain does of course make a great difference to the result: for example a good white grape concentrate fermented with a hock yeast will be readily distinguishable from the same concentrate fermented with a Graves culture; but control of sweetness or dryness is also necessary. Much research has been devoted to evolving recipes for wines made from easily available materials which do in fact very closely resemble well-known continental wines, and the appropriate yeast culture is used in each case; but for the beginner wanting to make his or her first gallon or so of sound, enjoyable wine from a proprietory concentrate or ready-formulated compound a reliable all-purpose wine yeast is perfectly satisfactory and is in fact sometimes provided or recommended by the manufacturers of the concentrates. To get the best out of your wine yeasts always use a starter bottle (p. 54) and a good nutrient, preferably non-acid and vitaminized, to ensure a quick start and thorough fermentation.

Beer Yeasts

These begin to ferment very much more quickly than wine yeasts, and a starter bottle is not really necessary though if used it does accelerate the whole process and minimize risk. A really potent starter can activate the brew within minutes of pitching (adding yeast), or it may take twelve hours. Yeast is fickle stuff.

Beer yeasts are of two main strains: top-fermenting and bottom-fermenting. The first is generally used for all brews except lager and works on the top of the wort, forming a dense, thick cap that eventually excludes the air. By forcing the yeast to attenuate the sugar in the wort instead of utilizing oxygen from the air, this helps to produce a dry beer of the full alcoholic strength required.

Bottom-fermenting yeasts, usually of the continental *carlsbergensis* strain, are used almost exclusively for lagers. Though frequently quick starters they take longer over the whole process of fermentation, partly owing to the lower temperatures at which the fermenting wort is kept. Amateurs used to the showy frothing of the more usual top-fermenters are apt to worry when they first use a bottom-fermenting yeast, believing that it has either failed to start or has done so but has subsequently expired. The quick method of finding out, which for some reason beginners seldom think of, is to take a long spoon, preferably of polypropylene, and trawl. If there is a healthy deposit of yeast at the bottom of the fermentation vessel all is well.

Liquid beer yeast cultures are usually sold as ale (or British ale) and stout, both top-fermenters, and lager, a bottom-fermenter. Granulated beer yeasts of various types are on sale and are very reliable and much quicker to start. The *carlsbergensis* granulated, though developed from a bottom-fermenting strain, is an excellent all-purpose yeast for all types of brews and is apt to start with a moderate but reassuring top ferment but to finish working on the bottom.

Baker's Yeast

This is a strain of yeast specially cultivated to leaven dough. It starts even more dramatically, quickly and frothily than a top-fermenting beer yeast, and because it can withstand concentrations of alcohol of up to 14 per cent by volume, which is more than sufficient to preserve wine, it can be used to ferment either wine or beer if the proper strains are unobtainable.

It is important to use a good grade of granulated baker's yeast rather than the fresh or pressed variety, as the latter is more difficult to disperse in the must or wort – hence the old technique of spreading it on bread or toast so that it floated and gradually fell away into the liquid – and more likely to pass on a bready taste.

Its other great disadvantages are its slowness to clear and the fact that it settles in a loose, cloudy deposit. If used for wine this habit makes racking (siphoning the wine off the yeast sediment) difficult and causes wastage; if for beer, the brew will be almost impossible to pour from the bottle without the yeast deposit rising and clouding it, and this of course means more wastage. It may also cause off-flavours if left long on the lees (sediment). When one considers all its undeniable bad points it seems strange that such excellent wines and beers can be made with it!

Reuse of Yeast

A gallon jar of wine may contain a deposit of yeast half an inch thick after the first racking, and a five-gallon brew of beer may leave a pound or two of creamy-looking yeast in the fermentation bin. In either case it seems a shame to waste all this eleemosynary goddesgoode, but though medieval serfs were forced to use it and modern breweries are equipped to do so the amateur need not and is not. The first, heavy deposit will be full of bitter hop resins and fine particles of malt if a beer yeast, and assorted biological debris if a wine yeast. Both will tend to deteriorate if kept and should be discarded.

Beer yeast from the secondary fermentation in bottle, pressure vessel or dispensing keg, and wine yeast left in the jar after the second or third racking, are, however, perfectly good to use again. The 'brewer's inch' from the bottom of any one of the forty pint bottles that go to a five-gallon brew of beer is ample to start another five gallons, and wine yeast will go even farther.

It is advisable for the amateur not to reuse any yeasts more than once or twice, as they soon lose their special characteristics and may ruin a fermentation with off-flavours if they are not skilfully kept. It is better to find the very small price of a fresh culture than lose a whole brew of beer or wine.

Since every process of brewing and wine-making is dependent on yeast this generous, cheap, hard-working and generally beneficent little fungus must of necessity creep into every section of any book on the subject and cannot be confined to one chapter.

5

BASIC INGREDIENTS

> If all be true that I do think
> There are FIVE REASONS we should drink;
> Good wine, a Friend, or being Dry,
> Or lest we should be by and by;
> Or any other Reason why.
>   – Dean Henry Aldrich: *A Catch*

Natural Bases

By far the most important component of any fermented drink is its natural base, that is to say the particular vegetable substance, be it malted barley, the grape or any one of a thousand others, whose delicate natural chemistry not only gives to each type of beer or wine its own characteristic flavour, aroma, colour and body but also makes possible the still mysterious processes of maturation.

Every such base naturally contains in greater or less degree all or some of the ingredients to be discussed in this section, but suitable additions and dilutions are necessary if properly balanced worts and musts are to be produced from them. All the main bases from which beer, wine, cider and mead can be made at home are dealt with under their respective headings.

Water

Water constitutes from 80 to over 85 per cent of unfortified wines and about 90 per cent of most home-brewed beer and it is therefore fortunate for amateur wine-makers and brewers that provided certain simple precautions are taken ordinary tapwater is usually perfectly suitable for their purposes. Unpleasant though it may be to drink by itself owing to excessive chlorination, water from the domestic tap is at least clean and non-toxic, but unhappily the same cannot still be said for rainwater. Instructions that specify it, usually for mild ales, stouts and flower wines, should be disregarded. They were originally formulated before we had polluted the atmosphere for miles around our cities with soot, acids, sulphur and other unpleasant by-products of chimneys and car exhausts which the rain collects as it falls.

The quality of the water used for brewing has always been of prime importance. Even the layman knows that the hard waters of Burton, rich in gypsum, have made its pale ales and bitters world-famous, and that the soft waters of Dublin have done the same for stout. The brewer's techniques of water treatment are based upon centuries of trial and error followed by over a century of scientific research.

Because wine has traditionally been made from the undiluted juice of the grape, the home wine-maker has no such store of traditional lore and modern research on which to draw. The juices of all other soft fruits are too acid to be fermented without dilution, and grape juice and other concentrates must also be diluted, so it is fortunate that wine depends far less than beer upon the nature of the water with which it is made provided that this is of the standard of purity required from domestic drinking water.

Water Treatment: Beer

Before the era of mass-production breweries and their nationally standardized products, it was a well-known fact that people strongly preferred beers brewed from the water found in their own localities. Brewers therefore made a point of drawing their water from the local supply and amateurs may still do likewise, treating it if necessary for: Unwanted Hardness and Chlorination.

Both these can be got rid of by boiling. If the water will not make a good lather and furs the kettle it contains undesirable bicarbonates. Boiling drives off the chlorine and precipitates the carbonates as sediment from which the water can be siphoned when cool. The water will now be sterile and free of chlorine and carbonates, but the oxygen and other gases dissolved in it will also have been driven off. Yeast needs this oxygen, so it is most important to reoxygenate the boiled water by rousing it well when it has cooled, that is, aerating it by vigorous stirring or shaking, or by pouring it from one vessel to another.

Hardening

This process, also known as Burtonizing, improves pale ales and bitter beers: it entails the addition of gypsum (hydrated calcium sulphate) and Epsom salts (hydrated magnesium sulphate), usually in the proportions of 3 of calcium sulphate to 1 of magnesium sulphate. A level teaspoonful of this mixture to the gallon of soft water will Burtonize it nicely. All suppliers sell water treatment ready made up and with full instructions for use.

Softening

Soft water containing some calcium sulphate and chlorides is best for stouts and mild ales, so treat as above to remove unwanted hardness and chlorine and add a teaspoonful of salt to a four- or five-gallon brew. Use real salt if possible (sea salt, *gros sel* or old-fashioned kitchen salt in blocks) rather than table salt, which contains other chemicals. On no account brew with water softened by a domestic water softener. For highly technical reasons such water is useless for brewing though perfectly good for wine-making.

Water Treatment: Wine

Though the final quality of wine is less dependent than that of beer on the water with which it is made, wine is far more likely than beer to be spoiled by the chlorine in domestic tapwater, which will ruin its flavour. The remedy is simply boiling, and if this at the same time precipitates unwanted mineral salts, so much the better. Proceed as directed for beer, not forgetting to rouse the water well when cool to reoxygenate it. Flower wines, whose delicate, elusive flavours are so easily lost, are better made with soft water or water which has been boiled, allowed to cool and reoxygenated. Here the domestic water softener can be a great help.

Distilled Water

Every advisory service for amateur wine-makers has a year-round trickle of plaintive inquiries from people who have tried, and failed, to make wine or beer from distilled water; a trickle which rises to a spate after any pollution scare.

Usually the fermentation starts but soon stops and cannot be restarted. The reason for this is that distilled water lacks both the dissolved oxygen and the minute trace elements that yeast needs. Even if aeration and the addition of nutrient salts could carry the ferment through to completion the finished wine might well taste flat and uninteresting owing to the absence of trace elements.

Sugar

The history of sugar as a domestic sweetener began in Great Britain in about 1750. Cane sugar had been known and used in India since time immemorial and there are records of its use in China in the seventh century A.D., but although one chronicler records that King John gave presents of wine, cloth and sugar, probably before his coronation in A.D. 1200, it is usually accepted that the first refined sugar was imported to England in the mid thirteenth century by Henry III. This must have come from the orient for no sugar was made in Europe until A.D. 1295, in which year Marco Polo arrived in Venice from Bengal with sugar-cane and the secrets of refining it. In Britain it remained far too expensive for general use until the West Indian sugar-cane plantations were developed by slave labour in the eighteenth century.

Until this time honey had been our only sweetening agent, and though it was of course used in wine-making because the juices of all our native fruits and berries, including most British-grown grapes, need the addition of some form of sugar before they will make satisfactory wine, honey imposes its own distinctive taste and aroma whereas refined sugar need in no way mask the flavour or bouquet of the fruit or other basic ingredient. It was therefore the advent of readily available refined sugar that at last made it possible to produce true wines in Britain, as distinct from what had been in effect pyments, melomels, cysers and other varieties of mead.

The chemistry of sugar is as complex as its use is simple. Briefly (see also the chapter on Fermentation, p. 17), ordinary household sugar, or sucrose, is first inverted, or split into glucose and fructose, by the yeast enzyme invertase; another enzyme, zymase, then attenuates the glucose and fructose to alcohol and carbon dioxide. The only information needed by the wine-maker concerns the type and quantity of sugar to use and how to use it.

Types of Sugar

Household Granulated

It is indeed fortunate for the home wine-maker and brewer that ordinary, white granulated sugar is not only one of the purest, cheapest and most readily available foodstuffs on the market but also the most suitable for practically all their purposes, either as it comes out of the packet or, preferably, in the form of standard syrup as described below. Unfortunately old books on home wine-making and brewing whose recipes stipulate preserving sugar, candy sugar, cane sugar and so forth are still being reprinted, but their instructions are outdated and granulated sugar can be substituted with advantage in almost every case. It is made from both cane and beet sugars, and these are indistinguishable from one another in the fully refined state.

Candy Sugar

Candy sugar was specified in a very large number of old recipes because until the introduction of refined loaf and preserving sugar and later granulated sugar it was the only pure form available. It is made by dissolving sugar in water and allowing it to crystallize. It is extremely hard, and because it takes a long time to dissolve in a cool liquid it is possible to feed sugar slowly to the fermenting must by dropping in a crystal every few days. For all other purposes household granulated sugar can be substituted for it.

Brown Sugars

Many types of brown sugar, including Barbados, Demarara and 'pieces', used to be included in recipes, usually to give colour and flavour to grain or vegetable wines or with the idea of producing an imitation Madeira or brown sherry. Such recipes were compiled when the only available ingredients for home wine-making in Britain were our native fruit, flowers, vegetables and grain in their seasons, baker's or brewer's yeast, honey and unrefined sugar. The home wine-maker is now so abundantly catered for that such recipes are best forgotten – and the cloying, unreliable brown sugars with them. They are still used by some home brewers in dark beer and stout, but it is better to obtain the required characteristics from a properly balanced recipe containing black malt or caramel for colour and the correct proportions of malt extract, crystal malt and glucose chips or polymer for body and strength, and these ingredients together with the right type and quantity of hops for flavour.

Treacle etc.

Save for such oddities as treacle beer it is advisable to use neither treacle nor golden syrup in wine-making or brewing.

Invert Sugar

When the invertase enzyme splits sucrose into glucose and fructose it is said to invert it, and the intelligent amateur invariably asks why this should be. Very briefly, a solution of sucrose bends a beam of light to the right while one of fructose bends it to the left. During the splitting process therefore the direction of the beam (despite token resistance by the glucose) will be reversed, or inverted. Invert sugar is dearer than granulated and as it contains some water 5 parts by weight of invert have to be used instead of 4 parts of granulated. Because the inversion has already been completed the yeast enzymes have one less process to perform, and for this reason it is widely believed that invert sugar gives a quicker and more thorough fermentation. Some acknowledged experts hotly dispute this, but whoever is right the fact remains that tons of it are used by breweries and home wine-makers, though most home brewers prefer brewing sugar or glucose chips.

Glucose

Glucose powder, glucose chips and glucose polymer are widely used in home brewing, and there is no doubt that, whether they speed fermentation or not, glucose chips certainly give improved body and character to most beers and stouts. The use of chips or powder is largely a matter of choice but most expert home brewers seem to prefer chips. As with invert sugar, 5 parts by weight can replace 4 parts of ordinary sugar in any brewing recipe unless white sugar is specifically called for.

Brewing Sugars

Brewing sugars can be bought from most suppliers and have been used by breweries for many years as a malt supplement. There are several brands, but most of them are mixtures of glucose or invert sugar and malt extract and are used in the same proportions as invert and glucose. The additional body imparted by glucose chips or brewing sugar is largely due to residual unfermentable solids that are not present in ordinary sugar.

Glucose Polymer

This is a form of glucose employed to give extra body to heavy beer and stout; it can be used for this purpose alone as instructed in a recipe or can replace up to 20 per cent by weight of malt extract. It has no sweetness, is only 10 per cent fermentable and is also sometimes used to give body to wine and liqueurs.

Caramel

Caramel is a preparation based on burnt sugar and is extensively used in the trade and by home brewers to give a dark colour and in some cases added flavour to brown ale, porter and stout.

Lactose

Lactose or milk sugar cannot be fermented by any of the yeasts that we use in Britain and although it is not as sweet as ordinary sugar it is therefore very useful for sweetening wine or beer. It is widely employed in brewing sweetish ale and stout, and until labelling regulations forbade it, one of these was in fact sold as 'milk stout'. Lactose can be included when the wort or must is compounded or it can be dissolved in finished wine or in beer before it is bottled. Food grade lactose is the most suitable for these purposes; B.P. (British Pharmacopoeia, i.e. dispensing grade) quality can be found but is said to cause hazes.

The Use of Sugar

The ways in which manufactured sugars of various kinds are used by the home brewer and wine-maker to supplement or replace the natural sugars of malt or fruit are dealt with elsewhere. Although the brewing procedure is straightforward enough if the home brewer checks all recipes by the rule-of-thumb alcohol potential values of his ingredients, wine-making recipes are still apt to specify far too much sugar and to instruct the reader to tip it all in in its normal crystalline state when the must is being made up. To follow them is to invite stuck fermentations and the production of liquors that are more like faintly alcoholic treacle than wine.

The perfect natural habitat for wine yeast is the juice of the ripe grape, which may contain as much as 25 per cent of sugar in a very sunny year indicating a gravity of about 95 and a theoretical alcohol content of $12\frac{1}{2}$ per cent, but 20 per cent of sugar is more usual and this would give a gravity of just under 75 or some $9\frac{1}{2}$ per cent of alcohol. Below this strength wine will not keep, and in bad, cold seasons the wine-makers have to resort to chaptalization, or the addition of extra sugar to the must.

Since yeast is thus intended by nature to live and reproduce in a must the gravity of which seldom exceeds 90 it is easy to understand that too high a concentration of sugar may not only inhibit the action of the yeast but may actually kill it, and if the yeast is introduced to a fermentation vessel in which large quantities of crystalline sugar have been added to the must it may well sink to rest on a bed of undissolved crystals covered by a layer of heavy, undistributed syrup, with disastrous results. All this can be prevented by never starting with more than 2 lb or at most $2\frac{1}{2}$ lb of sugar per gallon of must and feeding the rest as syrup in small quantities over the period of the fermentation, so that the yeast is always operating in a gravity which suits it. Even more important, the crystalline granulated sugar should not be used as it is but should be made into what is known as a standard syrup.

Standard Syrup

This is far the most important form of sugar used in home wine-making; *2 lb of granulated sugar dissolved in 1 pint of water produces 1 quart of standard syrup having a gravity of 300.* The sugar should be stirred continually with the water over a moderate heat until it is all dissolved, brought to the boil to ensure sterility, made up to the correct volume with boiled water to compensate for evaporation wastage, allowed to cool while closely covered and kept tightly stoppered as a stock supply.

This is not only the simplest and most accurate method of

adding sugar, since 1 pint of syrup contains exactly 1 lb of sugar and both the quantity and the volume can be accurately allowed for, but also much the best, for a brisk rousing will quickly mix the syrup with the must and ensure that there are no high-gravity layers or deposits to harm the yeast. It is also much better to feed with syrup, since the addition of crystals to a fermenting must may cause violent foaming.

Invert Syrup

If a strong sugar syrup is boiled with a little acid it is hydrolized, that is to say the sucrose is chemically separated into a mixture of glucose and fructose. This is the method used to make commercial invert sugar, and the amateur can easily follow it by simmering standard syrup to which 1 teaspoonful of citric acid per gallon has been added. After simmering for about forty minutes it will become a pale straw-coloured invert syrup, which should then be corrected for evaporation and stored as above. Unlike the commercial product this will still contain the acid, which should be allowed for when the must is compounded.

Acids

The paramount importance of a correct acid balance in wine musts has only lately been fully realized by home wine-makers, and even more recent is the realization that although the right degree of acidity can be achieved by the use of the three main fruit acids, citric, tartaric and malic, either separately or in conjunction, striking improvements in the bouquet and flavour of matured wine can be produced only by the addition of others, of which lactic acid is the most important. The most common cause of slow or stuck fermentations, dullness, and horrible, medicinal off-flavours has always been lack of acidity, especially in the wines of beginners who have relied on faulty recipes. Unless it deals with acid ingredients such as citrus fruits a 'no acid' recipe should be trusted no farther than a 'no yeast' one.

The two methods of ascertaining the degree of acidity in a

liquid are titration and the use of pH indicators. Titration means the measurement of the degree of acidity of the must by mixing known quantities of must, distilled water and phenolphthalein and finding out how much decinormal (N/10) sodium hydroxide solution is required to turn the mixture pink. The amount of free acid present can then be calculated in terms of parts per thousand of sulphuric acid, which then has to be converted into terms of the acid or acids to be used.

The pH symbol actually indicates the hydrogen ion concentration in a solution, but for highly complex reasons it is also a pretty reliable guide to the effective acidity of the must. Titration is moderately simple in theory but needs laboratory equipment to be carried out satisfactorily and is too complex and time-consuming for most people, whereas the determination of the pH factor, though its theory is beyond all but advanced chemists, is remarkably simple and satisfactory in operation and is widely used professionally.

For a few pence good suppliers sell little books of pH comparison papers. To ascertain the acidity of the must one of the narrow slips is torn out, dipped into it and then laid on a white surface so that its colour can be compared with those on the comparison chart supplied. It must be clearly borne in mind that the pH scale works in reverse as it were: the weakest acidity that it registers is pH 6·9 and the highest pH 0·3; anything over pH 7 is alkaline. The optimum indications are pH 3·4 to pH 3·2 for wine and about pH 5·4 for beer. Fermentation will not take place in a must more acid than pH 3, and if it is weaker than pH 4 some spoilage organisms that are inhibited by acid may breed in wine though they do not become dangerous during the shorter fermentation period of beer.

Acids Used in Wine-making

Citric

As its name implies, this is the main acid in all citrus fruits. For centuries these were the only sources of acid readily available to home wine-makers, and although B.P. (see p. 36) citric acid crystals are cheaper and better than lemon juice, especially if used in conjunction with a vitaminized yeast nutrient, many recipes still specify oranges and lemons where only their acidity and not their flavour is required. Citric acid promotes rapid and thorough fermentation, has a pleasant taste in solution and is still probably the best single acid for our purposes.

Tartaric

This acid is found in quantity only in grapes and of course in raisins, currants and sultanas, but despite this it is of no great assistance in fermentation or in the formation of bouquet as most of it will have crystallized out of the wine before maturation is complete. Any excess will cause white wine to become hazy when it is chilled.

Malic

This is the second main grape acid and is also common in other fruits especially the apple, from which (Latin, *malum*) it takes its name. Valuable though it is in every stage of fermentation and maturation, it is apt to impart a sour taste to wine if used alone and is therefore added in combination with other acids.

Succinic

All wines contain small quantities of succinic acid, as it is a product of their fermentation. It is of little assistance in the promotion of the ferment but helps to resist bacterial infections and has a most beneficial effect on the bouquet and flavour of the wine after maturation has continued for about two years.

Lactic

The main source of lactic acid is sour milk, so it may be surprising to learn not only that most wines develop it during the secondary or malo-lactic fermentation but also that it has a greater influence than any other acid on the final taste and aroma of the wine. Unlike the other acids mentioned, all of which are sold in crystalline form, lactic acid is supplied in a 50 per cent solution. One part in 1,000 of must is ample. This fortunately works out to just about 5 ml or 1 teaspoonful per gallon. Though its full benefits are felt only after a year's maturation or preferably two, lactic acid will improve any wine that is worth bottling.

Procedure

If a recipe calls for a given amount of acid and you have no means of checking acidity, follow the instructions given. Some acid is better than no acid at all, but although recipes for flower wines and others whose basic ingredient contains practically no acid are usually fairly accurate, the acid content of any fruit can vary so much from season to season that recipes should not be followed blindly and either titration or pH papers should always be used to regulate the acidity of the must. If lactic acid is used, first add 1 teaspoonful per gallon and then add citric, or even better a formula containing 20 parts citric, 50 parts tartaric and 30 parts malic (it is sold ready compounded) until a pH indication of between 3·2 and 3·4 is reached. The must should of course be well stirred after every addition or inaccurate readings will be obtained. If pH papers are not available and a recipe is to be followed that specifies only citric or other crystalline acids, ½ teaspoonful of crystals should be deducted to compensate for 1 teaspoonful of lactic acid solution.

Tannin

Anyone who has taught wine-making knows the confusion caused in many minds by the relationship between the words 'tannin' and 'tanning'. To clear this up, a tan is either a substance used for tanning leather or the colour produced by this process, and tannin is the substance's chemical name. It is commonly extracted from oak leaves, and the nouns tan and tannin, the verb to tan and the adjectives tawny and tenné all, like the Breton *tan*, derive from the Old High German *tanna*, an oak.

Tannin is an indispensable ingredient of good wine and occurs naturally in the skins of many fruits and berries, especially red ones. Red wines are fermented on the skins and pulp (stalks and pips also contain tannin) to extract the colour, so they usually contain a sufficient quantity. White wines that are made from the pressed juice of grapes or other fruit always require the addition of tannin; almost the only fruit juices to contain it are those of elderberries and some types of apples, and there is practically none in grain or flowers.

Tannin is not only valuable as a preservative and as an aid to clearing and maturation but its presence is also absolutely necessary if the wine is not to be dull and insipid. High-tannin red wines may need two years in the wood and at least as long in bottle before the tannin is precipitated out and its harsh astringency is mellowed, but the result is well worth waiting for. Lack of tannin ranks equal with lack of acid as the most common wine-making fault, and though more of it may be added at any stage the effect will not quite compare with that obtained from a well-balanced must. Excess tannin may be precipitated out by the use of white of egg or any protein finings, and if these are used to clear a wine that contains no excess the loss should be made good afterwards.

Because there is no practicable test for tannin content it is best to study the amounts specified in recipes for wines comparable to that which is being made and to accustom the tongue and palate to gauge its excess or deficiency. Broadly speaking, red wine fermented on the pulp or made from grape concentrate will need no tannin, others from $\frac{1}{8}$ to a maximum of $\frac{3}{4}$ teaspoonsful of powdered grape tannin per gallon. It weighs approximately 2 grammes ($\frac{1}{14}$ oz) per teaspoonful, and as it is now easy to obtain from any supplier the old alternatives of tannic acid, oak leaves, pear peelings or stewed tea are not worth bothering with. The powder is apt to clot if added directly to the must; it will dissolve in the end but it is better to beat it up in a little of the liquid and to stir this well into the bulk.

6

BASIC EQUIPMENT

> After Drinking Cure for the Heid-Ake.
> Take green Hemlock that is tender,
> and put it in your Socks, so that it may
> lie thinly between them and the Soles
> of your Feet; shift the Herbs once a day.
> – Hon. Robert Boyle:
> *Medical Experiments,* 1692

Most items of equipment are dealt with in other chapters, but there are a few basic tools of the trade whose nature and use should be more fully described.

The Hydrometer

This simple and inexpensive gadget is as necessary to the home brewer or wine-maker as a set-square is to a handyman and about as easy to use. It is simply a float that looks rather like a fishing float, with a 'quill' about 4 inches long on which is a scale that indicates the gravity, or density, of the wort or must. The scale is usually marked from 1·000 at its tip to 1·150 at its base, where it joins the float, which is so weighted that in pure water at 59–60 °F (15 °C) it sinks until the figure 1·000 is level with the surface. If the gravity of the water is raised by having something dissolved in it (in our case some form of sugar) the hydrometer floats higher in the liquid and exposes a higher figure on the scale. A glance at this and another at the tables that follow will show at once the total sugar content of the wort or must and the percentage of alcohol by volume that the finished beer or wine will contain if all this sugar is converted into alcohol. Some hydrometers are of glass and some of plastic; some have the alcohol potential scale conveniently printed alongside the gravity scale and some are designed to operate at different temperatures: a 70 °F (21–2 °C) hydrometer for example is useful to check the gravity of a fermenting wort or must. Special brewing hydrometers can be had, but one that reads up to about 1·150 will serve well for both beer and wine.

How to use the Hydrometer

Fill a sterilized hydrometer test jar (a tall, narrow glass jar) to within an inch or two from the top with wort or must. Check the temperature and adjust it by standing the jar in hot or cold water, then gently float the hydrometer in the liquid,

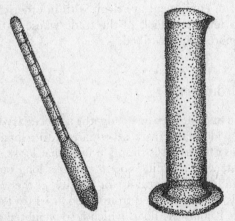

Hydrometer and test jar

place the jar at eye level and note the figure that is level with the surface. If for example this is 1·060 (G.60) it indicates only about 8 per cent potential alcohol and the tables will show that in order to raise the gravity to 90 to give 12 per cent alcohol, just right for a good table wine, another 13 oz of sugar per gallon must be added. For wine-making and brewing purposes we can forget about specific gravity and omit both the figure 1 and the decimal point that follows. Thus, a reading of 1·090 indicates a gravity (G.) of 90; 1·000 is G. zero and so forth. The gravity of the wort or must before fermentation has started is called the original gravity, or O.G.

The main uses of the hydrometer are:

1. To check that the wort or must before fermentation is of the right O.G. to give the required percentage of alcohol in the finished beer or wine.

2. To check from time to time, usually when the must is racked, that the fermentation is proceeding satisfactorily. The gravity should decrease at each reading, thus showing that more and more sugar is being converted into alcohol.

3. To indicate when the fermentation has stopped, i.e. when readings taken several days apart show no further fall in gravity. If this occurs at or around G. zero the fermentation will have finished normally, but if the gravity is considerably higher and the wine is still very sweet the ferment will have stuck and the hydrometer will have made it possible to take appropriate steps in good time.

4. To show the alcoholic strength of the finished beer or wine. If the wine had an O.G. of 90 its alcohol content would have been 12 per cent had the fermentation ended precisely at G. zero. It seldom does, so the final gravity should be subtracted from the O.G. to ascertain the drop in gravity. An O.G. of 90 falling to a final G.4 gives a drop of 86, equivalent to about 11·6 per cent alcohol. Because the gravity of alcohol is lower than that of water the final gravity of a strong, dry wine will read below zero, and for this reason most hydrometers are calibrated to 0·990, or 10 degrees of gravity below zero. Thus, if a must with an O.G. of 90 finished at G.0·995, or G.−5, the total drop from O.G.90 will have been 90 + 5 or 95, equal to 12·7 per cent alcohol. It is more difficult to estimate the O.G. for a beer of any given strength, partly because although the O.G. will be lower than that of wine the fermentation may cease in some cases at between G.5 and G.10 owing to the high propor-

tion of unfermentable material in solution, and this should be borne in mind when making up the wort.

If a must has been fed with a number of small quantities of sugar throughout the course of the fermentation, the gravity before and after adding the sugar and the amount of sugar added should be noted each time. The total of all the drops in gravity, or the total weight of sugar in the must will give the final percentage of alcohol. In practice probably the most accurate and least laborious method is to find the weight of sugar present in the original must from the O.G., to add to this the actual weight of all the added sugar and then to consult the tables to find the alcohol content of the finished wine.

The importance of the hydrometer as a reliable guide cannot be over-stressed, but it is a mistake to treat home brewing and wine-making as laboratory operations. All that is needed is a reasonably close approximation, but the ability to test the gravity of at least the O.G. within reasonable limits is vital.

This is no new-fangled idea: as far back as 1650 Sir Kenelm Digby, chef and mead-maker extraordinary, wrote in one of his recipes for metheglin: '. . . and when it is but blood-warm put in as much of the best honey as will make the Liquor bear an Egg the breadth of six pence above the water'.* He used an egg as a primitive hydrometer, and failing any other I would be quite happy to do the same. After all, if one is confident of getting good results, what does the odd degree or two of alcohol matter?

Tables

TABLE I.   TEMPERATURE ADJUSTMENT

Most hydrometers read accurately at 59–60 °F (15 °C); if the liquid is colder they will indicate too high a gravity, and too low a one if it is warmer. As the temperatures of worts and musts

* If Sir Kenelm was aiming at 10 per cent alcohol, the highest proportion that he could have hoped for with his recipe, his sixpence must have measured 15 to 16 mm across.

normally vary only between narrow limits no elaborate tables
are needed. The figures in the 'adjustment' column should be
subtracted from or added to the hydrometer readings at the
temperatures indicated.

Temperatures °F	°C	Adjustments	Examples
50	10	—0·6	G.90 becomes G.89·4
59–60	15	Nil	
70	21	+1	G.90 becomes G.91
77	25	+2	G.90 becomes G.92

TABLE 2. EQUIVALENTS

Gravity Drop at 59°F (15°C)	Potential Alcohol % by Volume	Weight of Sugar in 1 Gallon of Wort or Must lb oz		Type of Drink
25	3·1		9	light beer
30	3·8		12	,, ,,
35	4·4		15	,, ,,
40	5·0	1	1	medium beer
45	5·6	1	3	,, ,,
50	6·2	1	5	,, ,,
55	6·9	1	7	,, ,,
60	7·5	1	9	strong beer
65	8·1	1	11	,, ,,
70	8·8	1	13	,, ,,
75	9·4	1	15	,, ,,
80	10·6	2	2	light wine
85	11·4	2	4	,, ,,
90	12·0	2	6	,, ,,
95	12·7	2	8	,, ,,
100	13·3	2	10	medium wine
105	14·0	2	13	,, ,,
110	14·7	2	15	,, ,,
115	15·5	3	1	,, ,,
120	16·0	3	3	strong wine
125	16·7			,, ,,
130	17·3	3	8	,, ,,

How to Use the Tables

No such tables can be accurate as a chemist understands accuracy because of the number of unknown factors. In theory, estimation of alcohol percentage from the drop in gravity rather than from the O.G. to zero compensates for most of these but in fact the problem is a little more difficult, as witness the very wide variations between the tables and conversion formulae given in the books of writers all of whom are acknowledged experts in their field. Those given here can best be described as the offspring of theory tempered by experience. Try to remember this very simple formula for calculating alcohol percentage by volume in case you have not got the tables by you:

Beer range (G.25 to G.75) Subtract the final gravity from the O.G. and divide the result by 8. For example: O.G.50, final G.5. The difference is 45, which divided by 8 gives an approximate alcohol percentage by volume of 5·6.

Wine Range (G.80 and up) As above, but divide by 7·5 instead of 8. For example: O.G.100, final G. zero. The difference is 100, which divided by 7·5 gives an alcohol percentage of 13·3.

The Thermometer

A thermometer, like a hydrometer, is an absolute necessity to the home brewer or wine-maker and various types are sold to cater for his special needs. Some of these were designed originally for photographic processing and register from about 40° to 110 °F or the equivalent in Centigrade or Celsius, thus covering all the fermentation range; but the best, especially for brewers, are boiling-point thermometers graduated in Fahrenheit, upwards of a foot long to give a clear reading and to enable temperatures to be taken at the centre of a mash or liquid rather than at the surface. They are also provided with a loop, so that they can be suspended in a mash, and filled with spirit rather than mercury so that if one is broken in use the brew will not have to be thrown away. The glass will remain safely in the lees and can be flushed away with them after the wort or must has been racked off. Temperatures higher than boiling-point are needed only in the making of caramel, a messy and unrewarding process at best.

In this book the alternatives to Fahrenheit are given in brackets but this scale is so flexible and convenient that it will probably continue to be used by brewers, wine-makers and others who do not want to bother with fractions of degrees. A Fahrenheit/Centigrade comparison scale is on p. 307.

The Vinometer

The vinometer is designed to provide a quick and easy method of finding the alcoholic content of wines. It consists of a graduated capillary tube of glass with a small thistle-shaped funnel at the top, and the theory is that when a few drops of wine are placed in this and the appearance of a drop at the other end has shown the capillary tube to be filled the vinometer is inverted so that the wine drops back down the tube until stopped by its surface tension, which varies according to its alcoholic content. The calibration reading at the stopping-point is supposed to indicate the percentage of alcohol by volume.

The vinometer will give approximately accurate readings for very dry, light wines but unfortunately any sugar content will render the instrument hopelessly inaccurate and instructions to dilute heavy wine with its own volume of water and to double the resultant readings are really not very helpful.

The Fermentation Lock

This is of course the piece of equipment that has done more than anything else to make modern home wine-making trouble-free. Locks are of glass or plastic and of various designs but they all allow the carbon dioxide created by the fermentation to escape freely while they prevent any air from entering. All fermentation locks terminate in a glass or plastic tube which fits into a pierced cork or rubber bung which in turn fits the neck of the fermentation vessel. All types work efficiently, but the traditional glass lock in which the tube forms a U with a spherical bulb at each extremity is to be preferred to the cylindrical plastic kind, because even when the rate of fermentation has become almost imperceptible and the bubbles occur at very long intervals any difference in the level of the water in the two arms of the U shows that the must is still fermenting; when the water levels are the same the ferment has finished. This shape is also made in clear plastic and as it is not so likely to be broken it is probably the best buy of all.

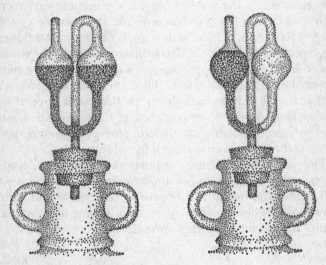

Fermentation locks fitted to jars. Uneven levels of liquid indicate an active fermentation

Glass fermentation locks are brittle and a cloth should be wrapped round the hand when they are fitted into the bung. Both cork and rubber bungs should be moistened first, and in any case they and the lock should be sterilized with sulphite solution before use and a little of this should also be added to the water in the lock – but not too much as it may be sucked into the jar when the bung is being removed. Some cotton-wool in the outer opening of the lock will deter suicidal insects.

The Bath Board

I have never seen this most useful piece of equipment described, but 'every home should have one' unless it has a fully-equipped winery or brew-house. It is simply a board or boards just long enough to go across the bath and strong enough to support a full 5-gallon carboy. Mine is made of three oak boards each 28 by 6 by $\frac{1}{2}$ inches, to the underside of which are screwed two oak battens, each 18 by 2 by $\frac{1}{2}$ inches. The battens are positioned to lie just inside the sides of the bath so that if the end of the board is accidently pushed it cannot slide far enough across the bath for one end to slip down into it. The 6-inch boards are spaced $\frac{1}{4}$ inch apart to permit drainage, so that spilth will run into the bath and not down outside it; the gaps should not be wide enough to allow small glass items such as U-tubes to slip through.

The bath board provides a working surface that is ideal for racking, bottling, compounding worts and musts and every other brewing and winemaking job. There is plenty of hot and cold water to hand, the drop from the board to the bottom of the bath is just right for siphoning and the inevitable spilth trickles down the plug-hole. Most important of all, this very simple gadget liberates the only alternative site, the much less convenient kitchen sink and draining-board. A bath-side chair or low stool is helpful especially for the tall. The board should be given a brisk scrub under running water and a rub over with sterilizing fluid before being put away.

The Press

A wine or cider press is a device for extracting the maximum amount of juice from any fruit pulp, but traditionally from grapes after they have been trodden or apples crushed by the cider mill. The juice can flow freely only after the fruit has been macerated in some way, but despite all warnings every season has its quota of beginners who break their presses or complain that they are useless after filling them with whole fruit.

The press in one form or another is as old as the making of wine or cider, and in every type the pulp must first have been wrapped in some material such as hessian and then subjected to pressure. Probably the first presses were operated by piling large stones on a hurdle resting on the package of crushed fruit. The Egyptians extracted the juice from a great sack of pulp by wringing it in a frame with ropes and levers, in much the same way as a washerwoman wrings the water from a sock, and the Romans either used wedges to tighten the press or simply crushed the package of pulp between two massive, hinged boards on the lever or nutcracker principle. This last method can form the basis of an improvised home press and was adapted by Worlidge in his weight-operated 'ingenio', but nowadays all presses rely on the screw for the exertion of the necessary pressure and various sound designs have been published for home-made presses operated by car jacks.

The best type of press made specifically for the home wine- or cider-maker is basically a very strong wooden box with an open top and slotted sides through which the pressed juice can flow into a wooden tray that forms its base and thence through a polythene tube into a suitable receptacle. Strong nylon pulp-bags are provided and after one of these has been filled, folded over and put in the press a heavy square of wood is placed on top of it. A flat steel cross-bar is then fitted into horizontal slots in the upper part of the press so that a long, screwed steel rod that runs through it can be turned by a cross-piece at its upper end to exert pressure on the wooden block and thence on the pulp in the bag.

The secret of successful pressing is to go steadily and to keep the juice running. It is easy to exert great pressure but this does not expedite the flow and may burst the bag or even break the press. Directly the juice begins to flow the pressure should be eased and increased only when the flow ceases, and if this process is carried out carefully the pulp will emerge from the

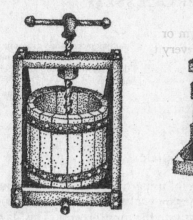

Domestic wine presses

bag as a hard, dry cake. Anyone who makes his own press should make absolutely certain that no metal ever comes in contact with the pulp or juice.

Alternative methods of extracting the juice from pulped or chopped fruit include steaming and the use of enzymes. The former used to be popular but the process takes a long time and requires special apparatus and some juices, especially those of apples and pears, are apt to be darkened by oxidation and to acquire a cooked taste that persists in the wine or cider. The enzyme process has already been dealt with, but although it is simpler and cheaper for the beginner to purée the fruit with an enzyme such as rohament P and to squeeze the juice out of it through a jelly-bag nothing can give the true amateur the same satisfaction as the use of his own miniature version of the age-old, traditional press.

7

SOME BASIC PROCESSES*

Champagne certainly gives one werry
gentlemanly ideas, but for a continuance,
I don't know but I should prefer mild
hale.

– Robert Smith Surtees,
Jorrocks' Jaunts and Jollities

Preparing a Starter Bottle

The only disadvantage of using true wine yeast or liquid beer
yeast cultures is that they may take a long time to become active
if they are added directly to the must or wort. This 'lag phase'
may be so protracted that beginners become convinced that
the yeast has failed, while more experienced wine-makers
hitherto accustomed only to the rapid, foamy fermentation of
baker's yeast are even more disconcerted and sometimes add
this as well in an attempt to speed things up, often with un-
fortunate results.

In the cultures in which they are sold both wine and beer
yeasts are dormant. Before they can begin first to breed and then
to produce alcohol they must be activated, but the average culture contains so few viable yeast cells, and these become so
widely dispersed if mixed directly into the must or wort, that
even when all conditions are favourable some days may well
elapse before there is any visible sign of fermentation. The lag
phase can last for a week or more if the temperature of the must
or wort is too low, if they are too acid or otherwise wrongly
formulated, if the must has been oversulphited or if the yeast

* Other basic processes not covered by this chapter, such as bottling and
storage, are fully dealt with elsewhere: consult the Index.

culture has a low live-cell count through having been too long in stock.

It is important to get a fermentation started as soon as possible, not only to cut out annoying and time-wasting delays but also to shorten the period during which the must or wort is at risk from air-borne spoilage organisms, for directly fermentation begins an increasing amount of protection is given both by the presence of a strong and growing yeast colony and by the production of inert carbon dioxide gas which soon displaces the lighter air and fills the headroom in the fermentation vessel.

The answer lies in the invaluable starter bottle. In this the yeast is introduced to a small quantity of nutrient solution in which it rapidly starts to breed and to attain a high concentration of live, active yeast cells. The effect of introducing such a starter to the must or wort is far more potent than the addition of a small culture of dormant yeast cells; in favourable conditions must may start to ferment visibly almost overnight and wort within a few hours.

Most of the packets, sachets or bottles in which proprietary yeast cultures are sold carry instructions for making a starter bottle but they usually stipulate much too small a quantity. The optimum amount of starter in wine-making is about 1 to 15, say $\frac{1}{2}$ pint of starter to 1 gallon of must, so if the recipes given with the yeast cultures are followed the amounts should be increased accordingly. A starter bottle should always be made when brewing with liquid beer yeast cultures and is usually preferable even for granulated yeasts.

To make a half-pint starter take a glass milk bottle or other suitable transparent container holding about a pint, sterilize it and either plug the mouth with plain, unmedicated cotton-wool or secure a small plastic bag over the neck of the vessel with a rubber band. The advantages of the latter method are that the contents may be shaken up without either soaking the cotton-wool or putting one's hand over the mouth, and that the starter can be seen to be ready when the gas fills the plastic bag.

Then:

(*a*) Use a commercial starter pack as instructed; or

(*b*) Follow the instructions on the yeast packet but increase the quantities if necessary; or

(*c*) (for beer or wine) Boil 1 tablespoonful of malt extract ($\frac{3}{4}$ if it is a dry extract), 2 teaspoons of sugar and half a teaspoon of lemon juice in $\frac{1}{2}$ pint of water. Let the liquid cool, closely covered, until it can safely be transferred to the milk bottle. Replace the cotton-wool plug and when the solution has cooled to about 75 °F (24 °C) add the yeast and a pinch of vitaminized nutrient, shake the bottle well, plug it and leave it in a warm place; or

(*d*) (for wine only) Proceed as above substituting for the malt extract and sugar *either* 2 tablespoons of the grape or other concentrate to be used and 2 teaspoons of sugar, *or* $\frac{3}{4}$ oz chopped raisins and 1 teaspoon of sugar, *or* $\frac{1}{2}$ pint of the wort or must to be used and 2 teaspoons of sugar. The vitaminized nutrient, lemon juice and yeast are added in each case.

It is always best to use, when possible, the malt extract, concentrate, must or wort methods since these accustom the yeast to grow in its destined medium right from the start. Instructions to use any available fruit juice for wine starters are still sometimes found, but to do so will not only get the yeast accustomed to the wrong medium but may also upset the balance of the must.

The starter bottle should be shaken occasionally to aerate the solution. When this has become cloudy and bubbles have begun to rise the yeast will be activated and the starter is ready to be stirred into the must or wort. Frothing, especially of wine yeasts, is not to be expected at this stage as they are too busy multiplying to attenuate much sugar into alcohol and the carbon dioxide gas that creates the foam. It is, however, as well to keep an eye on starters made from granulated beer yeasts: these may push out the cotton-wool plug and chase it on to the floor in under thirty minutes.

If a starter bottle and a good, vitaminized yeast nutrient are always used the risks of air taint and stuck fermentations will be reduced to vanishing point.

Racking

Racking, a word derived from the Provençal *raca*, the debris of pressed grapes, and *arraca*, to draw the wine off it, is the process by which fermenting worts and musts or finished beer and wine are drawn off their lees, a deposit of dead yeast and other organic matter that imparts an unpleasant taste if it is left for too long in contact with the wine.

Beer is normally racked only once or twice, either directly from the fermenting vat into casks, or, in home brewing, first into gallon jars, carboys, or other suitable vessels to accelerate the clearing process and finally into casks, pressure vessels or bottles. Wine, with its very much longer fermentation, should first be racked about four weeks after it has been placed under fermentation lock, thereafter at longer intervals whenever the deposit of lees warrants it, and finally as finished wine into bottles, jars or other storage vessels. Every time the wine is racked save the first, 50 ppm (parts per million) of sulphite (1 crushed campden tablet per gallon) should be added before the lock is replaced as it will help to preserve the colour of the wine, assist clearing and promote the production of glycerol which imparts body and smoothness. If the fermentation is sluggish the absorption of a little oxygen while it is being racked from one container to another may be helpful, but in the case of flower wines and others that rely on their delicate and evanescent aromas the outflow end of the siphon tube should be kept below the surface of the wine in the receiving vessel and splashing should be avoided.

The main secret of successful racking is to draw off the must or wine without disturbing the lees. This is rendered much easier by the use of proper wine and beer yeast cultures that (unlike baker's yeast) settle firmly on the bottom, but it is still not practicable to pour the wine, and for centuries atmospheric pressure has been employed either by siphoning or, in the old days, by the use of bellows to create air pressure in the cask and force the wine up through leather pipes. Today we use either automatic siphon-pumps also operated by bellows or a length of non-toxic polythene tubing, usually of $\frac{1}{4}$-inch internal diameter. Rubber tube is apt to kink and stop the flow. The suction end of the tube or pump should always be fitted with a U-tube so that the liquid will be drawn downwards, for no matter how much care is used a straight tube will always suck

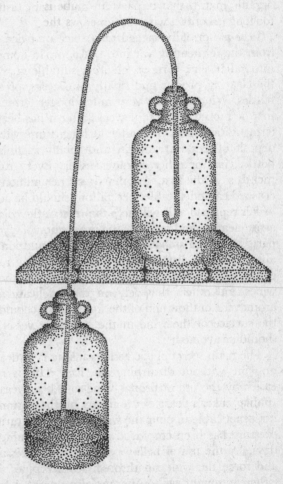

Racking or siphoning beer or wine off the lees, showing U-tube

up the lees. Some siphon-pumps have the end of the suction tube plugged and pierced horizontally and this arrangement acts very well. A yard of tubing giving a drop of about two feet is usually ample: too long a drop creates so powerful a suction that despite the U-tube the rush of wine will disturb the lees, which will then be sucked up. A siphon tap can be used to avoid spilth when the siphon outflow tube is being transferred from one bottle to another but this slows the flow. A simple, cheap, 'stop-go' bottling valve should shortly be available and has long been badly needed.

Fining and Filtering

Two of the criteria upon which both beer and wine are judged are their colour and clarity. The more brilliantly clear they are the better their colour can be appreciated and the more the drinker is predisposed to find them palatable. Conversely, however good they may taste and smell half the enjoyment of drinking them will be lost if they are cloudy and opaque. Wine and beer will normally 'drop bright' of their own accord especially if they have been properly racked. It is customary to add finings to beer to accelerate the process as this can be done without noticeable loss of quality but, despite the fact that the less one puts in to or takes out of wine by fining or filtering the better it will usually be, some form of treatment must be given if it remains obstinately cloudy after fermentation has ceased, and of the two methods filtration is usually the better.

Types of Finers

For many hundreds of years all kinds of animal and vegetable proteins such as isinglass, prepared from the swimbladders of sturgeons and other fish, gelatine, white of egg, ox blood, milk, casein and seaweed have been used to clarify beer and wine. Activated charcoal can also be used but it is messy, and although it can remove off-flavours and smells it also kills the normal bouquet and flavour and is recommended only as a last resort. Wine that has been treated with charcoal will be characterless but can be used for blending. One of the best stand-bys for the amateur is bentonite, a Montmorillonite earth; kieselguhr, a type of refined, powdered china clay, can also be used either by itself or in combination with Irish Moss. Various chemicals, some very poisonous, are used professionally to treat wine in bulk but any attempt to use them with small quantities would be not only useless but also extremely dangerous.

Protein Finers

Today excellent, professionally compounded wine and beer finers are available, usually based on isinglass, gelatine or Irish Moss, a dried and powdered preparation of the seaweed carragheen. These are sold complete with full instructions for use. Until very recently it was thought that protein finings combined physically with the microscopic haze particles to create nuclei of sufficient mass to precipitate them to the bottom, but it is now known that their action is electrical. The haze particles all carry the same charges and thus repel each other so that they can never combine to achieve a mass sufficient to sink them. The colloidal particles of protein finers carry an opposite charge, so that they attract and coagulate with the haze particles and precipitate them. All this is mentioned only to explain why over-fining can only make matters worse. Only just enough finers are needed to cope with an equivalent amount of haze, for if any particles of protein finers remain in the wine after the haze has been dealt with they will all have similar electrical charges, will repel each other and will create and stabilize a new haze. Further attempts to clear this with the same finers will of course make it worse, but it can be dispersed by the use of pectinaze.

Bentonite

The best of all non-protein finers is bentonite, a fine earth whose particles carry negative charges and can absorb a very large proportion of water.

Enzymes

Unfilterable and normally unfinable hazes can be caused by pectin in fruit wines and starch in beer or grain wines. They can be cleared by the enzymes that attack them: pectinaze for pectin and amylase for starch.

The Use of Finers

Two things to remember when using any kinds of finers are, first, to forget all you may have read about isinglass, egg-whites and so forth, and buy a properly prepared product and use it in exactly the stated dosage. It will be better and cheaper in the long run. Second, always to rack the fined wine immediately it has cleared and the bulky lees have had time to form a fairly compact layer, otherwise the proteins may start to decompose and give it off-tastes. Even if the finings are added in cask, beer is not in contact with them long enough for this to occur. Bentonite will take longer to settle and since it is inorganic may be left to do so without ill-effects. If too much is used or it is left in the wine for several weeks it may impart an earthy taste such as is sometimes noticeable in the less expensive, bulk-shipped foreign wines.

Fining Beer

There are two main ways of fining beer: one is effected when it is cold, and the second when the wort is boiling.

In the first method, which can be used for every type of brew, a reliable proprietary finer is added as instructed, preferably a few days before the beer is to be bottled and after it has been racked into jars or a carboy; alternatively the finings can be added after the beer has been racked into a cask or pressure barrel, which is then thoroughly agitated to mix them. The bulky lees do not matter so much in cask but are a nuisance if the finings are added just before the beer is bottled. Bentonite is much used on the continent but protein finers are best for home brewers. They are sold either in colloidal form as a thick, almost jelly-like liquid, or dry, to be made up with water. The latter are both cheaper and better, as heat – even a hot summer's day – will cause ready-mixed finings to liquefy and become useless, a process that cannot be reversed by cooling, whereas dry finings can be made up as they are needed.

The second method is to add a small quantity of Irish Moss to the boiling hops and wort usually about fifteen minutes before the end of the boil. This will start the clearing process right away by what is called the 'hot break' or 'copper break' and will continue it later. At least one supplier sells Irish Moss properly compounded with kieselguhr B.P., which helps its action.

Fining Wine, Mead and Cider

Save that these are never fined when hot the same criteria apply as for fining beer, and the main points have already been made. Dry or ready-mixed protein finers, pectinaze and amylase are all sold with full instructions which should be carefully followed. Protein finers work very well but have one drawback in that they react with tannin, remove it all from the wine (all these remarks apply equally to mead and cider) and leave it flat and without zest. White wines are low in tannin and some should be added before they are fined; more should be added to all wines after they have been fined and racked off their lees.

Bentonite does not have this effect and will often clarify wine when everything else has failed, so it is useful to prepare a batch and keep it in store. Unlike proteins it does not deteriorate through heat or any other cause but rather improves with storage. There are many grades, of which best Wyoming is the only one suitable for wine-making. If it is simply mixed with the bulk it will form lumps of useless, apparently insoluble goo. The best method is to make up a 5 per cent dispersion, or mixture, by putting 1 pint of cold, preferably boiled water into a domestic mixer or liquidizer and adding 1 oz of bentonite very gradually to create a thick, creamy slurry free of lumps and of almost the same appearance and consistency as a potter's slip.

Bottle this, leave it for at least twelve hours and always shake the bottle before it is used.

There is little danger of over-fining with bentonite, but as it creates very bulky lees that take some time to settle it is best to use only just enough, usually 1 to 2 teaspoonfuls of the mixture per gallon according to the cloudiness of the wine. The appropriate dose should be beaten up in a pint or so of the wine which is then thoroughly stirred or shaken into the bulk. Bentonite usually acts within forty-eight hours, but if the wine is still hazy after the lees have settled it can be racked off them and treated with a little more.

The same technique should be adopted in adding all types of finers; they should all be most thoroughly dispersed in the bulk after first being beaten up in a small quantity of the wine or beer to be cleared. All instructions stress this.

Filtering

Wine may be filtered if it is to be drunk very soon after fermentation has ceased or if it refuses to clear. Filtering is preferable to fining as it does not remove the tannin, but on the other hand there is some risk of air taint or oxidation owing to the length of time during which the wine is exposed to the air. Various special filters are now sold which are designed to avoid these risks, but rapid filter papers or a filter bag and filter medium are quite adequate for beginners.

Filter Papers

These are circular and either of the laboratory or special rapid types. The first are so slow in action that the wine is exposed to the air for a dangerously long time. The fast papers are excellent for most purposes but if real brilliance is required the first quart of the wine should be thoroughly mixed with 2 teaspoonfuls of bentonite slurry as above or ½ tablespoonful of kieselguhr B.P. filter powder before filtration. The amount depends on the thickness of the wine, but it must be remembered that the filter paper has a very small surface and that too much medium will clog it.

Place a polythene funnel in the neck of a gallon jar and fold a filter paper in half, then in quarters and so forth as shown on the packet, so that when opened up the paper fits the funnel

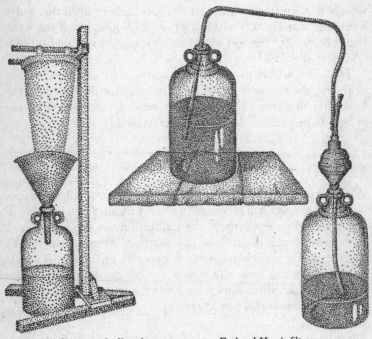

Adjustable filter stand, filter bag, funnel, 1-gallon jar. In use a plastic cover protects the whole apparatus

Enclosed Harris filter

but does not lie flat against its sides. Pour the wine gently into the paper to about ½ inch from the edge. The bentonite or filter powder will build up a layer on the surface of the paper but until this has formed the wine will run cloudy. When it runs quite clear this first filtrate is returned to the bulk for refiltering. During the whole filtering process the wine should be protected by a sheet of paper or transparent plastic laid across the mouth of the funnel.

Filter Bag and Filter Medium

The best method of filtering, excluding perhaps the specially designed apparatus already mentioned, is the use of a filter bag and filter powder. The bag may be of fine nylon or it may be an ordinary jelly-bag such as is used to strain off juice from fruit pulp, used with filter powder. Until fairly recently asbestos pulp was used but this is now suspect as a health risk and most suppliers no longer sell it.

The bag should hold at least 1 gallon and have loops so that it can be suspended as near as possible without touching it to a large funnel inserted in the neck of a gallon jar. To filter a gallon of wine, beat up 3 heaped tablespoonfuls of filter powder very thoroughly in a quart of it, using a properly sterilized domestic mixer or whisk. Pour this into the bag and quickly fill it to within 2 inches of the top with unfiltered wine. This will ensure that the filter medium is distributed throughout the bulk and will form an even layer on the inner surface of the bag as the wine runs out. It will be murky at first but as the layer builds up it will become brilliantly clear. At this point switch the gallon jar for a clean one and return the first filtrate to the bag. A bath board is ideal for this process as there tends to be a small amount of spilth. Once the wine is running clear several more gallons may be filtered without the addition of any more powder.

It is possible to filter small quantities through a funnel in which the filter layer is built up on a cottonwool plug, but this method was more suitable for use with asbestos pulp and even so was very slow and messy. A filter bag is best, preferably suspended from a stand designed so that the whole apparatus can be completely covered and protected from air taint by a large, transparent polythene sack. Kieselguhr filter powder is very cheap but it should be labelled B.P. grade.

Filter bags should be sterilized by being boiled, or moistened with sulphate solution before use and rinsed out and dried before they are put away, or they may develop mould. It is better to filter than to fine but remember that the wine will need several weeks to recover. If neither process clears it and it has no off-flavours or smells such as are caused by metal contamination (casse), it must have a pectin or starch haze that can be treated only by the appropriate enzymes.

Clearing Unfilterable Hazes

Pectin Haze

As already mentioned this is due to an excess of pectin in fruit, especially apples, and vegetables, especially parsnips. The better a fruit gels when made into jam, the more likely it is to develop a pectin haze.

TEST. Put 1 teaspoonful of the hazy wine and 3 of methylated spirits into a small clear glass bottle and shake well. After fifteen minutes or so hold it against the light and if the haze has been caused by pectin, spots or chains of jelly and possibly a white deposit will be seen.

CURE. Use pectinaze or some other form of pectic enzyme formula as directed and the haze should start to disappear within twelve hours if the wine is kept warm.

PREVENTION. Add a pectic enzyme formula such as pectinaze to all fruit and vegetable musts after preparation but before fermentation on the pulp. This will not only prevent pectin haze but also assist juice extraction and fermentation. Never boil pectin-rich fruit or vegetables, as heat not only helps to create the haze but also destroys any natural pectic enzymes that may be present. Chop, mince or crush them well and add the water at not more than fermentation heat – 75 °F (24 °C). Pectic enzymes work best at about this temperature but are destroyed at over 150 °F (67 °C).

Starch Haze

This is caused by an excess of starch in beer through faulty mashing, or more usually in grain or potato wines.

TEST. Carry out an iodine test as explained on p. 115.

CURE. All good stockists sell commercial preparations of the starch-destroying enzyme amylase, and one of these should be used as directed.

PREVENTION. When brewing make sure that the mash has plenty of diastatic content (see Brewing with Malt Grain, p. 114) to convert the starch into fermentable sugar. Starch haze in grain and potato wines can be guarded against to some degree by using as little grain or potato and as much of other ingredients such as raisins, sugar or grape concentrate as possible.

Oxidasic Haze or Darkening

These can occur if over-ripe fruit has been used or if sleepy or bruised portions have not been removed.

TEST. If there is no reaction to the tests for pectin or starch and the wine has no harsh off-taste, the haze is probably oxidasic.

CURE. Sulphite at 50 to 100 ppm (1 or 2 crushed campden tablets per gallon) according to severity.

PREVENTION. The normal addition to any fruit must of 1 crushed campden tablet per gallon twenty-four hours before yeasting and again every time save the first that the wine is racked usually prevents this type of haze from forming.

Casse

A haze, sometimes coloured, caused either by leaving the wine in contact with metal or by metallic salts absorbed from the soil by fruits or berries.

TEST AND ACTION. If there is no reaction to pectin or starch tests or to sulphiting and the wine has a harsh, unpleasant taste it may be suffering from casse. There are tests for iron and other metals but no cures, and as the metallic salts created may be poisonous the wine is best thrown away. The addition of citric acid may cure the haze but not the condition that caused it.

Bacterial Hazes

The types of hazes already dealt with prevent the wine from clearing at any stage. A haze that develops in clear, finished wine at normal temperatures is almost certainly caused by bacteria or other spoilage organisms.

TEST. The home wine-maker has no way of telling what micro-organisms are present, but lactic bacteria are among the most common offenders and these make the wine viscous and give it an unmistakeably oily or ropy appearance, though its taste may not be affected.

CURE. Beat the wine up really well, preferably in a domestic mixer or liquidizer, then add 100 to 150 ppm of sulphite (2 to 3 crushed campden tablets per gallon) according to the severity of the infection, and beat it up again. Return it to the jar, and after a short time the wine should clear and be racked off the lees and filtered or fined. I' the wine is fined it must of course be racked once more, but this, like filtering, will help to dispel the heavy dose of sulphur dioxide that it now contains.

PREVENTION. Proper sulphiting throughout (see under Oxidasic Haze Prevention, above) and an acidity of between pH 3·2 and pH 3·4 as recommended for all wine musts should inhibit the activity of this bacterium, and the scrupulous cleanliness and sterility of all apparatus including bottles and corks are all-important in the prevention of any kind of infection.

Cold Haze

This type of haze is produced when severe cold, as in refrigeration, causes solids which are normally held in solution and help to give body to beer and wine to be thrown into suspension. For this reason commercial bottled beers are chilled and force-filtered before they are bottled.

TEST. Try the hazy beer or wine. If it is good but chilled the haze will have been caused by cold.

CURE. Restore to normal temperature. Wine seldom throws a cold haze but if it does it should be racked off the lees if any have formed.

PREVENTION. Severe fining or filtration would help but might impair the quality of the beer or wine. Tartaric acid should not be used in white wines that are to be drunk chilled.

Bentonite

Many unfilterable and otherwise unfinable hazes will respond to bentonite prepared and used as described on pp. 62 and 63.

Sulphiting

The urgent necessity of sterilizing their fermentation and storage vessels was recognized by the very earliest wine-makers of whose techniques authentic records survive. Although they knew nothing of micro-organisms they quickly learned that their wine-soaked timber, stoneware and leather vessels would spoil any wine contained in them unless they were kept absolutely clean between vintages.

They may have noticed that moulds, the only visually identifiable spoilage organisms, did not grow on certain substances, but whatever it was that gave them the necessary clues the Greeks impregnated their goatskin winesacks with resin and the Romans coated their containers with pitch, both of which inhibited bacterial growth. The next advance was the discovery of the power of sulphur fumes to sterilize spots that could not be reached by other means. The wine-makers used to burn the sulphur in cressets in the great fermentation vats or in iron spoons poked through the bungholes of casks and barrels so that the fumes impregnated the wood and sterilized it. The fact that some remained to be absorbed into the must helped to make it resistant to moulds and wild yeasts but unfortunately the process could also result in raw, molten sulphur spilling into the storage vessels and remaining there to produce in the wine a proportion of dissolved hydrogen sulphide, the 'sulphuretted hydrogen' used in stink bombs. Wine was therefore *chambré* or opened and allowed to 'breathe' at room temperature for some time so that the volatile gas could escape, and though modern vintners employ less rugged techniques to sterilize their containers this still remains the best way of serving red wines.

Today both professionals and amateurs use the sulphur dioxide gas given off when sodium metabisulphite is dissolved in water and a little acid to sterilize all vessels and equipment, while the amateur also uses sodium metabisulphite in the form of the well-known campden tablets or crystals to sterilize the must. One or two standard 7 grain (0·44 gr.) campden tablets in one gallon of must give exactly the right strengths of 50 or 100 ppm (parts per million). Fortunately the gas given off is highly volatile, and after twenty-four hours the must or pulped fruit to be fermented is both sterile and free of sulphur dioxide and is ready to receive the yeast. This process is known as sulphiting. Because the efficacy of the sulphite increases according to the acidity of the medium in which it works, 1 campden tablet per gallon is usually sufficient for the musts of acid fruits such as sloes, lemons, gooseberries, rowanberries, elderberries and garden black-currants, while stone fruits, the milder berries such as raspberries, loganberries and blackberries, and apples and grapes may need 1½ or even 2. Flowers and leaves have very low acidity, as have ripe pears, and especial care should be taken to sterilize the musts made from them. The acid content of fruits varies so very widely according to the amount of sunshine and warmth they have experienced that no tables can be reliable, and it is always best to adjust the acidity of the must to between pH 3 and pH 3·5 (just over pH 3 on the pH comparison paper is near enough) by the addition of water or acid and to add 1 tablet, or 2 if the fruit is bruised or otherwise in bad condition. If the must is diluted by the addition of more water at any stage the acidity should be checked again and readjusted.

Over the centuries during which sulphur in one form or another has been used in wine-making, true wine yeasts have built up a considerable tolerance for it and concentrations of from 50 to 100 ppm which will effectively kill or inhibit the growth of most bacteria, moulds and wild yeasts serve only to slow up the growth of wine yeasts until the volatile gas has evaporated out of the must. Towards the end of a fermentation, however, when most of the sugar on which the yeast feeds has been used up and it has been further weakened by its struggle to survive the resultant high concentration of alcohol, the addition of one campden tablet to each gallon of wine will effectively prevent further fermentation. If the jar is then stoppered or the wine bottled, a small quantity of sulphur dioxide will remain in the wine and help to preserve it and stabilize it against the sometimes disastrous secondary fermentation in bottle that can otherwise occur in hot weather. Fortunately sulphur dioxide does not possess the nauseating smell of the hydrogen sulphide which is released by free sulphur, and any slight odour will vanish if red wines are *chambré* and white wines are chilled.

It is also advisable to sulphite at the rate of 1 campden tablet or its equivalent per gallon every time the wine is racked, for this not only inhibits the growth of any airborne spoilage organisms that may have been picked up during the siphoning process but also allows the sulphite to confer other benefits on the wine, including added smoothness, better colour and improved clarity. Fermentation in the presence of sulphite induces the yeast to produce a larger proportion of glycerine (glycerol is a member of the alcohol group) which renders the wine smooth, helps to give it body and acts as a buffer against minor harshnesses. Oxidation through exposure to light or by other means causes red wines to lose their clear colour and to become brownish and dull, but sulphite is an anti-oxidant and not only prevents this but improves the colour of both red and white wines. Sulphite also hastens and improves the clarification of wine through its ability to alter the electrical charges of certain minute particles that cause haze, thus allowing them to precipitate out.

Handy though campden tablets are in supplying the correct dosage they are difficult to dissolve and should always be crushed in a little of the must or wine before they are added to the bulk; the butt-end of a plastic-handled table knife and an egg-cup make a good pestle and mortar for this job. If wine-making is to be undertaken on any considerable scale it is much easier to use the sulphite in solution. To make a 10 per cent solution dissolve 1 lb of sodium metabisulphite crystals of B.P. grade in $\frac{1}{2}$ gallon of warm water, and when they are completely dissolved make the volume up to 1 gallon with cold water and stopper the container tightly. Use this, or any smaller quantity prepared in the same proportions, as a stock bottle, drawing off the solution as required. The addition of up to 4 oz per gallon of citric acid increases the sterilizing power of the sulphite but greatly diminishes its keeping qualities, so up to $\frac{1}{2}$ oz of acid may be dissolved in every pint drawn off; but acid must never be added to the stock bottle especially as this solution will also be used for adding to the must. 5 ml (1 teaspoonful) of 10 per cent solution is the equivalent of 1 campden tablet. The 10 per cent solution diluted with its own volume of water is still a more than adequately strong sterilizer and is more pleasant to work with, but the weaker the solution is, especially when it is acidified, the shorter the period for which it will keep. It can be diluted yet once more to a $2\frac{1}{2}$ per cent solution for use in fermentation locks to ensure the sterility of the liquid which is in direct contact with the air in the fermentation vessel; it is a mistake to use too strong a solution as the slight vacuum created in the jar by the extraction of the pierced bung and lock may cause the liquid to be sucked back into the must.

In brief, the campden tablet or its equivalent in sodium metabisulphite crystals is an absolutely necessary part of the amateur wine-maker's equipment. Some professional brewers use a similar technique but the home brewer can forget sulphiting save for the sterilization of equipment. The fermentation of beer is so quickly over and the beer drunk so soon afterwards that the resins of the hop are perfectly adequate preservatives.

Section II

HOME BREWING

8

THE HISTORY OF
HOME BREWING

I have fed purely upon ale; I have eat
my ale, drank my ale, and I always
sleep upon ale.
– George Farquhar: *The Beaux' Stratagem*

The origins of brewing are lost in the mists of prehistory, but
man seems to have devised some method of producing alcoholic liquor from grain at least as soon as he learned to cultivate
crops and settled down to look after them and to leave evidence
of his early skill in his kitchen middens. In early times all brewing was of course carried out at home or, as in the case of some
African tribes today, as a communal undertaking.

Archaeologists who have deciphered early Sumerian writings
believe that brewing began between the valleys of the Euphrates
and the Tigris and that ale was drunk in Babylon well over
6,000 years ago. Whether the Sumerians passed the craft on to
the ancient Egyptians or not, there is evidence that they were
brewing a thousand years or so later, and it is certain that both
these great nations integrated ale and brewing into their
religions and their class structures and that by 2,000 B.C. they
had both developed laws to regulate the management of ale-
houses and breweries and the quality of the beer that they
sold.

History records that the Babylonians had almost as many
different types of beers as we have, but it was the Egyptians
who introduced the use of bitter herbs, possibly including hops,

to counteract the mawkish sweetness of ale brewed solely from grain and to improve its keeping qualities. All early brewers probably used any grain that was to hand, but the Egyptians certainly brewed with barley and experts now believe that they were the first to cultivate it. One of the first fermented drinks resembling ale was made by soaking a kind of leavened bread in water mixed with honey and spices. This handy method of brewing is still used by the Egyptian fellaheen. Though the name of the brew is *boozah* it seems to have no etymological connection with our word booze, which derives from the Middle English *bousen*.

The Egyptians passed on their knowledge of brewing to the Hebrews and Greeks; the Romans inherited the technique from them, and classical literature is full of references to brewing and beer, of which incidentally Lucullus thought highly. The Romans are said to have brewed with hops and to have introduced hopped beer into Britain during their occupation, and one of the Latin words for beer, *cerevisia*, has been perpetuated in the universal name for brewer's yeast, *saccharomyces var. cerevisiae*.

Whether or not the Romans brought us the hop they certainly found plenty of unhopped ale when they arrived here in 54 B.C., for the Britons, the Picts and the Scots had been brewing from time immemorial and the Druids had already been recognized as masters of the craft, an example to be followed devoutly by later priesthoods. In the first century A.D. a Greek writer referred to British ale in anything but enthusiastic terms and described it as being made from wheat, but five hundred years later we were certainly growing barley specifically for brewing, and well before the Norman conquest the alehouse was a familiar feature of the British scene. The first inns developed naturally from the then universal practice of home brewing; a brewer, or more probably a brewster, would become locally celebrated for his or her skill and would find that while a big brew took little more time or trouble than a small one the surplus could be profitably sold to neighbours. In those insanitary days brewing must have been a pretty chancy business, and other things being equal the cleanest house would most consistently produce the best ale.

During the Middle Ages many civilized arts and crafts not directly connected with war or religion declined to vanishing-point but brewing was not allowed to die out. In England honey was used to strengthen and sweeten ale as it had been in Egypt, Greece and Rome, and a heavily spiced Welsh ale was popular until it was enacted in 1484 that ale should be brewed only from malt, water and yeast and the use of honey was banned. It is worth noting that certain restrictions on home brewing were enforced in feudal times: in England villeins had to pay a tax to their lords for permission to brew, and in some parts of Europe the monasteries had established a monopoly and forbade anyone to brew at home while the monks had any ale to sell. The first national tax to affect brewers was imposed by Henry II in 1188 to finance a crusade; this exacted the value of one tenth of all moveables including the equipment of brewers whether private or otherwise.

In the fourteenth century alehouses were still natural extensions of home brewing; innkeepers who brewed their own ale could sell it almost without restriction whereas those who bought theirs from breweries were permitted to sell it only to resident guests to be drunk on the premises. At the beginning of the fifteenth century the importation of hopped ale, or beer as it was called, from the Low Countries signalled both a historic point in the development of British brewing and the start of a century of violent controversy between beer-lovers, supported by returning troops who had become addicted to it in Flanders, and the ale faction, who referred to the hop as a poisonous and noxious weed. It has been alleged that the anti-hop campaign was organized by powerful politicians who had a vested interest in the sale of gruit, a herbal compound based on bog-myrtle and extensively used for flavouring ale. Whether this was so or not, hops themselves were not imported for another fifty years although beer was already becoming well liked. Long before this, beer, meaning ale brewed with hops, had become clearly differentiated from any other malt brew; the word itself had existed in Old English as *beor* and in Middle English as *bere*, but after apparently dropping out of the language was returned to us via the German and Dutch *bier* by the troops returning from the Low Countries after the Hundred Years War. The Old English *ealu*, for ale, was of equal antiquity but had its origins in Scandinavia and the Slavic countries, whereas the roots of *beor* were Germanic.

Whatever the other reasons for the long fight against the hop, there must have been a great reluctance among the common people to allow this foreign herb to oust their beloved ale, for it had always been intimately associated with every joyful occasion in their remarkably bleak lives. All drinking parties and celebrations were 'ales' and many of them used to be held in the churches, which were at that time the usual sites for social gatherings. There were church-ales, bid-ales, Whitsun-ales and in fact 'ales' for every kind of occasion, and it should be stressed that the word simply meant a function at which ale was drunk, and not a different type of brew for each. Some of these meetings, such as give-ales, were for raising funds, and a scot-ale was a medieval bottle-party to which everyone had to make his 'scot', or contribution. This has given us the phrases 'scot-free' and 'to pay one's shot', while bride-ale has become 'bridal'.

Various governments tried for hundreds of years to put a stop to 'ales', but with the support of the church, which profited by them, they managed to survive until their final suppression by Oliver Cromwell gave rise to the heartfelt cry: 'Shall there be no more cakes and ale?'

During the fifteenth century the commercial brewers of both ale and beer were officially recognized; the former received their Royal charter in 1437 and the latter in 1493. Since 1484 ale brewers had been forbidden by law to use anything but malt, water and yeast, but none of these things affected home brewers, who still produced by far the greater volume of ale and beer. By the close of the century the number of ale conners, or ale tasters as they were called outside London, had greatly increased. They wore leathern breeches and for one of their tests they sat unmoving for half an hour in a puddle of ale or beer spilled on the head of a cask. If their breeches stuck to the wood when they got up they condemned the beer because its malt sugar content showed that it had not been properly fermented and was deficient in alcohol. Lay writers delight to describe this test but usually wrongly, owing to their belief that the stickier the ale was the stronger it must have been.

Hops were first planted in Kent in 1524 and surviving records show that they were very soon used by home brewers, who could now brew in larger quantities and therefore more economically, since the hopped brew kept far longer than ale. Commercial brewing benefited from the incursion of highly skilled monks after the dissolution of the monasteries, and breweries, inns and alehouses proliferated. During the ensuing centuries the continuing growth of commercial brewing reaped the usual crop of new laws and taxes and the increased cost of beer which resulted was a great stimulus to home brewing.

The eighteenth century saw the introduction of isinglass finings, the thermometer and the hydrometer, but the home brewer or brewster and the alewife still judged mashing temperatures by the length of time a hand could stay in the water, by watching its surface as it came off the boil until it was tranquil enough to give an unbroken reflection, or by mixing given proportions of cold and boiling water as is often done today. Fermentation temperature was assessed by the finger or elbow and the gravity and strength of the wort by tasting it.

The Industrial Revolution struck a serious blow at all the traditional rural skills including home brewing and wine-making, and early in the nineteenth century the number of breweries had enormously increased and the malpractices of some of them caused the passing of the Act of 1816 which ruled once again that the only ingredients were to be malt, hops, water and yeast. It was not until 1847 that another Act permitted the use of sugar. William Cobbett inveighed against 'the intoxicating and stupefactive compositions of the porter

quacks and beer doctors' which were ruining the health of the
public, and later, in 1821, he wrote:

> To show Englishmen, forty years ago, that it was good for them to
> brew beer in their own houses, would have been as impertinent as
> gravely to insist that they ought to endeavour not to lose their
> breath; for in those times, to have a *house* and not to brew was a rare
> thing indeed.

At the time he wrote, home brewing still accounted for about
half the beer drunk in Britain, but thereafter its decline was
rapid and in 1830 the proportion was estimated as one fifth.
Even so, the brewers were already demanding that home brewing should be taxed, and in 1880 Mr Gladstone's Inland
Revenue Act brought this about. Its results on the home
brewer were described in the chapter on legality, but it had
two other important sections, one of which permitted commercial brewers to use any ingredients they chose as long as they
were not poisonous while the other established the system, still
in use, of calculating taxation on the original gravity of the
wort before fermentation, not, as is so often thought, on the
alcoholic strength of the finished beer.

Thus began the eighty-three dark years that temporarily
extinguished home brewing. From the date of the Act to the
present day taxation has caused the price of a pint of commercial beer to rise on average by well over 2,000 per cent (from
about ½p to 14p) while at the same time its average strength has
plummeted from nearly 7½ per cent alcohol by volume to
about 3½ per cent – a drop of over 50 per cent. The result is,
of course, that home-brewed beer is not only infinitely cheaper
and better but also far easier to brew, for it easily withstands
invasion by wild yeasts and other spoilage organisms from which
the commercial brewer is finding it more and more difficult
to protect his weaker brew. He deserves our sympathy, not our
blame, but it is interesting to reflect that much of the 'pub
beer' that we drink today has almost precisely the alcoholic
content of the 'near-beer' that was the first drink Americans
were allowed towards the end of prohibition.

From 1963, the year in which home brewing was freed from taxation, the craft has flourished. At first the public either could not believe that it was legal or were unable to find out how to brew or could not find the necessary ingredients, but gradually all these difficulties were overcome, until today practically all the materials used by breweries are put up in small quantities for the home brewer and available almost everywhere, and there are also canned 'instant beer' compounds and many items of equipment specially produced for him, even to thermostatically controlled heaters and pressure containers with carbon dioxide injectors.

The equipment takes up only the space needed for an ordinary dustbin, the best wort concentrates can be prepared in a few minutes, and their fermentation produces very little smell, so that every year more and more people are becoming home brewers. Thanks to sensible legislation Britain is far ahead of the rest of the world in both the techniques and the merchandise of the craft and is building up a flourishing export trade with all countries in which home brewing is lawful.

9

MALT AND HOPS

Malt does more than Milton can
To justify God's ways to man.
– A. E. Housman:
A Shropshire Lad

Malt

All true beers are based on malted grain and though most
grains can be, and are, malted, the word 'malt' by itself now
refers only to malted barley. The object of malting is to render
the contents of the barleycorn soluble and fermentable. The
barley is first cleaned by being sieved and is then dried gently
and stored for some weeks to prepare the dormant grain for
sprouting. It is next steeped for two days or more in several
changes of water, after which it is spread out in a thick layer
on the malting floor to 'chit' or sprout, for it is during germina-
tion that the enzymes which render the contents of the grain
soluble and fermentable are produced or activated.

This process continues for a week or more, during which the
temperature and humidity of the sprouting barley are carefully
controlled by the maltsters. By this time the acrospire (leaflet)
has reached about three quarters the length of the grain and the
heat is now increased so that it withers and growth is stopped.
After about twelve days in all the 'green malt' is moved to
kilns, where it is first dried slowly for some days after which the
heat is raised to complete the process. The degree of heat
applied depends on the colour required; the minimum necessary, some 200 °F (93–94 °C), is used for lager malt and for the

pale malt which is the base of nearly all beers, while increasing temperatures produce amber, crystal, brown and black malts. The darker the malt the less fermentables it yields and the fewer of its enzymes remain active. The darker malts are valuable mainly for the colour and flavour that they impart and 'patent black' malt, which is heated almost to combustion point, was originally developed and patented solely as a colouring agent.

After the malt has been kilned the rootlets are sieved off and it is stored for a while in sealed bins before being milled, or lightly cracked between steel rollers. This is the final process, and the grist, as it has now become, is ready for the mash tun.

The malting process seems fairly simple on the face of it and has been carried out in all parts of the world for thousands of years. The ancient Egyptians malted their brewing grains and to this day the most remote and primitive African tribes steep their maize or millet and carry out a crude but effective kilning with the aid of hot stones. Yet the underlying principles of malting, depending as they do on the complex reactions of enzymes whose very existence was undreamed of until the nineteenth century, could not possibly have been known to them. One can only surmise that in every case it was found that sprouting grain was pleasantly sweet and crisp to eat when partially roasted, and later that the roasted grain would ferment if left in warm water.

The enzymes produced during the malting process include cytase, which attacks the cellulose walls of the starch granules in the barley thus freeing the starch together with the diastase which converts it into fermentable sugar (maltose) and dextrins. When the malt is mashed the enzymes of the yeast take over and convert the maltose into alcohol and carbon dioxide gas, and the dextrins help to give body and flavour to the brew.

Hops

The history of the hop since its introduction to Britain is virtually the history of British beer. The hop plant, or bine, is a strong climber and is grown in the hop gardens of Kent, Worcestershire and Herefordshire on a framework of wire and twine stretched between tall poles. There are both male and female plants, and only the cones, or flowers, of the female plant are used by the brewer. In warmer countries no male hops are planted as the seeds of the fertilized female plant are not wanted by the brewer, but because fertilization gives protection against ailments to which hops are prone in damp climates such as ours a few males are set to windward of each English hop garden to pollinate it.

When the cones have been stripped from the bines they are dried, packed tightly into very large sacks called hop pockets and kept in cold storage and in the dark, for strong light soon oxidizes hops and turns the delicate primrose-green of the flowers to brown.

The main function of the hop is to give flavour and aroma to the beer by its bitter resins and its fragrant essential oils. Almost equally important are the preservative qualities of the resins (humulon and lupulon) and their ability to promote both clarification and good head retention.

For the last century or so practically all the hops grown in England have been goldings or fuggles or varieties of them. Goldings are principally used for light ale, pale ale and bitter, in which their delicate flavour and aroma can be appreciated to the fullest advantage, whereas fuggles are more suitable for mild ale, brown ale and stout. Northern brewer is a type of hop used in strong, dry stout and in blends for lager when imported hops are unobtainable. It is a very bitter hop and in use is roughly equivalent to twice its weight in fuggles. Other very bitter types used in blending are bullion and brewer's gold. Among the best-known varieties of goldings are East Kent and Whitbread; the former is sometimes specified in recipes as E.K.G.

To brew a typical continental lager it is best to use not only a proper lager yeast but also imported hops grown for the purpose, of which the best known are Styrian goldings, Hallertauers and Saaz. The better suppliers stock all or most of the hops named above with the possible exceptions of Saaz, brewer's gold and bullion. English goldings with a touch of northern brewer will produce a very pleasant lager if imported hops are not available.

When buying hops first look at the label, which should tell you the weight of the contents and the type of hop and should carry some assurance that they are from the latest available crop. Owing to the complexities of the hop market and the fact that hops of one year's crop are never on sale until the next year dating presents difficulties but the legend 'latest crop' on a sealed pack put up by a reputable supplier should be sufficient. Next look at the colour, which should be pale primrose. Retailers like hops to be put up in transparent polythene packs so that the customer can see what he is buying, but on the other hand hops should be kept in the dark to avoid discoloration through oxidation; but if the shopkeeper has been careless and the outer layer is faintly browned this will make no appreciable difference to the brew. If the hops are badly discoloured refuse them. When the expert chooses hops he rubs a handful from the hop pocket between his hands, sniffs their aroma and notes the amount of resins adhering to his palms as sticky, golden dust. The home brewer buying a small packet cannot do this but he should count his blessings; for some years after 1963, when home brewing was made legal, most of the few retailers in the business sold imported, compressed hops having much the colour and fragrance of brown paper, and it was some time before named hops warranted from the latest crop appeared on the market.

Various forms of 'instant hop' have been sold for many years, including hop extract containing both the resins and essential oils of the hop; hop essence or hop oil, a distillate of the essential oils used for imparting extra aroma before the beer is racked into casks or bottled; and several kinds of dehydrated and powdered hops which, though widely used by breweries especially on the continent, are difficult to pack or store in small quantities for the home-brewing trade. Hop extracts must be boiled with the wort in the same way as hops.

It will be noticed that a teaspoon used for measuring hop extract is difficult to clean owing to the thin film of extract adhering closely to it, and care must be taken to ensure that the extracts are not wasted by being left clinging in the same way to the sides of the boiler. Only a very small amount is used, and this should be added drop by drop to a quart or so of the wort while this is being vigorously agitated with a fork. The wort and extract should then be poured back into the bulk, without being allowed to settle, and briskly stirred into it. Hop essence is used at the rate of only 1 drop per gallon or thereabouts, but even so the same procedure should be adopted.

The proper method of adding hops to a brew is to boil them briskly in the wort for an hour or more, adding a small proportion near the end of the boil for the sake of the essential oils, most of which have been boiled out of the main batch. Another method that is sometimes advocated involves the making of an infusion in water, either by boiling the hops for 20 to 30 minutes or by pouring boiling water over them and leaving them to infuse in a closed vessel for 10 minutes. In the first case the boiling liquid is usually strained on to malt extract and sugar, after which the hops are boiled once more in some fresh water and the process is repeated. In the second the 'hop tea' is poured off and set aside while the hops are boiled with the wort in the usual way to extract the resins. The liquid is added later when the wort has cooled, and 'hop tea' protagonists contend that in this way all the essential oils are preserved.

No subject can provoke more passionate argument between home brewers than the merits of these 'hop tea' methods versus orthodox boiling. Brewing theory supports boiling, if only because all worts which include malt extracts should be boiled, but in practice both methods seem to produce excellent beer.

10

METHODS OF
HOME BREWING

> Blessing of your heart, you brew good ale.
> – Shakespeare : *The Two Gentlemen of Verona*

Brewing from Beer Kits and Cans

In the early nineteen-sixties, when the renaissance of home
brewing in Britain was just beginning after more than eighty
years of legal proscription, it was no easy matter for anyone
outside the trade to assemble all the necessary ingredients,
reliable instruction manuals were still virtually unobtainable,
and canned concentrates for the amateur were yet to be evolved.
For the beginner, the only way out of all these difficulties was
to buy a beer kit.

Beer Kits

Such kits are called 'box kits' or 'dry kits' to differentiate them
from canned compounds, and are still sold by the thousand.
They are now attractively packed and widely advertised and
range from well-balanced selections of sound ingredients
accompanied by simple, well-thought-out instructions to sad
mixtures of aged hops and stale, cracked malt all jumbled
together in ill-sealed bags and partnered by twists of baker's
yeast and instructions whose incomprehensibility is equalled
only by their optimism. Good or bad, they are usually designed
to make either 2 gallons (16 pints) or 5 gallons (40 pints) of

home brew and will contain some or all of the following ingredients and additives:

A can of malt extract or packet of dry malt extract
A bag of whole or crushed malt grains
Hops either in a separate bag or mixed with the malt, or in the best kits put up ready for boiling in a muslin bag which in turn should be enclosed in a polythene bag with its mouth properly sealed, not just tied up
Beer yeast, but this is sometimes baker's yeast
Some kits contain also yeast nutrient and beer finings or brewing salts (usually a compound of nutrient, water conditioning salts, acid, etc.) and combined headers and finers. Glucose polymer may also be included to add body to the brew.
Full instructions should be included in all kits.

The use of a beer kit of this type demands almost as much work as full-scale brewing for the malt extract, malt grains and hops have first to be boiled together in a vessel holding at least a gallon for about 45 minutes, after which the hops and the remains of the malt grains must be carefully strained off and the wort poured into the fermenting bin. Hot water is then poured over the hops and grains which have been put into a straining bag or nylon sieve to extract the last of the wort. This also goes into the fermenting vessel and the specified amount of sugar or glucose chips is dissolved in the hot wort, after which cold water is added as instructed until the right volume, temperature and gravity are arrived at. The instructions should be so specific that there is no need to use a hydrometer to ascertain the gravity of the wort.

The yeast and other additives are now stirred in and the fermentation, racking and bottling carried out as instructed.

Canned Worts and Extracts

The nearest thing to instant beer is a can of concentrated wort compounded to produce a named type of beer after simply dissolving it in hot water, adding cold water and sugar or glucose chips according to instructions and then fermenting it with beer yeast. Concentrates of this kind are made by boiling the wort with the hops, dehydrating it until only 18 to 20 per cent of its water content remains and then canning it. Other kinds of canned concentrates are compounded from malt extract mixed with hop extract and are often coloured and flavoured to produce different types of beers. Both usually offer a choice of lager, light ale, bitter, brown ale and stout and are supplied in sizes which will make either 2-gallon (16 pints) or 4- to 5-gallon (32 to 40 pints) brews, and both can make excellent beer. The worts have been boiled with the hops and are therefore sterile, while the hopped malt extracts should be boiled before fermentation. Worts are usually described as such on the label.

There can be no doubt that both for the totally inexperienced home brewer and for the expert with no time to spare a can of a well-formulated wort concentrate such as Brucan is preferable to any boxed kit. This is not to say that every can will produce better beer than any kit, but a reliable canned concentrate is not only cheaper but so much simpler in use that the beginner is more likely to get good results from it than from a kit the contents of which have to be boiled, strained and in fact subjected to all the processes of normal brewing save the mashing of the malt. These entail at least an hour of hot kitchen work, as against the fifteen minutes of preparation needed by a canned wort concentrate.

Choosing Kits and Cans

Both kits and canned, preformulated extracts are stocked by specialist suppliers, multiple stores, chemists, health food stores, grocers and other shops. The beginner's first purchase is best made from either a specialist shop or some other store making a feature of home brewing and wine-making, for either of these will not only offer the widest range of reliable kits and cans and all the necessary equipment but will also provide helpful and friendly advice. It is worth remembering that this will be given all the more willingly and at greater length if it is not sought at the busiest time of the day or two minutes before closing time.

Prices of different brands to make the same gallonage of beer vary quite widely. The price of the kit or can is by no means an infallible guide to quality, but all those that you will find in the type of shop indicated will make drinkable beer, and only experience can show which you prefer. Having made your choice make sure before you leave the shop that you understand the instructions and have the necessary equipment, campden tablets, yeast and other additives. Other things being equal, a can incorporating the word 'wort' on the label is usually the best choice.

Equipment

The beginner will find that one of the greatest advantages of starting to brew from kits or with canned, preformulated concentrates is that very little special equipment is needed and its cost is negligible. Much of it is usually already to be found in the kitchen. Another great saving is that practically all the necessary ingredients are provided so that nothing has to be bought in excess of what is to be used immediately and there is therefore no wastage.

The necessary items of equipment are:

Fermentation Vessels

The best, cheapest and easiest to find are buckets or bins of white or light-coloured polythene. Avoid dark colours, especially grey or black, as some of these contain materials that can affect the brew. All fermentation vessels should have close-fitting lids; buckets can usually be found with deep, flanged lids and bins with covers that lock on with a twist. The capacity of the container can either be slightly larger than that of the intended brew to allow for the yeast head, or the brew can be made using all the ingredients but with about half a gallon less water for a two-gallon brew, or one gallon less for a four- or five-gallon brew, and topped up with the required amount after the first

Polythene fermentation bin

violent fermentation is over. Many expert brewers prefer the latter method as this ensures the smallest possible air space during most of the time that the brew is in the fermenting vessel, but given well-fitting lids the risk of air-borne contamination is so slight that either method will do.

Boiler

If concentrated brewer's worts are used no boiler is necessary, but for kits or for malt extracts that must be boiled any really clean or grease-free saucepan or fish-kettle holding a gallon or more is suitable.

Stirrer

A great deal of stirring is necessary when the concentrate and the sugar or glucose chippings are being dissolved in the water and later when the yeast and other additives are mixed in, so that a good, long, non-metallic stirrer is needed right from the start.

Siphon

This is used to rack the beer, that is to say to transfer it into another vessel to settle further, or directly into casks or bottles, without disturbing the yeast sediment. A yard or so of food grade, non-toxic polythene tubing or an automatic siphon pump will answer the purpose excellently. Both should be fitted with U-tubes.

Funnels

White polythene are best and cheapest. The handiest sizes for

Polythene funnel

brewing and wine-making are 8½ inches for pouring into jars and larger vessels and 5½ inches for bottling.

Thermometer

No other measuring instruments are needed at this stage; a hydrometer, for example, is unnecessary because if the instructions are followed carefully the gravity of the wort must be correct, but the success of a brew depends so much on the temperatures at which the yeast is added and at which the beer is kept at subsequent stages that a thermometer is a good investment.

Bottles and Barrels

See the sections on bottling, p. 132, casks, p. 140, and other dispensers, p. 138. It would clearly be rather extravagant to buy pressure barrels or other dispensers to receive your first, trial brew, and oak casks are not to be recommended for beginners unless they have experienced friends to advise them on preparation and maintenance, so bottles are the answer. Bottling and the various types of closures available are fully explained elsewhere. Here again the cheapest method is the best to start with, provided that it is also safe and efficient, and this means proper beer or cider bottles either of the now almost obsolete screw-stopper type or crown-cork bottles which can be stoppered with very cheap, deep-dome polythene pressure caps applied by hand. Metal crown caps need capping tools and are not necessary at this stage.

Additives

Additives are all those substances that have to be put into the concentrate in order to cause or promote fermentation, increase alcoholic strength, speed up the clearing process, aid the retention of a good head and in any way improve the final product. The two basic necessities are of course water and yeast, and unless an uneconomical and indeed normally unnecessary amount of concentrate is used some form of sugar is also needed. A one-pound can of good concentrate contains the necessary malt and hops for two gallons of beer, but the sugar content of the malt when fermented would produce only about 2 per cent alcohol by volume, a very wishy-washy brew. The home brewer usually aims at 4 to 6 per cent, and the addition of sugar or glucose chips provides the extra alcohol.

Yeast

Chapters 3 and 4, on yeast and fermentation, explain the way in which the yeast cell converts sugar into alcohol and describe the varieties of yeast used by brewers and wine-makers. For the concentrate it is best to buy a sealed packet of granulated beer yeast, making sure that it is clearly labelled as such and is not in fact granulated baker's yeast. A good granular beer yeast starts quickly and strongly and is the best choice for a beginner; liquid cultures and tablet yeasts are quite satisfactory if used with a starter bottle (see p. 54) but are slower to act. Lager requires a bottom-fermenting yeast if it is to be made in the approved manner and lager yeast cultures are usually sold in liquid or tablet form. Although there are very good lager concentrates it is better to start with one of the other varieties, as lager should really be fermented at low temperature under fermentation lock and this takes longer than ordinary brewing and is rather more complicated. Be sure to use enough yeast to start the brew fermenting quickly; a quarter of an ounce of a good granulated beer yeast is enough for a two-gallon brew and half an ounce for a four- or five-gallon batch.

Sugars

Most instructions specify ordinary household granulated sugar. This is perfectly satisfactory for a first brew and indeed many home brewers use it exclusively, but glucose chippings ferment more quickly and produce better beers, free from the slight 'cidery' taste that ordinary sugars sometimes give. Brown sugar is sometimes specified for brown ale and stout.

Water

The professional brewer's name for water is 'liquor', and as explained in Chapter 5 its hardness or softness, in other words its mineral content, is of the utmost importance to him, but for the beginner it is simply what comes out of the tap. All water used for home brewing from kits and cans should in theory be boiled first to sterilize it but needless to say it seldom is, nor do most instructions demand that it should be.

Other Additives

Clear instructions will be given by the manufacturers if additives other than water, sugar or glucose chippings, and yeast are to be used. Very good beer can be made with these three basics and a well-formulated concentrate, but there is no doubt that if it can be managed without too much additional cost or complication the addition of several other harmless substances can cut fermentation time and improve the product.

They include yeast nutrient salts, vitamins, in some cases a trace of acid to speed the ferment, and finings to make the finished beer drop clear more quickly. Water-conditioning salts, usually based on the natural mineral content of the famous Burton-on-Trent water, can certainly improve the brew, heading liquid or powder will help it to retain a creamy head and glucose polymer will add body. Some or all of these may be incorporated in the canned concentrate itself or they may be offered in separate packs as optional extras. One supplier compounds nutrient salts, acid, vitamin B and water conditioner in one packet as 'brewing salts' and headers and finers in another, both put up in the right quantities for 2- or 4- to 5-gallon brews.

Procedure

Sterilization

Make up a stock bottle of sterilizing fluid from some of the campden tablets as instructed. Wash all equipment and containers with clean hot water, using soda if necessary but no detergents, then rinse or wipe them with sterilizing fluid. Disposable kitchen paper or tissues are excellent for wiping and for swabbing working surfaces. Rinse the sterilizer out of containers with clean cold water before using them.

Preparation of the Wort

Whatever the concentrate its preparation will be even simpler than the instructions suggest. These vary slightly for different brands but the processes are substantially the same from opening the can to 'pitching' (adding yeast), and the instructions might well read:

Remove the wrapper on which the instructions are printed from the can, for reference.

Warm the can in hot water so that the contents will pour more easily. (This is especially important when using high-concentrate brewer's worts.)

Open the can and pour the contents into the fermentation vessel.

Add a given amount of hot or boiling water and stir well.

Add the sugar or glucose chippings and stir until dissolved.

Add a given quantity of cold water and stir again. (The proportions of hot and cold water should be calculated by the manufacturers to bring the wort to the volume required at a temperature of about 70–5 °F, 21–4 °C.)

Cream the yeast, if granulated, in a little of the wort; add this and stir in well. Alternatively add the contents of the activated starter bottle if a liquid culture has been used.

Stir in any additives to be used at this stage, such as yeast nutrient or brewing salts.

Leave the wort in the closely covered fermentation vessel in a warm place for a week, or until the fermentation is quite finished.

From opening the can to pitching with yeast and leaving the wort to ferment, in other words the entire preparation, should have taken between fifteen and twenty minutes. The next stage is bottling, and if the instructions given on the can are not perfectly clear the procedure described in the next chapter, Bottling and Storage, should be followed.

The beer should be crystal clear and ready to drink in two to three weeks from bottling. Later on the admittedly laborious chore of washing, sterilizing, rinsing, filling and capping bottles can be avoided by using pressure vessels or other types of dispensers.

Brewing with Malt Extracts

It was pointed out earlier that whereas wort concentrates are sterile it is advisable to boil other malt extracts to sterilize them. Since the method of brewing to be described in this section involves boiling in every case there will be no need to differentiate between them.

Ingredients

Malt Extracts

It is a very simple matter to make really excellent beer from malt extracts and many types are now sold specifically for home brewing in cans or other packs containing from 1 lb to 56 lb. Extracts in both syrup and dry forms are prepared in various shades and flavours to make suitable bases for most kinds of beers and stouts; the darker dried extracts are sometimes described as caramelized. Dried extracts are rather dearer than syrups but, as the latter normally contain about 20 per cent water, that much less by weight is needed when the dry extracts are used. The term 'malt extract' will always indicate syrup unless dried extract is specifically called for.

Some syrups are described as diastatic. This refers to their power to render starchy additives fermentable during mashing, but as this process is not employed when brewing from extracts alone it makes no difference at this stage whether the extract is diastatic or not.

The chief difference between brewing with malt extracts and the use of preformulated concentrates is that the hops and other ingredients are not already included and have to be added to the wort, but the amateur who wants to develop distinctive brews to suit his own taste will not begrudge the extra time and work entailed. Some advanced amateur brewers still affect to look down on anyone who does not brew exclusively from malt grain but all professional breweries use large quantities of extracts, partly to help them maintain the standard and volume of their output at times when malting barley is scarce or of poor quality.

The main functions of malt extract are to help determine the character of the brew and to provide fermentable sugars which will be attenuated (converted) into alcohol. Upon the type of extract used depend the colour and body of the beer and much of its flavour and aroma, and the higher the proportion of extract to sugar the heavier and more fully flavoured the brew will be. Some home brewers prefer to use extract alone, with no sugar, especially in stouts, but this materially increases the cost.

Hops

The two main functions of the hop in brewing are to flavour and preserve the beer (see p. 86), and several varieties can now be bought by the home brewer each of which gives its special flavour and aroma to the brew and combines with the malt extract to produce its individual character. The beginner cannot do better than to use English goldings for pale ale and bitter and fuggles for mild ale, brown ale and stout. Alternatively, most stockists keep a special blend of these two hops that is excellent for almost any type of beer. Hop extracts can be used very successfully and should in any case be kept in stock for use when good hops are hard to find. Breweries use large quantities of extracts. The amount of hops added depends so much on personal taste that it is difficult to give any hard and fast rule, but a simple method that will ensure that the resulting brews are at least pleasantly drinkable is (for 4-5 gallons):

> for light brews (3-4 per cent alcohol), use 2-3 oz hops
> for medium brews (4-6 per cent), 3-4 oz
> for strong brews (6-8 per cent), 4-6 oz.

In each case use the smaller amount if sugar equals or exceeds malt extract by weight; use the higher figure if malt exceeds sugar. After the first brew consult your palate but be careful not to underhop any brew that is to be kept for more than a few weeks.

Yeast

Use a good granulated or liquid culture of beer yeast, not

baker's yeast. A rate of $\frac{1}{4}$ oz granulated yeast for brews up to $2\frac{1}{2}$ gallons and $\frac{1}{2}$ oz for $2\frac{1}{2}$-5 gallons will be ample.

Carbon Dioxide

Carbon dioxide and alcohol are produced in almost equal weights by any alcoholic fermentation, but whereas the gas is a waste product in wine-making, save in the case of sparkling wines, it is a very important ingredient in brewing for upon it depends the proper conditioning of the brew.

Most commercial beers have the natural carbon dioxide gas removed by the chilling and force-filtering which they undergo. The keg beers that have replaced draught beer from the wood have it pumped back under pressure as part of the process that raises the beer from the metal keg in the pub cellar to the bar, while bottled beers are carbonated in the same way as fizzy lemonade at the time of bottling. One of the great attractions of home-brewed beer is that it is naturally conditioned through the absorption of its own carbon dioxide produced during the course of fermentation, particularly during the secondary fermentation in the bottle during which considerable pressure is generated. The carbon dioxide injectors used by home brewers in conjunction with pressure vessels such as the Brukeg are not normally intended to carbonate the beer but to substitute the gas for the air which would otherwise replace the beer drawn off and might well cause souring. As it is introduced under moderate pressure it also prevents the naturally-produced gas already absorbed in the beer from bubbling out, thus maintaining the true natural conditioning and sparkle of the brew to the last glass.

Procedure (for a 4-gallon brew)

It is a very simple matter to brew with malt extract, and whatever recipe is followed the ingredients and equipment needed and the procedure to be followed are the same. For quantities see Table 3, pp. 112-13.

Ingredients

> Malt extract
> hops
> sugar or glucose chips
> yeast
> citric acid
> water

Yeast nutrient (or brewing salts), finings and heading liquid (or headers and finers), and water conditioner are optional.

Equipment

> Boiler/fermentation bin/polypropylene spoon or stirrer/nylon sieve or other fine strainer/hop bag or length of butter muslin/ sterilizing fluid/thermometer/preferably a hydrometer and test jar

Bottling equipment will include screw-top or crown cork bottles of any size to hold four gallons of beer between them, or other suitable pressure containers, screw stoppers, crown caps and capping device or hand-inserted polythene pressure stoppers, siphon with U-tube, bottle brush, gallon jars or carboy and large (jar size) and small (bottling) funnels.

Brewing

First repeat to yourself the brewers' and wine-makers' incantation: 'Keep it clean; keep it warm; keep it covered.' Next open the can of malt extract and make a starter bottle as explained on pp. 54–6. The process is hastened if the yeast granules are creamed in a little of the liquid, using a cup and the back of a spoon, both wiped with sterilizing fluid and rinsed. Even if the starter bottle is not fully active when you come to use it the fermentation of the wort will still be greatly accelerated. Wash out the bin and sterilize it thoroughly (do not use detergent as this is very difficult to remove completely), using the bottle brush to ensure that all the surface is reached by the sterilizing fluid, not forgetting the inside of the lid. Wash all the other implements and the working surface and wipe them with a clean rag or better still kitchen tissue well moistened with sterilizing fluid. Rinse all the equipment in clean water and put the bits and pieces into the bin, with the lid closed, until you are ready for them.

Put the hop bag or muslin into the boiler with a little water, put on the lid, bring to the boil for a few minutes to sterilize it, drain away the water, wring out the hop bag and put it in the bin for protection. It saves time to start this operation first, but the risk of forgetting the boiler while you are busily sterilizing the rest of the equipment is considerable, and when you smell the hop bag or muslin toasting it will be too late.

Put about 6 quarts of water in the boiler (not more than 2 gallons, but the amount depends on the size of the boiler) and set it to boil. Fill the hop bag or muslin with the hops, keeping back a good large pinch, say $\frac{1}{4}$ oz, and tie firmly. Add the malt extract to the hot water in the boiler and stir until it is dissolved, then put in the full hop bag, add 1 teaspoon citric acid for all brews and 1 teaspoon of salt for stout, replace the lid, raise to the boil and boil briskly for 45 minutes. This will sterilize the wort and extract the bitter, preservative resins from the hops, but it will also evaporate the volatile esters and essential oils that give the beer the delicate aroma of the hop flower. To restore this, stir in the hops that were kept back, replace the lid and boil for another 2-3 minutes only.

Take the thermometer, hydrometer and test jar out of the bin and put them on a sheet of kitchen paper with another sheet over them. You will need the strainer right away. Rinse the bin again, place in it the sugar or glucose chips and pour the hot wort in through the strainer. Gently press the hop bag, pour more boiling water over it in the boiler, press gently once more and add this liquor to the hot wort, stirring it until the sugar is quite dissolved.

Add cold water to make the wort up to four gallons, cover the bin closely and leave the wort to cool. When it has fallen to about 70 °F (21–2 °C) stir it well and check the gravity with the hydrometer. This is intended to be read at 59 °F, so 1 ° of gravity should be added to the reading to compensate for the temperature difference – not that it really matters to anyone but an exciseman.

Now add the yeast, sprinkling it on the surface, or the activated starter bottle, rousing well in either case, put the bin lid on carefully and closely and leave the wort in the warm to ferment. The first ferment may well be violent so it is wise to stand the bin in a basin to catch any overflow.

The bitter resins of the hops seem to be concentrated in the first, frothy yeast heads, and to skim these removes excess bitterness. They are quite different in appearance from the smooth, creamy yeast cap that forms later and normally sinks to the bottom of the fermenting vessel when the strong upward flow of carbon dioxide gas caused by the ferment dies down. The brew may be stirred after skimming, but thereafter leave it alone to ferment in peace while its undisturbed yeast cap can promote the production of alcohol and a thorough attenuation by excluding oxygen.

The fermentation of ordinary brews should be completed in under a week for light beers and rather longer for those of higher gravity if the temperature remains at between 60° and 70°F (15° and 21°C), but will take several weeks for lager made by the traditional method with an initial fermentation temperature of 40°F (5°C) even though this is allowed to rise slightly during the later stages. When hydrometer checks have shown that the fermentation is complete, or practically so, proceed as described in the next chapter, on storage and bottling.

The Formulation of Recipes

Quantities

It will be noticed that brewing recipes are usually given for batches of 2 (or 2½) and 4 (or 5) gallons, and this is probably because these quantities weigh what the average brewster or brewer respectively can comfortably lift, because 2 gallons is the smallest amount worth brewing and because 4 to 5 gallons will last the beer-drinkers of an average family for a convenient length of time during which they can always have their beer at its best while having to brew only at reasonable intervals. The eventual compromise will of course be brews of 10 and 20 litres or almost exactly 2¼ and 4½ gallons, but until all our equipment has been replaced it is simpler to give quantities and weights in the old style and leave the reader to use the conversion tables on pp. 304–7 where necessary.

All brewing recipes in this book are for 4 gallons; simply halve the quantities for 2 gallons and increase them by one quarter for 5-gallon brews. Because the final clearing process is facilitated by the use of gallon jars or a 5-gallon carboy it is best to avoid batches involving fractions of a gallon.

Formulation

The basic principles for recipe formulation are given at this stage because there are so far only four main ingredients to deal with: malt extract, sugar, hops and water, so that the process is remarkably uncomplicated. Additional data on malt grains and cereal or other additives will be found later in this chapter.

All figures and proportions given are merely rule-of-thumb, satisfactory working approximations. Mathematically accurate formulae would be not only confusing but also quite unnecessary, for the margins of error in the quantities or proportions of malt extract and sugar within which the home brewer can still produce a perfectly drinkable beer are very wide. Care must, however, be taken over the addition of hops. Under-hopping is an error that can be cured but a badly overhopped brew is acrid and fit only to be poured down the sink.

Before attempting to formulate a recipe it is important to have a clear idea of the points that you are looking for in your ideal brew. There is more to a drop of good wallop than might at first appear and among the main factors to be considered are:

TYPE. There are hundreds of different types of brews but most recipes, including those for malt extract, are based on the beers that are best known to us. These are: bitter, light (or pale) ale,

mild ale, brown ale, stout, light and dark lager and the specially
strong brews such as barley wine and Russian stout.

CHARACTER. Beers of the same types may have very different
characters, as every beer drinker knows; a weak, flat, under-
hopped bitter is very different from a strong, foaming bitter
redolent of the hop – but they are both bitter beers. Some of the
factors that determine character are:

(*a*) *Appearance*. The visual features on which a beer is judged
are its colour and clarity and the nature and durability of its
head. Its *colour* gives the first indication of its type and can range
from palest gold to black. It is determined by the kinds and
proportions of malt grains or extracts, cereal additives, sugars
and caramel in the brew. *Clarity*, or brilliance, is achieved in
home brewing by temperature control (good cellar work) and
the use of finings, especially in the stronger beers that take longer to clear. Careful formulation also helps greatly when mashing but is not so important when brewing with malt extracts.
The *head* is a most appetizing feature of the appearance of a
beer. It is greatest in bottled beers containing a large amount
of dissolved carbon dioxide under pressure, rather less in commercial keg beers or home-brewed beers stored in the pressure
vessels designed for the amateur and used with carbon dioxide
injectors, and least of all in draught from the wood.
Whatever the size of the head, the ability of its bubbles to
stay unburst for the longest possible time is all-important. This
is known as head retention and is due to many complex factors
including hop resins. Home brews usually have better natural
head retention than chilled and force-filtered commercial
beers, but breweries usually add a little harmless heading liquid
to put matters right. The home brewer who likes a tenacious
'cauliflower head' can do the same.

(*b*) *Flavour and Aroma*. Whatever its appearance, one likes or
dislikes a beer mainly on the grounds of its taste and smell.
These preferences are matters of personal taste, and that is why
the reader is encouraged to experiment and is given a sound
set of rules on which to do so rather than a list of cast-iron

recipes. Both these features can be determined by the kinds and proportions of the malt or malt extracts, hops and sugars in the brew. Proper maturation is another important factor, especially when brewing strong beers which taste simultaneously harsh and mawkishly sweet if drunk too soon.

Both malt or malt extract and alcohol have what is called a buffering effect against the bitter taste of the hop; in other words they mask it so that the stronger the beer, and the higher the proportion of malt or extract to sugar, the greater the quantity of hops needed. Many expert brewers would therefore indicate even more hops than are recommended for the all-malt, 8 per cent alcohol brew listed in the table on pp. 112–13, but a palate and nose for very hoppy beers have to be acquired by many people used only to commercial brews.

(c) *Body*. More easily recognized than described, 'body' is the apparent weight and fulness of the brew on the palate: a good, strong stout has more body than a light ale. Body, like head retention, is more readily achieved in home brews than in commercial beers from which everything filterable has been removed. It is due to unfermented residues of malt and sugar, alcoholic strength and other factors too technical to go into here. It can be improved by the use of glucose chips instead of sugar in malt extract brews, by the addition of glucose polymer, by raising the proportion of extract or by using extract alone, with no sugar or glucose. Various additives can also be used when mashing. Stout, porter, brown ale, bitter, the heavier lagers and all specially strong brews should have plenty of body.

(d) *Alcoholic Strength*. This is determined by the amounts of malt extract and sugar in the brew and by the proportions of malt grains and other cereals added when mashing or when using crystal malt (see tables on pp. 119 and 112–13). A hydrometer check on the gravity of the wort will indicate the probable alcoholic content of the brew. Some commercial beers contain as little as $2\frac{1}{2}$ per cent alcohol by volume, but home brewers usually aim at from 4 to 6 per cent for normal drinking, the heavier beers being reserved for cold weather. Barley wine and other 'specials' can contain up to 12 per cent alcohol and are stronger than many wines.

(*e*) *Condition*. This term covers the results of priming, fining and maturing and the absorption of carbon dioxide gas into the beer. If these processes have been properly carried out and the beer has been fully matured at the appropriate temperatures it should be star-bright, without harshness or undue sweetness, and should tingle on the tongue even after it has been left for some time in the tankard.

*

When a product is to be judged on qualities of which so many, including the all-important ones of taste and smell, are matters of personal preference, it is necessary to find an objective approach to the problem of formulation. The appearance and condition of all brews should be satisfactory if instructions on procedure are followed so that the formulator is left to choose between the type of brew or its alcoholic content. Type is the obvious and usual choice, but an analysis of published recipes has produced so many examples of excessively or even impossibly high potential alcohol contents lurking beneath the innocent labels of 'bitter', 'brown ale', 'stout' and so forth that, because many readers of this book may well be beginners who cannot calculate the potential alcoholic content of a recipe at sight, those given here are tabulated according to strength. This system will not only ensure that you do not unwittingly brew near-beer on the one hand or skull-splitter on the other, but will also provide a base from which experimental brews can very easily be developed with a pretty accurate foreknowledge of their strength and characteristics.

The temptation to brew inordinately strong beer is often powerful at first but should be resisted. The strength of a brew should suit the type of beer to be made; the addition of extra sugar or malt extract in an attempt to strengthen recipes designed for long drinks only spoils them, for specially strong brews need careful formulation and brewing and long maturing. An unbalanced strong beer made with too much sugar and too little body 'drinks thin' and no amount of maturing will improve it much. Malt extract alone or with sugar or even glucose cannot provide enough body for really successful strong brews but are quite satisfactory up to about 8 per cent alcohol, which is after all more than twice as strong as most commercial beers.

Our rule-of-thumb methods may well result in the actual percentage of alcohol by volume in the resultant brews being a degree or so more or less than the tables indicate, but so small a variation will be both unimportant and undetectable by anyone save (possibly) an expert. The tables that follow are based on figures already given. If they are memorized the strength of any malt extract recipe can be assessed almost at a glance.

If fermented right out in (*in* – not added to) 1 gallon of wort:

1 lb white sugar gives	5% alcohol by volume
1 lb glucose, glucose chips, invert sugar or brown sugar gives	4% ,, ,, ,,
1 lb dry malt extract gives	5% ,, ,, ,,
1 lb syrup malt extract gives	4% ,, ,, ,,

If for example the recipe for a 4-gallon brew of 'basic beer' reads:

sugar	2 lb
malt extract	2 lb
hops	2 oz

we omit the unfermentables, in this case hops only, and calculate the amount of alcohol produced by the malt extract and sugar in 1 gallon. As 1 lb of malt extract produces 4 per cent, 2 lb would give 8 per cent. Similarly 1 lb of sugar gives 5 per cent, so 2 lb would give 10 per cent, to make a theoretical 18 per cent in all in 1 gallon. Divide by 4 for a 4-gallon brew and we find that its strength is $4\frac{1}{2}$ per cent alcohol by volume.

This method is extremely simple and sufficiently accurate. Factors such as incomplete attenuation on the one hand and the addition of extra sugar for priming on the other have been deliberately omitted and have a habit of cancelling each other out in practice.

In the table that follows the rough guide for hop addition already given has been adapted to take into account the buffering effects of malt and alcohol.

Brewing with Crystal Malt

Malt grains and mashing are dealt with in the next section, but crystal malt requires a separate section because it is prepared in such a way that it needs no mashing and can therefore be used either with malt extract brews or in the full brewing procedure with other malt grains. It is known as crystal malt because of its distinctive amber-toffee colour, still evident when the grain is cut or crushed to expose the kernel. It has a delightfully nutty, sweet taste and is so brittle that the grains can be crushed between the finger and thumb through the transparent polythene of the sealed packet which is the only reliable way of keeping malt really fresh and crisp in small quantities.

If it is to be used with malt extract the crystal malt is first cracked or milled and then simply boiled with the hops and extract. Mess and straining can be avoided if the cracked malt is put into the hop bag with the hops, but if this is done boiling water should be poured over the bag, which is then lightly squeezed, several times after the wort has been strained off in order to extract all the soluble matter from the malt.

Crystal malt used with discretion gives colour, flavour, body and smoothness to most beers whether brewed from malt extracts or malt grain, but because its flavour is strong and some of the sugars it contains are difficult to ferment right out, too large a proportion can produce a brew that is almost sickly-sweet.

Patent black malt grains, mainly used for colouring stout, leave no residual sweetness, so that crystal malt is a useful ingredient in stout and brown ales when these are preferred slightly sweet. In theory 1 lb of most malt grains and other cereal additives should produce about 3½ per cent alcohol, but this is calculated on a degree of perfection higher than most home brewers, who have to deal with small quantities, can bring to the processes of mashing and sparging, or extracting all the soluble sugars from the malt by washing with boiling water. In the case of crystal malt not all these sugars are fermentable, and a figure of 3 per cent would be a close enough approximation.

All the malt extract recipes given in Table 3 (pp. 112/113) can be improved by the addition of crystal malt. Add 8 oz to Nos. 1, 5, 7, 8, 9, 10, 11, 13, 16, 17 and 18 and balance the recipes by deducting 6 oz of sugar. Add 4 oz of crystal malt to Nos. 2, 3, 4, 6, 12 and 15 and deduct 3 oz of sugar if you feel meticulous.

It may have been noticed that none of the recipes in the table specify more sugar than malt extract, though the instructions given with kits and cans very often do so, partly to keep down the price of the beer made from them and partly because at least one canned, preformulated wort is more highly concentrated than the average malt extract. Readers in search of a brew even more economic than those in the tables can experiment with higher ratios of sugar but if so they will find that glucose chips, though rather dearer than household sugar, will give the brews body and help them to avoid the thin, cidery taste that is known as sugar tang.

Brewing with Patent Black Malt

Patent black malt can be used with malt extract brews to give certain types of stout their dark colour and distinctive burnt, woody flavour, for these can be extracted almost equally well by boiling with the hops as by mashing.

This malt derives its name from the patents originally taken out on its method of manufacture, which involves heating it until it begins to fume. The process kills most if not all of its

TABLE 3. 4 GALLON BREWS

Types of Beers	O.G.	Alcohol % by Volume	Malt Extract		Sugar (lb)		Hops	Notes
			lb	type	white	or glucose	oz	
1 mild	32	4	3	dark	1	1¼*	3	
2 'basic beer' 222	35	4½	2	any	2	2½	2	
3 light ale	,,	4½	3	light	1¼	1½	2	
4 lager (light)	,,	4½	4	lager/light	½	¾	3	lager yeast
5 bitter	40	5	3	bitter/light	2	2½*	4	
6 pale ale	,,	5	2	light	2½	3	3	
7 stout	,,	5	4	stout/dark	1	1¼*	4	add caramel if needed and 1 teaspoon salt
8 milk stout	,,	5	3	stout/dark	2	2½*	3½	add 12 oz lactose, and caramel if needed

9	better bitter	48	bitter/light	3	2½	3*	4	
10	brown ale	"	dark	2	3½	4¼*	3	add caramel if needed
11	'basic beer' 333	50	any	3	3	4¼	3	
12	strong pale ale	55	light	2	4	5	4	
13	best bitter	"	bitter/light	3	3½	4½*	4½	
14	extra stout	"	stout/dark	7	—	—*	5	add 1 teaspoon salt and caramel if needed
15	lager (strong)	"	lager/light	6	1	1¼	5	lager yeast
16	'345' strong ale	62	dark	3	4	5*	5	
17	strong dark lager	"	lager/dark	6	2	2½*	5	lager yeast and caramel
18	'8-X'	"	dark	8	—	—*	5½	caramel if needed

* Glucose or glucose chips preferred.

enzymes and so carbonizes it that it has little fermentable matter left. It should not be cracked or milled or it will disintegrate to a fine, black powder which may render the brew very slow to clear. If you like a traditionally dry stout try adding 8 oz to No. 7 and 1 lb to No. 14, with or without cracked crystal malt, varying the amounts in subsequent brews, if necessary, to suit your own taste. Only very small quantities of patent black malt should be used to darken any brew that is intended to be slightly sweet; in such cases caramel is preferable.

Brewing with Malt Grain

Unless some form of extra sugar is added to the wort the alcohol in beer is derived from fermentable malt sugar (maltose), while its body, flavour and power of head retention are largely provided by sweet, soluble but mainly unfermentable dextrins. Both of these are converted from the starch of the malt by its own enzymes, known collectively as diastase, during the process of mashing, but before this can take place the malt must be cracked or crushed, after which it is called grist.

Testing the Malt

If malt is to be bought in 1 lb packets to supplement malt extract, and if the malt seems fresh and your methods of mashing are adequate, 1 lb of pale malt in 1 gallon of wort can be relied on to yield a gravity of between 25 and 30. Before buying malt in bulk, however, it is wise to test it first.

It is best always to use ordinary household equipment including kitchen scales and measures, for brewing is essentially a cheerful, domestic operation. For this reason the sample should be large enough to compensate for any minor errors in weighing or measuring, and as the objective is to measure the gravity of 1 gallon of wort in which 1 lb of grist has been mashed, a sample mash of 4 oz of grist in 1 quart of wort will be just right.

Put 1 pint of water at 160°F (74°C) into the top half of a double boiler and stir in the 4 oz of grist. This is not a steaming operation, so the bottom half of the boiler can be as full as possible without spilling when the top is replaced. The introduction of the grist will bring the temperature of the mash down to about 150°F (65–6°C), and the gas or electricity should then be regulated to keep the mash at as near 150°F (65–6°C) as possible for two hours, stirring occasionally. With a little practice this can easily be managed with accuracy but it is best to leave the thermometer in the mash and consult it frequently. After the two hours add another 1 pint of water at 150°F (65–6°C), stir the mash well and return it to the double boiler for another fifteen minutes. Strain the wort off the mash and bring it to the boil to sterilize it and destroy the diastase. Bring it up to 1 quart with cold water to counteract evaporation wastage, cover it and leave it to cool. When the wort is at 60°F (15°C) test its gravity.

Use a small saucepan in a larger one if no suitable double boiler is available, but take care that their contents do not slop into each other.

The Iodine Test

Add 2 drops of domestic iodine solution (brown not colourless) to 2 drops of cold water. Add 4 drops of wort and mix. If the mixture turns blue, starch is still present and mashing is not complete. Make this test before boiling the wort so that mashing can be continued if necessary. The easiest method is to pick up the drops of liquid on the end of the thermometer, which must be washed between immersions, and mix them in a white egg-cup.

Cracking the Malt

All types of malt grains are crisp and brittle when fresh and are easily cracked or crushed by the home brewer in any suitable type of domestic mill, liquidizer or grinder or by putting them in a stout polythene bag and using a rolling-pin or bottle.

The polythene bag stops fragments of grist flying about, and a tray or large baking dish will serve the same purpose. Ready-crushed malt is available but make sure that it is properly sealed in polythene bags, otherwise it may be stale, or 'slack' as the term is, and not worth using. Whatever method is used only light cracking is necessary; if you have to use a liquidizer remember to fine the brew or it may be slow to clear. Patent black malt should not be cracked.

Mashing

This is the most crucial process in brewing. In breweries the grist and any cereal additives such as flaked maize are first mixed in the mash tun with hot water at an exact temperature until they form a thick, porridgy mash which gives the diastatic enzymes sufficient moisture in which to work while subjecting them to the minimum of dilution. Next the temperature is held steady for from two to eight hours, and finally the perforated bottom of the mash tun is opened, revolving arms sparge (sprinkle) the thick mass of the mash with hot water to wash out the last of the dissolved maltose and dextrins, and the sweet wort containing them is run off.

The four factors that will decide the nature of the brew are the composition, temperature and acidity of the mash and the type of water available, and the professional brewer exercises great skill in adjusting these so as to brew standard beers from raw materials that may vary widely from batch to batch.

Composition of the Mash

The mash is composed of a mixture of different malts and other grits in proportions that will produce the required colour and other characteristics of the beer to be brewed. The alcoholic strength of the brew will be determined by the gravity of the wort and the amount of malt extract, sugar or glucose added to it later. The gravity of the wort depends upon the types of malts used and the proportion of grist to water. Since dark malts are used mainly for their colour and flavour it is best to base any calculations on pale malt.

Extraction rates vary according to the freshness of the malt and the kinds of grits included, but if fresh and crisp and bought from a reputable supplier 1 lb of pale malt grist or 1 lb of grits should yield a gravity of 25 to 30 in 1 gallon of wort. Allowing for unfermentable solids and other factors we can therefore add to the rule-of-thumb figures already given for sugars and malt extracts:

1 lb of pale malt grist or 1 lb of other grits in 1 gallon of wort will give approximately 3 per cent alcohol by volume.

To brew 4 gallons at $4\frac{1}{2}$ per cent alcohol an O.G. (original gravity) of 40 is needed, and a mash of $5\frac{1}{2}$ lb should produce this.

It is interesting to experiment with various cereal additives at a later stage but the beginner can produce splendid beer without them and will do best to keep to malt extract, malt and sugar or glucose chips for his first brews. The diastase in the malt or malt extract can convert only a limited amount of extra starch and unconverted starch causes cloudy brews, so it is wise to restrict the proportion of other cereals in any recipe to not more than 25 per cent of the weight of the malt or malt extract.

Temperature

Enzymes are extremely sensitive to temperature, and because the diastatic enzymes produce maltose most efficiently at 130 °F (54–5 °C) and dextrins at 150 °F (65–6 °C) the brewer can control the proportions of these in the wort by slight variations in the temperature of the mash and thereby cause quite striking changes in the nature of the beer. In practice mashing is carried out between 145 °F and 155 °F (63 ° and 68–9 °C), but whereas in the British method of infusion the mash is started and held throughout at or near 150 °F (65–6 °C), American and continental breweries use the decoction method which involves bringing the mash up to this temperature slowly, in a series of steps. The British method gives a perfectly adequate production of maltose as well as of the dextrins to which our native brews owe their characteristic body, flavour and good head retention, whereas the decoction system tends to produce thinner, harsher beers, many of which are best drunk very cold.

Though the diastase can continue to convert starch into maltose and dextrins for up to eight hours if the mash is held at the same temperature, practically all its work is done in the first two, after which the sweet wort is run off and the mash sparged with water at about 170 °F (77 °C). The wort is then boiled with the hops, a process which destroys the diastatic enzymes by heat and thus stabilizes the wort, in which no further conversion can take place. It is important never to have the mashing water much above 170 °F (77 °C) or the diastase may be weakened or destroyed, though 165 °F (74 °C) is a safe water heat at which the home brewer may add the grist, as this will bring the temperature down.

Acidity

The acidity of the wort is important, and here again the optimum conditions for the production of maltose and dextrins differ, the former needing pH 4·7 and the latter pH 5·7. It is best to aim for pH 5·3 and to check this with pH comparison papers. It is not necessary to be exact – pH5 or just over is near enough – but if the acidity of the wort is too far out the enzymes will be unable to work properly and the brew will certainly suffer.

Water

Water, or 'liquor' as the brewer calls it, has a great effect upon the character of the beer brewed from it, so that certain hard-water areas have become famous for their light ales and bitters as have some soft-water districts for their stouts. Tapwater can be hardened or softened as may be necessary, and the methods are described in the chapter on water.

Mashing at home

Such good beer can be brewed without mashing that one is tempted to give the beginner Mr Punch's famous 'advice to those about to marry – don't!' The main problem is to keep the mash at a level 150 °F (65–6 °C) for at least 2 hours if it is a stiff one of 4–5 lb of grist per gallon or for up to 8 hours if it is a thin mash of 1½ lb per gallon. Aided by steam-heated mash tuns, breweries use the first method and sparge the mash afterwards, but the home brewer will find that a larger version of the double-boiler method described under Testing the Malt (p. 114) is probably the best way to deal with a stiff mash, as any form of direct heat may cause it to stick to the heated surface and burn on. After the grist has been mashed for 2 to 2½ hours the wort is strained off and the mash must then be sparged with water at about 170 °F (77 °C). The water can be sprayed from the rose of a small plastic watering-can and must be allowed to percolate through the mash in order to wash out the remaining maltose and dextrins. A special receptacle for sparging the mash can be made by punching small holes in the bottom of a plastic bucket; alternatively as much mash as possible can be scooped up in a large domestic strainer, held over the wort bin, sparged and discarded (birds and most pets like it) until it has all been dealt with. Be very careful not to over-sparge, as this may cause a starch haze in the beer that will not respond to fining.

The home brewer usually finds it more convenient to use the thinner mash as this will not burn on to an immersion heater, but because the enzymes are more diluted they need a longer period in which to work and the mash must be kept at or near 150 °F (65–6 °C) for eight hours. The best method is to put the mash in a well-lagged plastic mashing bucket or bin and to insert a thermostatically controlled immersion heater. For larger batches a thermostat can be arranged to control an electric boiler. A thin mash of this kind need not be sparged and the wort can simply be strained off.

If no thermostat is available a rough and ready method is to use a 50-watt immersion heater on its own, for this will keep a mash of rather less than 2 gallons at approximately the desired heat if it is contained in a 2-gallon plastic bucket which is closely covered and carefully wrapped up. In theory this method should not work well because the surrounding air temperature varies so widely from summer to winter unless there is central heating, but in practice it operates effectively enough. Whichever method is used, the mash must be started at full heat, not brought up from cold. If the grist is added when the water is at 160–5 °F (71–4 °C) the temperature of the mash will drop to about 150 °F (65–6 °C). Thereafter it should never be allowed to rise above 160 °F (71 °C).

Cereal Additives

There is scarcely a cereal which has not been employed in brewing at one time or another. Comparatively recent introductions are syrups made from malted wheat, maize and other grains in the same way as malted barley becomes malt extract, and these syrups are increasingly used by both professionals and amateurs. Cereal additives are not only economical sources of starch but are also valuable in that some of them can impart body, smoothness, flavour, improved head retention and so forth to the brew. All of them should be used with care and in moderation, or the result can be singularly nasty beer containing unconverted starch that may cause a haze similar to that produced by over-sparging, or even prevent proper fermentation.

Most of them are already processed to aid in the extraction of their starch; they may be flaked, rolled, milled, kibbled (kibbled maize is English for the American cracked corn) or torrified (torrified maize is in fact popcorn). Save for syrups and roast barley they should all be boiled for twenty minutes or so to release their starch content and allowed to cool to 150 °F (65–66 °C) before they and the water they were boiled in are added to the mash, which then proceeds as usual.

Maize is by far the most useful additive, especially in light ale, lager and bitter. It gives body and flavour and confers some protection against haze, and is very largely used in continental and American beers, including lager, which are brewed by the decoction system and tend to be thin and harsh. The maize corrects these faults but the large quantities used give the beer a flavour that is not always to the British taste.

8 oz of flaked maize boiled in $\frac{1}{2}$ gallon of water is ample for the average 4-gallon brew.

A small addition of flaked or torrified *barley* gives a pleasant, clean tang to light ale, pale ale or bitter. Roast barley added directly to the mash confers a distinctive dry, woody flavour to stout as well as deepening its colour.

Long ago a great deal of strong ale was made from malted *wheat*, but today this grain is converted into a wheat syrup of which quantities are used by both breweries and home brewers. It can be added directly to the mash or boiled with the wort, can be substituted for not more than one third the amount of malt extract or its equivalent, is cheaper than malt or malt extract and gives smoothness and body.

Another very useful wheat derivative is brewer's grade wheat flour. This is readily convertible when added to the mash and improves almost any brew, giving better head retention and clarification as well as the typical wheaten smoothness and body.

The legendary mum was a strong ale made from malted wheat with bean and pease flour added to the mash.

Other additives include processed *oats*, *rice* and *rye*. Like those described above they are sold by most suppliers, but save in special brews and for experimental purposes their value to the home brewer is minimal.

Adding the Hops

After the sweet (unhopped) wort has been run off the mash the husks of the malt will have been strained out but it will still be cloudy. It is next transferred to the boiler and the hops are added. The method is the same as that described on p. 88, but whereas only fuggles, English goldings or a blend of the two were used at that stage in proportions based on the tables given, the home brewer can now begin to experiment with other varieties if he wishes, including imported Hallertauers, Styrian goldings and Saaz for lagers and northern brewer and varieties such as Whitbread goldings for special brews. Remember that the quantities used may differ slightly from those given in the tables for fuggles and goldings.

Boiling

The wort is now to be boiled with the hops and it is most important that it should be boiled both briskly and thoroughly. Breweries boil the wort quite fiercely under slight pressure for 1½ to 2 hours, but perhaps partly because under kitchen conditions hopped wort at a rolling boil in an open vessel generates lots of steam and a powerful brewery smell, some home brewers cut the boil to well under an hour. The breweries' long boiling period is partly to guard against any possibility of a haze forming in bottle. The slightest haze renders commercial bottled beer unsaleable, but though undesirable it is not of such vital importance to the home brewer especially as his stock is not usually so long on the shelf.

Important though it is to extract the flavour, aroma and resins from the hops, boiling the wort does far more than this. It also sterilizes the wort, stabilizes it by destroying the malt enzymes, precipitates out substances that would otherwise cause hazes in the beer, and if it is boiled in an open vessel it strengthens the wort and raises its gravity by evaporating part of its water content. If the boiler has a lid most of the water condenses on it and drops back into the wort. The addition of a little Irish moss to the wort when at the boil will accelerate and improve clarification.

In some countries it is still illegal to add sugar to the wort, which has to be boiled until its gravity is high enough for brewing even strong beer. The home brewer may care to experiment along these lines but the usual procedure is as described below.

Completing the Wort

Measure into a sterilized fermentation bin the amount of sugar or glucose to be added and strain the hot wort on to it. Stir the mixture until the sugar is quite dissolved and then make the wort up to the required volume with cold water.

When the wort has cooled to about 75 °F (24 °C) test its pH. If the acidity of the mash has been properly adjusted that of the diluted wort may be too low, so correct it to approximately pH 5·3 with a little lemon juice or a teaspoonful or less of citric acid. Just over pH 5 and well under pH 6 is quite good enough. If yeast nutrient is to be used now is the time to add it, and it should be a vitaminized brand. Before pitching with yeast fill the hydrometer test jar to within 1 inch or so of the top, cover it, and stand it in cold water to cool. Add the yeast to the wort, stir it in well and cover the bin. Check the O.G. of the wort in the test jar at 60 °F (15 °C) and refer to the comparison tables on pp. 112–13 to make sure that the beer will be of the desired strength. If the gravity is too low add sugar as indicated by the tables; if it is too high resign yourself gracefully to enduring a rather stronger brew than you planned or dilute the mash with a little water if the fermenting vessel is large enough.

Before putting the fermentation bin in its warm corner enter all the data and your comments on the log card and attach it to the bin. Thereafter proceed as in the chapter on brewing with malt extracts.

11

SELECTED RECIPES

The secrets of originating successful new recipes are to use the finest raw materials available and to experiment sensibly along accepted lines, so that while a new brew may or may not turn out to be the nectar for which one hoped it will in any case be an enjoyable drink. The recipes that follow from my own cellar-book are therefore offered as exercises in improvisation rather than as formulae to be followed exactly. In this section some trade names will be given as the recipes are of specific brews that have turned out well. For example, I have so many test brews to make in the way of business that when there is no time to mash I often base experimental batches on Brucan, a hopped wort concentrate preformulated to make lager, light ale, bitter, brown ale or stout and needing a minimum of preparation. Brew It Yourself Ltd brand granulated beer yeast is used throughout; this is developed from a *carlsbergensis* bottom-fermenting strain and is as good for lagers as for other brews. Unless otherwise stated all other ingredients are also of this brand.

Light Ale (4 gallons)

Brucan light ale type	1 large can (1 kilo)
light dry malt extract	2 lb

```
sugar as invert syrup    1 lb
yeast                     ½ oz
citric acid
yeast nutrient
Irish moss
```

Day 1. Compounded basic wort to 3 gallons using the Brucan only, no malt extract or sugar, and pitched at 70 °F (21 °C) with ½ oz yeast.

Day 2. Vigorous fermentation; skimmed and stirred.

Day 3. Boiled the malt extract in 1 gallon of water for 25 minutes with 3 heaped teaspoons of Irish moss. Stirred in syrup while hot; when cool added this to the fermenting wort and roused well. Corrected acidity to pH 5·4.

Day 6. Transferred to carboy under lock; fermentation slowed.

Day 9. Beginning to clear down; racked off yeast and returned to cleaned carboy.

Day 14. G zero and beer so clear that after racking, priming and fining (to settle secondary fermentation) it was krausened (see Glossary) with a little fresh yeast before it was bottled. This was to try the effect of using dry malt extract instead of the larger part of the usual sugar on a syrup malt extract base and in addition to see if the addition of the ingredients progressively made any difference.

No O.G. was taken as it was simpler in this case to calculate the alcohol percentage from the ingredients on the basis of the final gravity – about 5½ per cent.

This beer cleared so quickly that some was drunk too soon and was slightly cidery, but after three weeks in bottle the yeast had compacted to a firm paint layer and the brew was outstandingly good.

Stout (4 gallons)

```
dark dry malt extract    4 lb
caramel                  ½ oz
roast malt               8 oz
patent black malt        8 oz
sugar as invert syrup    2 lb
```

> northern brewer hops   4 oz
> vitaminized brewing salts
> heading liquid
> Irish moss

Day 1. Wort, cracked malt and sugar boiled in 2 gallons of water for 1 hour. Irish moss and 3½ oz hops added at start of boil; rest of hops 5 minutes before its end. Yeast and brewing salts added at 75 °F: O.G.62. Fermentation started overnight. Immersion heater set at 75 °F.

Day 2. Skimmed lightly and stirred.

Day 4. Ferment apparently stopped but wort very thick: G.10.

Day 6 Racked into gallon jars under lock.

Day 9. Cleared down; G.4. Bottled.

A very good stout at its best after three weeks in bottle.

Pepys's Rowan Ale (4 gallons)

Samuel Pepys mentioned in his diary that he had tried ale brewed with rowanberries and found it the best that he had ever drunk. After some experimenting this recipe proved excellent, with a fine colour and a clean, dry tang.
Mashed at 150 °F (65·5 °C) for 2 hours:

> light malt   1 lb
> crystal malt   ½ lb
> roast malt   ½ lb

Meanwhile boiled together for 1 hour:

> dark malt extract   2 lb
> glucose chips   2 lb
> wheat syrup   1 lb
> dried rowanberries   2 oz
> goldings   4 oz
> Irish moss   3 teaspoons

Usual method. The two worts were then strained and mixed.

Day 1. Pitched with beer yeast.

Day 2. Strong ferment; skimmed off dark froth.

Day 4. Skimmed again.

Day 6. Ferment over. Racked into 5-gallon carboy and filled headroom with carbon dioxide from B.i.Y. injector. Fitted lock.

Day 9. Racked into pressure vessel at G.5. Added Brufina finings; primed with 4½ oz standard syrup, fitted injector.

Splendid colour, clear and good at two weeks, better at three.

Easy Rowan Ale (4 gallons)

> Brucan brown ale wort 1 large can
> glucose chips   2 lb
> crystal malt   ½ lb
> dried rowanberries 2 oz
> yeast
> finings (Brufina)

Simmer the cracked crystal malt with the glucose chips and berries in 2 gallons of water for 40 minutes, strain on to the Brucan and proceed as usual.

Pepys also mentions having drunk horseradish ale but comments only that it was supposed to be good against the stone, from which he suffered, so I have not experimented with it yet.

Brapple (4 gallons)

A light, summery drink made with any basic light ale recipe plus, in this case, a particularly good apple concentrate made from a balanced mix of sweet and tart apples.

> light malt extract (dry) 2 lb
> apple concentrate   1 litre (or 1 quart)
> goldings hops   4 oz
> crystal malt   ½ lb
> pectinaze
> glucose polymer   8 oz
>   (No brewing salts as these contain acid and tannin which
>   are supplied by the apple concentrate)

Crack the malt and simmer it with the dry malt extract, 3½ oz hops, glucose polymer and apple concentrate for 35 minutes, then add rest of hops, boil 5 minutes more, strain into bin and sparge as usual. Add cold water to 4 gallons and if necessary adjust the gravity to about 40 by adding sugar. Pitch with beer yeast and proceed normally.

Brapple is best drunk at least four weeks after bottling, as despite their having been fermented together the ingredients take some time to blend properly; if drunk too soon after it has been bottled Brapple merely tastes like a cidery beer.

Bitzerbrew (4 gallons)

One of the best beers I have ever brewed, this was made to use up the bits and pieces left over from a series of test mashes. They were:

light malt	1 lb
lager malt	$\frac{1}{2}$ lb
roast malt	$\frac{1}{2}$ lb
crystal malt	$\frac{1}{4}$ lb

These were all mashed together until the iodine test was negative: just over 2 hours rising slowly from 140 °F to 150 °F (60 to 65.5 °C).

Meanwhile the following had been boiled in 2 gallons of water for 1 hour:

glucose chips	2 lb
wheat syrup	1 lb
fuggles	4 oz
dried rowanberries	$\frac{1}{2}$ oz
Irish moss	

The O.G. was 65, equivalent to about $8\frac{1}{2}$ per cent alcohol by volume, but as in most strong beers the amount of unfermentable solids was so high that the hydrometer could only indicate the gravity. I expected so little from this Bitzerbrew that the final gravity was not even taken.

The beer was allowed to clear, racked into a 5-gallon pressure vessel and primed and fined – and after three weeks I drew off a foaming pint of a memorable, dark golden, star-bright beer.

Pale Ale (4 gallons)

Edme D.M.S.	
(diastatic malt syrup)	2 lb
pale malt	2 lb
maize flakes	1 lb
goldings	4 oz
glucose chips	3 lb
glucose polymer	½ lb
Irish moss	3 teaspoons
yeast	½ oz
citric acid	

The malt was crushed and mashed for 2 hours with the flakes, the malt extract boiled for 1½ hours with 3½ oz of the hops, the Irish moss put in 15 minutes and the rest of the hops 5 minutes before the end of the boil. Good hot break. Both worts were strained and sparged on to the glucose chips and polymer in the fermentation bin and made up to 4 gallons and 70°F (21°C). O.G. 44. Acidity was adjusted with citric acid to pH 5·4, as mash. On the third day gravity down to 8; racked into carboy under lock. On the fourteenth day perfectly clear and G. a shade over zero; unusual with so many unfermentables present. Racked into pressure vessel, primed and klausened with ½ teaspoonful yeast from active brew.

A pale, full-bodied beer that seemed stronger than its probable 5 per cent alcohol content.

Heavy Pale Lager (4 gallons)

light, dry malt extract	3 lb
Brucan hopped lager wort	1 large can
yeast	
vitaminized yeast nutrient	
salt	
citric acid	

Day 1. The dry malt extract was boiled for 30 minutes in 2 gallons of water; this was then poured on to the Brucan and made up to 4 gallons at 70°F (21°C), when the acidity was

corrected to pH 5·4, the nutrient and 2 teaspoons of salt were added and the wort pitched with ½ oz of yeast. O.G. 52.

Day 2. Temperature 65 °F (18 °C). Strong fermentation, lightly skimmed dark spots from yeast head.

Day 3. Temperature reduced to 60 °F (15 °C). Fermentation slowing.

Day 5. Transferred to carboy under lock.

Day 15. Fermentation apparently ceased; G.10; beer beginning to clear down.

Day 20. Racked (G.8), primed, fined and bottled.

After six weeks in bottle in coolest available spot (about 60 °F) and not more than an hour's chilling, this very heavy, almost creamy lager was at its best, and seemed stronger than its theoretical alcohol content of about 5·5 per cent should warrant.

Well-hopped Bitter (4 gallons)

light malt extract	4 lb
cracked crystal malt	1 lb
goldings	4 oz
glucose chippings	3 lb
Irish moss	3 teaspoons
brewing salts	large B.i.Y. pack
yeast	½ oz

Day 1. The malt extract, cracked crystal malt, glucose chippings, hops and Irish moss were boiled together for 45 minutes, ½ oz of hops being reserved for the last 5 minutes. The wort was strained off, the hops and malt sparged, the wort made up to 4 gallons at 75 °F (24 °C) and pitched with ½ oz yeast after the brewing salts had been stirred in and the acidity checked. (Had white sugar been used the hot wort would have been strained on to this but glucose chippings are best sterilized by boiling.) O.G.56. Heater fitted, set at 70 °F (21 °C).

Day 2. Brisk fermentation; skimmed head lightly and stirred.

Day 6. Beginning to clear down.

Day 8. Into carboy under lock. Clearing well.

Day 14. Racked, primed, Brufina and a little heading liquid added and transferred to pressure vessel. Final Gravity 4.

After three weeks clear and good; fine colour and head. Perhaps too hoppy for some tastes.

Best Bitter (4 gallons)

Edme D.M.S. malt extract	4 lb
wheat syrup	1½ lb
crystal malt	½ lb
English goldings	3 oz
Irish moss	
citric acid	
yeast	
yeast nutrient	

Day 1. Mashed the D.M.S., crystal malt and wheat syrup for 30 minutes. pH 5·4. Added Irish moss and 2¾ oz of hops and boiled all together for 55 minutes, plus 5 minutes' simmer with rest of hops. After straining and sparging and making up to 4 gallons, the gravity of 41 was rather lower than expected but the addition of 4 oz sugar as invert syrup brought it to G.50 for a brew of about 6½ per cent alcohol. The vitaminized nutrient was stirred in, acidity corrected and the yeast pitched at 75 °F (24 °C).

Subsequent days. The course of fermentation and maturation was substantially the same as in the previous recipe and resulted in an excellent bitter beer.

12

BOTTLING AND STORAGE

Hops and Turkies, Carpes and Beer,
Came into England all on a year.
 – Traditional. Variously quoted and
ascribed

Until comparatively recently beer was sold commercially either in bottles or from oaken barrels, but today draught from the wood has given place to 'keg' beers forced from metal containers by compressed carbon dioxide gas. The passing of the old-style draught beer is regretted by many, but the cost of oak barrels made and maintained by craftsmen combined with the modern demand for lighter, gassier beers to make the change inevitable. The storage and service of home brew have followed much the same pattern; while bottled beer is still very popular the modern trend is towards pressurized plastic containers of various capacities.

Preparation

It used to be common practice to bottle the beer or to rack it into casks or other containers soon after fermentation had stopped or when the gravity had dropped to the bottling marks shown on special brewing hydrometers. Both methods led to so high a concentration of yeast in the beer that it took far too long to clear, while the heavy yeast deposit rose to cloud it directly a bottle was opened or a pressure dispenser operated. The latter method could also lead to burst bottles, for bottling marks vary from G.5 to G.8 according to the make of the hydrometer. Not only is this confusing, but the gravity of a heavy, strong brew containing a high proportion of unfermentable matter might never fall to a gravity of 8, let alone 5, while a light beer made from malt extract and the maximum quantity of granulated sugar could still have enough fermentation potential left at a gravity of 5 to burst bottles. The remedy for both these faults is to interpose a clearing stage between the fermentation vessel and the bottle or other storage container.

When the primary fermentation appears to have ceased and the beer has started to clear, lift the bin carefully on to a table, draining board or bath board and siphon the beer into gallon jars (a carboy is better for larger brews) to just below their necks, using a U-tube to avoid disturbing the yeast sediment. Then fit fermentation locks or cotton-wool plugs to the necks of the jars in case fermentation has not quite finished and leave them in the cool to finish clearing. If finings are used they should be added as the beer is being siphoned into the jars; this will help to ensure a thorough mix.

After one to two weeks the beer will have thrown a further deposit and have dropped clear. Take hydrometer readings for two or three consecutive days to ensure that fermentation is complete, then siphon the beer off the new lees in the jars or carboy into the fermentation bin or some other sterilized container and add the priming sugar, and the caramel and heading liquid if these are to be used. Never prime at the rate of more than 1 teaspoonful of sugar per quart, which corresponds to $\frac{1}{2}$ oz per gallon. Better still, use $1\frac{1}{4}$ teaspoonfuls of standard or invert syrup per quart or $\frac{3}{4}$ fl. oz per gallon. Two ounces of sugar or 3 fl. oz of syrup will prime a 4-gallon brew. Instructions can still be met with that specify up to 3 oz of priming sugar per gallon but those who have no liking for burst bottles or wildly ebullient beer should stick to the easily-remembered ratios given here. If sugar is used it should be dissolved in a little warmed beer before it is added to the bulk.

The beer should then be well stirred until the priming sugar or syrup is thoroughly mixed in.

Containers

Bottles

The bottles that contain the primed beer will be subject to considerable pressure as the secondary ferment caused by the priming sugar proceeds. It is therefore very important indeed that only proper beer or cider bottles are used. Screw-topped

Beer bottles: half-pint crown-capped;
and pint quart screw-stoppered

spirit bottles or wine bottles with their corks tied or wired down are not designed to withstand pressure and have been known to explode in the hand with serious results. Any standard size can be used but half-pints and pints or their nearest metric equivalents are more convenient to use than quarts as the larger bottles are seldom poured out all at once and must consequently be resealed and left for a day or two until the disturbed yeast has settled again.

The old-style screw-stoppered bottles were very useful to home brewers but are now almost unobtainable. If they are used the rubber sealing rings should be periodically inspected and replaced if they are cracked or badly stained; they are still stocked by specialist suppliers. Both rings and stoppers should be washed, sterilized and rinsed before reuse.

Three types of caps may be used with crown cap bottles: the standard metal cap; the reseal metal cap with a plastic liner which can be used several times if it has been carefully removed and which can be replaced by hand sufficiently firmly to hold pressure while the yeast settles between drinks; and the plastic, inverted-dome cap which is applied by a firm pressure with the heel of the hand and can be reused almost

Beer bottle closures: screw stopper; plastic
pressure closure; crown cap

indefinitely. All types should be thoroughly washed in running water before use; the plastic caps may be immersed in sterilizing fluid and then rinsed but sulphite solution should never be in contact with metal. Beer bottles sealed with the plastic cap should be inverted afterwards to wet the seal.

When bottles or other containers were filled directly from the fermentation bin it was necessary to use a siphon and U-tube to avoid disturbing the lees and the switching of the siphon tube from bottle to bottle led to considerable spilth; but if the method outlined above is used a jug or other dipper, sterilized inside and out, and a small funnel can be employed. A better method still is to transfer the beer to a spare pressure vessel or other container with a tap and place this on the bath board or on a table. A length of polythene tube is attached to the tap so that it reaches nearly to the bottoms of the bottles and as the beer enters them below the surface there is none of the usual wasteful fobbing (the brewer's term for foaming).

Both types of standard metal crown caps must be affixed with a special tool and there are several of these on the market, from the simple lump of metal with a hole in it which is placed over the cap and hit with a hammer to the lever-action bench capper. The knock-on capper often causes broken bottles and wasted beer as it must be hit hard and held perfectly straight to effect a proper seal and misjudgements are inevitable. The best tools for the home brewer are the bench capper or the twin-lever hand capper which grips the neck of the bottle below the cap as the handles are pressed down. One of these is

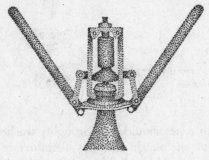

Lever-type crown capper

provided with a magnet which holds the crown cap in place as the tool is placed over the bottle.

Care of bottles

All bottles in use should be washed out as soon as they are emptied as this saves a great deal of work later on and the probability of mould infection. They should be stored upside down and need only be rinsed, sterilized, rinsed again and drained before reuse. All others should be thoroughly washed and brushed out in very hot water before they are sterilized. If the bottles are clean and drained the sulphite solution may be poured from bottle to bottle, each being thoroughly shaken, and then back to the stock bottle.

Storage

When the bottles have been filled and stoppered they should be stored upright in bottle cartons or crates so that the divisions between the bottles can protect the others from the unlikely event of a burst. The cartons or crates should be left for a day or two at room temperature to encourage the secondary fermentation to start and then moved to the coolest place in the house so that clearing and conditioning may proceed slowly, naturally and thoroughly. A sharp to-and-fro twist to each bottle when the beer has almost cleared will dislodge any yeast that has clung to its sides. Lager should in theory be stored in bottle for two months or more at $34\,°F$ ($1\,°C$) but in practice a month to six weeks in the coolest spot available produces a very good brew. It is possible to 'lager' the brew for longer periods only when very low temperatures can be maintained or the yeast will autolyse (deteriorate) and impart off-flavours to the brew.

The beer may drop star-bright very soon after bottling if finings have been used, but it will still be two to three weeks before it is properly conditioned and the yeast has formed the ideal, compact paint layer on the bottoms of the bottles. The clearer the beer was when it was bottled the less yeast it contained and the longer the secondary or conditioning fermentation in bottle will take. On the other hand, if too much yeast is in the beer when bottled it will condition quickly but take longer to clear. Perfection comes with practice but the quality of the beer should not be affected save that if too much yeast is present in the bottles clouding will occur when they are opened. If the process is properly carried out and only a paint layer of yeast remains on the bottoms of the bottles the beer should pour clear almost to the end.

Pressurized Containers

The 5¼-gallon pressure keg and the carbon dioxide cartridge injector for use with it were introduced in 1969 and are now used by many thousands of home brewers. The modern 'Brukeg' holds 5¼ gallons and easily withstands the pressures necessary to keep the natural fermentation gas in the beer. or to carbonate an unprimed brew.

The 'Brukeg' Pressure Container is designed specifically for home brewers. It has a visible contents scale and a separate base to insulate the brew from floor vibration and temperature changes

This is normally primed in the keg, and as the priming head dies away the pressure is kept up by admitting gas from the injector so that the beer retains its natural conditioning and remains clear and foaming down to the last pint, with a head approaching that of bottled beer. Since no air is admitted the beer will keep perfectly for months and the labour of washing, sterilizing, rinsing, filling and capping all the bottles needed for a 5-gallon brew becomes a thing of the past. If the keg is used for a smaller brew a short blast from the injector before the cap is screwed on will blow out the air in the headroom and replace it with carbon dioxide gas, thus obviating any risk of air taint.

The Carbon Dioxide Injector

This is a device for pressurizing either the 5-gallon pressure barrel or any other suitable container with carbon dioxide gas. It is fitted through a hole made in the screw cap, uses either

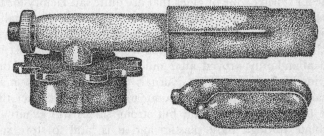

The Mk IV Duplex carbon dioxide injector. This allows beer to be stored and dispensed under controlled pressure and free from air taint. A pressure gauge may be fitted alongside this model.

ordinary soda-siphon sparklets or the larger, 12-gramme bulbs and incorporates a safety-valve. Given a normal brew, priming and temperature, one or two ordinary sparklets are usually enough. A sensitive control valve admits gas as it is needed and the amount of head on the beer can be increased by raising the gas pressure.

Pressure Dispensers

Several different designs of low-pressure beer dispensers exist, most of which are designed for or can be adapted for use by the home brewer. They range in capacity from 7-pint pipkins to small plastic barrels holding a gallon and upwards and are usually designed to look well on a home bar.

All types work on similar principles and all can be used to

carbonate clear, unprimed beer if several sparklet bulbs are used and the container is regularly shaken over several days. It is far better, however, to prime the beer in the usual way or to fill one of these dispensers with lively, clear beer from a big pressure keg or several quart bottles if it is to be shaken about en route to a party.

Plastic Containers (unpressurized)

There are many polythene and polyurethane containers specially made for storing wine or cider that are quite satisfactory for the storage of unprimed draught beer. They include 5-gallon semi-rigid cubes supported in strong cartons and fitted with taps, and rigid tap barrels holding from 2 to 5 gallons. It has been abundantly proved after much stormy debate in home brewing and wine-making journals that such specially-made containers convey no taste or odour to their contents once they have been well washed out, but strong smells will eventually percolate through most plastics and it is fatal to store such containers in the same cellar or outhouse as paraffin, carbolic, onions, paint, fertilizer and so forth. Plastic vessels of this type will not hold pressure and if it is desired to prime the beer stored in them they should be fitted with vented caps or fermentation locks.

Treatment of Plastic Containers

All new plastic containers should be filled with a solution of hot water containing a handful of soda per gallon and left overnight, then rinsed thoroughly before use. This will dispel any smell the plastic may have when new. A weak sulphite solution may be used to sterilize plastic containers and to keep them sweet in storage, but neither strong sulphite nor boiling water, detergent or soap should ever be employed.

Oak Casks

These are only for the dedicated home brewer. They produced

good draught when handled by expert cellarmen in pubs, where their contents were sold in a few days at most and whence they returned to the brewery to be steam-cleaned and immediately reused. They are, however, heavy and difficult to condition and to keep sweet, and since they do not hold the priming head pressure well and air must then be drawn in to replace the beer that has been run off the remainder cannot be kept for long without becoming flat and sour.

If nothing but a cask will do it is best to try to get a recoopered brewery 'pin' (4½ gallons). The bunghole should be carefully sniffed to make sure that the pin is sweet, for casks left holding dregs or rainwater may be infected with mould and become incurable 'stinkers'. Wash the cask out with relays of hot (not boiling) and cold water until the water runs out clear; then pour in a quart or so of weak sulphite solution and rock the cask vigorously so that it reaches every part. Bung it, leave it overnight and then repeat the washing process to remove the sulphite. No soap or detergent should ever be used. The cask is ready for use but will not be at its best until it has been seasoned by one or two batches of beer. If the cask appears dry watch it carefully for leaks and if any appear leave it full of water until the wood has swollen again.

Casks should never be left unsupported on their sides when full or they will leak. A stillage or stand should be provided which takes the weight of the cask at its two ends. The cask should be placed with the bunghole on top and the tap hole at the bottom in such a position that the tap can be driven in with one blow of a heavy mallet and a jug can thereafter be placed below the tap. The beer can conveniently be primed and fined in the cask, which is then rolled briskly around to rouse it. Wooden shives (shallow bungs) will be needed and both hard and porous pegs: these latter are inserted in a hole bored in the shive, the hard peg while the pressure of the priming head is to be retained and the porous peg when this pressure has fallen and air has to be admitted. It is important that the cask be stored in a cool cellar at between 50° and 60°F (10° and 15°C). To keep it sweet it should be used continuously and washed both outside and in with hot water between batches. If it is left unused it should be thoroughly washed,

Wooden barrel tap

partly filled with a weak sulphite solution and bunged tightly enough to exclude all air.

Stone-ware Tap Jars

These are now seldom used, though the old books advocate them. They are heavy, difficult to clean and have no advantages over the lighter and better designed containers now on the market.

13

TO SERVE BEER

St George he was for England,
And before he killed the dragon
He drank a pint of English ale
Out of an English flagon.
— George Keith Chesterton:
The Englishman

Beer can be drunk as soon as it has dropped clear but is all the better for a good three weeks' conditioning, or twice as long for lager. By that time the yeast should have formed good, compact lees and attached itself to the bottom of the bottle or other container but it is nevertheless most important that it should not be disturbed. The first half-pint or so from a pressure vessel or from a pipkin or other container fitted with a dispenser will contain the yeast nearest to the tap or central downtube respectively, after which the beer should run clear and foaming to the last pint if the vessel is not moved. Bottles should be lifted carefully from their crates or cartons, brought to the table without disturbing the contents and held firmly upon it while they are unstoppered.

It is best to pour the beer first into a large jug that will hold the contents of the bottle and the head. Incline the jug and the bottle gently towards each other so that the beer slides smoothly down the inside of the jug without undue foaming and keep pouring at the same rate, without stopping, until the last of the bright beer has been poured and the yeast is approaching the neck. The rest of the beer will be yeasty and thick but is said to be an excellent tonic. It is known as the 'brewer's inch' — and brewers should know what is good for them.

The temperature at which beer is served depends on personal taste and of course the weather, but lager and light ale are certainly better when cold and moderately chilled beer is much easier to pour without disturbing the yeast. Because home brew has not had all the goodness and body frozen and force-filtered out of it, too sharp a drop in temperature may cause it to develop a haze due to matter in solution being thrown into suspension, and it is therefore best to cool it only an hour or so before it is to be drunk; preferably in the quiet type of refrigerator, not the motorized kind that shudders periodically and churns up the yeast.

Drinking Vessels

Beer can be drunk with anything and out of anything. Beer glasses came in fairly late, for until comparatively recent times ale and beer were usually cloudy and best drunk from opaque vessels of leather, silver, pewter or earthenware. Glass shows off the brilliance, head and liveliness of a star-bright pale gold or deep amber brew as nothing else can, but stout, porter and perhaps brown ale seem to taste better from pewter.

No detergent should ever be used to wash beer glasses or tankards as it is extremely difficult to remove entirely and even an imperceptible film will kill the head and make the beer flat and lifeless. All drinking vessels should be washed in hot, soapy water, well rinsed under the cold tap and very thoroughly dried until they shine. Tankards should never under any circumstances be treated with metal polish, which leaves a disgusting and almost permanent tang on silver or pewter. It is, however, a mistake to think that pewter should be left drably black; if it is polished with the traditional wood ash, whiting or in extreme cases very fine sand or brick dust (all mixed to paste with water) it will gradually take on a really beautiful smoky lustre which is well worth the effort required.

All jugs and drinking vessels should come to table at as nearly the temperature of the beer as possible. Cold beer poured into a warm glass or tankard loses not only its refreshing coolness but also much of its life; its head soon subsides and it no longer tingles deliciously on the tongue.

Finally, let me repeat that beer goes with anything, from audit ale with saddle of mutton or stout with oysters to a fine draught bitter with a gammon of bacon and the first of the broad beans or a frosted glass of cool lager with strawberries and cream.

14

AILMENTS OF BEER

Beer drinking don't do half the harm
of lovemaking.
    – Eden Philpotts: *The Farmer's Wife*

Home-brewed beer usually contains a sensible 5 per cent or
more of alcohol by volume and is a healthy liquid very capable
of looking after itself, so that the home brewer suffers from few
of the worries that beset the professional who often has to use
sulphite and other means of keeping his tax-thinned fluid free
from infection. Given scrupulous cleanliness, sterilization of
equipment and a carefully protected wort there is little that
can go wrong with home brew. The most usual ailments are
described below.

Hazes

Hazes in beer are of several kinds. In the unlikely event of a
haze being caused by bacterial infection the beer will self-
evidently be unfit to drink and must be scrapped. If, as is
usual, it is caused by some slight error in the management of
the mash or fermentation or by a sudden drop in temperature
and the beer smells and tastes good the sensible thing is to forget
the haze and drink it out of a tankard. If a cure is necessary the
beer should be left until there is no sign of liveliness from either
dissolved carbon dioxide or secondary fermentation and then
fined, preferably with bentonite rather than the usual protein

finers. If this has no effect the haze is probably caused by excess starch and should be treated with fungal amylase 2209 10 per cent. The beer must then be racked off the lees, reprimed and rebottled.

Yeast-Bite

This gives the beer an acrid bitterness. It may be mistaken for the effect of overhopping the first time it is encountered, but whereas hop bitterness quickly leaves the palate that of yeast-bitten beer seems to cling to the mouth and throat. If it is not too bad the addition of lactose may make an improvement. Yeast-bite is probably the most common ailment of home-brewed beer since two of its main causes are lack of air and excess of heat during fermentation, and home brewers are often instructed to tie sheets of plastic tightly over fermentation bins and to use immersion heaters set to $75\,°F$ ($24\,°C$) so that the temperature of the fermenting wort may well rise to over $80\,°F$ ($26-7\,°C$).

Mustiness

If the beer is left too long on the yeast deposited by the secondary fermentation in a cask or pressure vessel the yeast autolyses and gives the beer a musty, mousy flavour which is sometimes inaccurately described as yeast-bite. Throw it away and be more careful next time!

Mycoderma Candida

If wine or beer is left too long in a vessel with too much head-room it is likely to be infected by this bacillus, and if it has already formed a white film on the surface of the beer the brew will be fit only to pour away. The usual phrase is 'down the sink' but this is a dangerous method of disposing of infective liquids. Pour it down the lavatory pan together with a good dose of disinfectant or bleach and close the lid before you pull the chain, then sterilize the bin and all other equipment that has been anywhere near. This infection can be prevented by topping up all vessels, since the bacillus cannot live in the absence of air. If you have an injector even the small space remaining can be filled with a squirt of carbon dioxide.

Acetification

If the common-sense rules of hygiene are not observed or beer is left exposed to the air it may become infected by acetic bacilli and start to turn to vinegar, or alegar as acetified beer used to be called. There is no cure, but given modern equipment and knowledge the condition is extremely rare. It is mentioned here mainly because the extreme dryness of beer that has been allowed to ferment right out before bottling is often mistaken for it with a consequent waste of good ale, though no one who has ever tasted or smelt an acetified brew could ever make such an error. The cure for an overdry brew is simple: all its sugar has been converted into alcohol and carbon dioxide and the judicious addition of lactose to the priming sugar will put matters right without causing violent refermentation.

Section III

HOME
WINE-MAKING

15

THE HISTORY OF WINE-MAKING

Choose you wine after this sort; it must
be fragrant and redolent, having a
good odour and flavour in the nose; ...
it must be cold and pleasant in the
mouth; and it must be strong and
subtle of substance. And then moderately
drunken it does quicken a man's wits,
it doth comfort the heart, it doth scour
the liver; ... it doth rejoice all the
powers of man, and doth nourish them ...
– Andrew Boorde: *Dyetary*, 1562

From prehistoric times to the present day the art of wine-making has been so closely entwined with the religion, mythology, magic, medicine and social customs of every tribe and nation from the tropics to the temperate zones (saving only the Australian aborigines) that in a book such as this it is quite impossible to take more than the briefest glance at its long and fascinating history.

The first wine was almost certainly made from the small ancestor of the grape we know, for even today this is almost the only berry or soft fruit from which wine can be made simply by pressing out the juice and leaving it to be fermented by the yeast that grows on its skin. The conditions needed to bring about this sequence of events must often have occurred naturally and have been observed, reproduced and improved upon by man, for the first evidence of systematic wine-making is derived from large deposits of grape pips excavated from kitchen middens and estimated to be some ten thousand years old. Further archaeological evidence supported by early wall and cave paintings suggests that vineyards were being planted about two thousand years later and that the vine was the first plant to be cultivated systematically. If this is so man's early taste for wine may well have led him to take one of the most important forward steps in his history, from the life of a nomadic hunter or herdsman to that of a settled grower of crops.

There is evidence that the arts of viticulture and wine-making were first developed in the area between the Black and Caspian seas, whence they spread southward down the valleys of the Tigris and Euphrates and were brought to increased perfection by the Persian, Egyptian, Greek and Roman civilizations in turn. From Italy they spread to the whole of western Europe and there were vineyards in France by 54 B.C. when the Romans invaded Britain.

A tremendous amount of documentation and pictorial description of early wine-making exists, some dating from the time of the Pharaohs whose wall paintings show every aspect of the craft in great detail, and some from ancient Greece and Rome whose poets and authors wrote exhaustively on the growing of grapes and the making and drinking of wine. Because wine was as essential a part of the religious rites of the great ancient civilizations as it is of Christianity and Judaism today, its preparation has been to some extent the prerogative of the priesthood from the earliest recorded times, and our own monastic orders maintained this tradition until Henry VIII abolished them and plundered their monasteries in the mid-sixteenth century.

The Romans drank great quantities of wine but diluted it well with water, as did the Greeks and as indeed the inhabitants of most wine-producing countries do to this day save for their finest vintages. One reason for this may have been that until the discovery of the use of cork for stoppers air could not be effectively excluded and most wine had to be drunk very young and rough. The Romans regarded those who drank their wine neat as gross topers, but some of their diluted potions would have seemed odd, if not revolting, to our palates for they mixed into them every kind of spice and flavouring. Wine mixed with sea water – even 'old sea water' – was highly esteemed, but it is not certain whether this diluent served as a preservative, an aperient, a means of stimulating further thirst, an emetic or a built-in hangover cure.

It is usually assumed that most of the early historical evidence refers to wine made from grapes, but it is also true that wine has been made from the diluted and sweetened juices of innumerable other fruits and berries in nearly all warm or temperate zones from the remotest ages and that when the Romans arrived in Britain we had already been making our own wines for centuries as well as mead and ale.

The Romans may well have planted vineyards when they first invaded Britain but they must have been dug up in A.D. 85 when all those outside Italy were destroyed by imperial decree. In A.D. 280 Rome allowed us to grow vines once again, and from then on we have always had at least a few vineyards. Norman references to vines were quite specific, but although several vineyards were listed in *Domesday Book* monkish Latin was less precise than Norman French and the use of the same word for both vineyards and apple orchards has caused much confusion, as described in Chapter 27 on the history of cider. After the departure of the monks in the sixteenth century British viticulture fell into a decline from which it is only now recovering. Today we have many amateur and several commercial vignerons such as Sir Guy Salisbury-Jones, whose vineyard in Hampshire produces the famous Hambledon white wine and is visited by large numbers of home wine-makers on open days.

No one who has tasted his product could deny that really splendid wine can be made from grapes grown in Britain, but in this country, as on the continent in less sunny years, both amateurs and professionals have to resort to chaptalization, or the addition of sugar to the must. It therefore seems unlikely that any very good wine could have been made in Britain in Roman or medieval times without some form of chaptalization, for as late as the seventeenth century Hyclutt wrote in his treatise on animals and plants introduced from newly-discovered lands:

. . . it may serve for pleasure and some use, like as our vines doe, which we cannot wel spare, although the climat so colde will not permit us to have good wines of them.

We can take it therefore that from the very earliest times honey must have been added to provide the necessary sweetness and alcoholic strength since sugar was not yet in use here, and though the careful use of sugar can help to produce excellent wines in which the full flavour and bouquet of the grape are retained honey superimposes its own strong character so that much of the wine made by the early vignerons must in reality have been more like a pyment, or mead fermented with grape juice.

Sugar became generally available in Britain not much more than two hundred years ago. Before this, honey was our only sweetener and thus a necessary ingredient of all our wines and there could have been only the most nebulous of dividing lines between wine made with honey and mead flavoured with fruit-juice, flowers, herbs or spices.

The comparatively short period between the coming of cheap sugar and the beginning of the Industrial Revolution must have been the first golden age of home wine-making, for Britain was still an agricultural community, abundant wild and culti-vated fruit and flowers were there for the picking, and wine-making was still as much a regular household task as baking or brewing. From the smallest cottage to the greatest country house the mistress and daughters of the house, the cook, the still-room maids or all of them together made not only wine but also cordials and simples from traditional recipes. Although wine had been imported from the continent since Roman times it was still often cloudy, sour or grossly adulterated, and for many years our native wines were much preferred save by the wealthy few who could afford to import their own and ensure that they got the best.

At the time of the Industrial Revolution formerly self-sufficient small-holders and agricultural workers were lured by apparently high cash wages to exchange a healthy sufficiency in the country for the squalor and poverty of urban slums. The countryside was depopulated and its traditional skills were soon almost forgotten. Owing to a peculiarly crass piece of legislation designed to help our farmers at the expense of foreign wine-growers and brandy distillers, crude gin was extremely cheap and there was little to be gained by the new townspeople through making their own wine when fruit, sugar and even yeast had to be bought.

At the same time good, cheap wines had begun to come in from France, Germany and Portugal. The upper classes set the fashion by importing in cask and maturing and bottling in their own cellars, and from sovereign to squire it was almost mandatory to lay down a pipe of port at the birth of the heir which would be first drunk when he came of age. From on high came that fatuous ukase: 'claret [pronounced *clart*] is the only drink fit for a gentleman', but the nobility and gentry also consumed oceans of port, madeira, brown sherry, champagne and Rhine wines, and the fashion that they set was faithfully followed by the professional classes, merchants, shopkeepers and those of their clerks and other employees who could afford to do so. 'Country wines', now so called to distinguish them from the genteel, imported variety, were much blown upon and ceased to be made in most fashionable, and even more would-be fashionable households, and contemporary commentators lamented that even in the cottages tea and gin were replacing nutritious, home-brewed beer and harmless home-made wine.

All this took place very gradually, from about the mid eighteenth to the late nineteenth centuries, by which time Great Britain was not only completely industrialized but also the most prosperous country in the world and the hub of the greatest empire in history. For the last twenty years of the nineteenth century the actual spending value of money rose steadily year by year, imported wines and all other drinks were extremely cheap, and home wine-making simply was not worth while save in remote country districts. In the early years of the present century prices and taxes were both beginning to rise, and it may have been partly on this account that, in the country at least, almost every farm and cottage once more had its store of home-made wine. That it had not yet returned to the still-rooms and dining-rooms of country houses was probably because the palates of the well-to-do had become accustomed to the more subtle bouquets and flavours of vintage, or at least sound wines from the continent and that for the first time in this country a taste for dry wine was spreading. The appreciation of dry imported table wines swiftly became a part of the peculiarly British wine snobbery that also began to flourish at this time, so that the sweetness of nearly all home-made wines counted as another point against them.

That they were sweet, and often sickly-sweet, nobody who can remember them would deny. Before the First World War I lived as a small boy in the Worcestershire and Shropshire countrysides, and summer walks with my nurse or a maid often ended in a field golden with cowslips which I was encouraged to pick by the promise of a cowslip ball to play with. This was made by threading the stems together with the blossoms outwards and after a game of catch it went into the basket with the rest to be made into wine by the cook, who 'took it for her nerves'. I was sometimes given a sip and enjoyed it, but children in Edwardian days had a passion for sweet things that is not shared by the present generation of youngsters. At least three pounds of sugar must have gone to the gallon and probably more, and though I must have had hundreds of sips, and later glasses of all kinds of home-made wine in my youth I cannot remember one that was not sweet or over-sweet, though some were certainly also quite strong. Probably they were never seen in our dining-room or those of our friends because they were too syrupy to drink with food and not strong enough to compete with fortified after-dinner wines such as port and madeira. In earlier days this had not been so, for skilled housewives and still-room maids used far less sugar but fortified the wine and checked its fermentation by the addition of brandy.

Somehow the basic arts of wine-making survived the sugar shortages of two world wars and the agricultural depression that came between them, but by 1945 very few home wine-makers were left and the fate of our native country wines seemed to be finally sealed by the great resurgence of wine snobbery that followed the post-war reappearance in this country of good imported wines.

We should be thankful that cheap foreign travel has now shown us all that wine is something to be drunk, not merely talked or written about. If sensible people want wine they will have it, and as enjoyable wine is so ridiculously expensive when imported but so very cheap and simple to make at home it is easy to understand why home wine-making is now more popular in Britain than ever before.

16

METHODS OF
MAKING WINE

> To happy convents, bosomed deep in vines,
> Where slumber abbots, purple as their wines.
> – Alexander Pope:
> *The Art of Sinking in Poetry*

Making Wine from Kits and Cans

Many different wine kits are now sold both by specialist shops
and by mail order. Some are better than others, but most of
them have the advantage for the beginner that, although it is
naturally more expensive to make a gallon of wine from the
contents of a boxed kit than to make it from ingredients bought
separately over the counter, the kit contains smaller quantities
of these than are normally supplied and provides all that are
needed with no superfluities, while the items of apparatus may
be used again and again.

Most kits are based either on a can or sachet of grape juice
concentrate which will produce one gallon of red, white or
rosé wine, or port or sherry types, or on one of the many compounds preformulated in the can to make a number of named
types of wines. Besides this basic ingredient a kit should contain
at least:

> full and clear instructions
> a suitable wine yeast
> yeast nutrient
> campden tablets (or sodium metabisulphite crystals)
> fermentation lock

pierced bung for a gallon jar to take the lock
3 feet of non-toxic polythene siphon tubing
U-piece for above
6 each of the following per gallon
　corks, or preferably red or white polythene Vintop
　stoppers which can be inserted by hand
　Viskap shrink-on neck and cork capusles
　labels

Unless the kit includes a polythene fermentation vessel, a 1-gallon glass jar will be necessary; these used to be sent with mail-order kits but the days when this could be done economically and safely are long past.

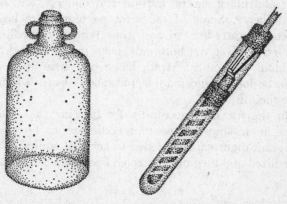

Standard 1-gallon fermentation jar and thermostatically controlled immersion heater

As with beer kits, price is not necessarily a guide to value and it pays to shop around and ask advice; a helpful shopkeeper may well make up a kit out of stock items for much less than the cost of a boxed and advertised one. The more expensive kits may contain items such as filter bags which, though useful to have if wine-making is to become a regular hobby, should not really be necessary if only a trial gallon is to be made; some kits may also still contain asbestos filter medium and if so it is advisable to replace this with filter powder (kieselguhr B.P.) as it may constitute a health risk.

Wine Compounds

Canned compounds from which many different types of wines can be made are based either upon fruit juices alone or in combination or, more usually, upon grape concentrates blended, coloured and flavoured to produce very fair approximations to many well-known wines. Both types are put up in cans sufficient to make 1 gallon of wine.

Among the pleasant wines to be made from fruit juice concentrates are peach, apricot, currant and morello cherry, currant and black cherry, currant and bilberry, and currant and elderberry. Some of the most popular types based on grape concentrates are red and white port, dry, medium and sweet sherry, claret, red burgundy, hock, sauternes and French and Italian vermouths. Mead, based of course upon honey, can also be found, and manufacturers are always adding new types to their lists.

As in the use of concentrates for brewing the basic skill required lies in knowing how to use a tin-opener, but also as in brewing fastidious care is needed to keep all equipment clean and sterilized and the must protected from airborne contamination.

Equipment

You will need a stirrer, the two funnels and thermometer as already described (ch. 6), and a siphon, but because this has to reach only the bottom of a 1-gallon fermentation jar instead of that of a 5-gallon vessel the smallest size of automatic siphon-pump (described as 'jar size') is best, fitted with a U-tube or other device designed to prevent the disturbance or sucking up of the yeast sediment. Alternatively, a yard of polythene tubing and long U-tube will do excellently.

Fermentation Jar

The standard vessel in which to ferment small quantities of wine must is the glass one-gallon jar with a one-inch mouth and two carrying ears. This is a basic item of equipment and is stocked by all shops catering for home brewers and wine-makers.

Fermentation Lock

Cheap and invaluable, this can be of glass or transparent plastic, as already described (p. 50). The glass locks are of three different patterns, all 'bubblers'. The plastic ones are either bubblers or of an even cheaper, cylindrical type. The bubbler pattern is the better, since by comparing the level of the liquid in the two bubbles it is possible to know when the jar's contents have completely ceased to ferment. This is not easy when the cylindrical type of plastic lock is used.

Pierced Bung

This is a tapered cork or rubber bung that fits the mouth of a standard one-gallon fermentation jar. It is pierced with a hole in which the stem of the fermentation lock is inserted.

Bottles

There are many kinds of wine bottles, each traditionally associated with a different type of wine as explained in Chapter 19, but all that the beginner need concern himself with is the acquisition of six clean wine bottles of any kind to hold his first gallon of wine. They should preferably be of clear glass for white wines to show off their colour and clarity and of green glass for red wines to prevent their being faded to brown by the action of light.

Closures

A corking gun is needed for the insertion of standard, cylindrical wine bottle corks, but the beginner should try to avoid buying even such minor items of equipment as a corking gun

Wine bottle

until he has tasted his first wine and decided to continue with this rewarding hobby. For his first batch, red or white polythene Vintops are perfectly suitable; many experienced winemakers use nothing else. They are inserted by hand, last indefinitely and are almost as cheap as corks.

Additives

These are very similar to those used in brewing: mainly water, sugar and yeast. The compounders will usually have incorporated any extra additives such as acid, nutrient salts or grape tannin into the formula, but occasionally they will be asked for in the instructions. Campden tablets will be needed for sterilization as already described, for the fermentation lock and for adding to the wine according to instructions.

Yeast

As was seen in Chapter 4 on yeast there are innumerable different cultures of wine yeasts of which twenty or more are commonly sold by suppliers. For his first gallon the beginner may use either an all-purpose wine yeast of a well-known brand or the type of yeast most suitable for the wine he proposes to make; a bordeaux yeast for a claret, or a hock, burgundy, port or sherry yeast as the case may be. A liquid culture of a well-known brand is probably safest.

Water

As only a gallon of wine is to be made it is advisable to boil all the water used. This will not only sterilize it but will also cause the unwanted mineral salts always present in hard water to precipitate out.

Sugar

Ordinary household granulated sugar is the kind on which all instructions are based, and there is little if any advantage to be gained for the beginner by experimenting with invert sugar or syrup.

Yeast Nutrient

Many experienced wine-makers, myself included, always add yeast nutrient to a must whether it is specified or not, but this can be done safely only if the nutrient is non-acid. Some proprietory nutrients contain a large proportion of acid which is not only unnecessary but will also upset the acid balance of the must. The nutrient should also contain vitamin B. It is worth reading the label to make sure of these two important points. If the instructions say merely 'add nutrient', use the dosage indicated on the nutrient label.

Acid

The section on acids in Chapter 5 explains that although citric acid can be faulted theoretically it is very satisfactory in practice. For this reason, and because it is easy to obtain and is also used in making up sterilizing fluid, it is usually specified in the instructions if any acid has to be added.

Tannin

This is usually already added, but if it is required use powdered grape tannin as instructed on p. 42.

Procedure

Selection

As advised in Chapter 10 on home brewing, go in the first instance to a shop whose proprietor or manager is able and willing to explain anything you do not understand. When choosing a wine compound it is even more important to compare prices than when selecting a brewing concentrate, for the prices of different brands vary even more widely, and here again personal experience rather than cost is the best guide to value.

Sterilization

Make up a sterilizing solution as explained on p. 72.

Preparation

Whereas the instructions for the use of concentrates for brewing are very much the same for all brands, those issued with winemaking compounds are so diverse that it is not possible to give an example that will approximate to all of them. Some directions are printed on the inside of the label so that unless you can persuade the shopkeeper to enlighten you it is necessary to buy the can in order to tear off the label before you can find out what you have let yourself in for and what extra additives you need, if any. Leave the compounds which instruct you to buy apparatus such as filters alone for the time being, and start with one that is not so demanding.

Whatever is said or unsaid 'on the can', begin by making up a starter bottle from the yeast you have bought, following the instructions given with it or those on p. 56. When the yeast is activated make up the sterilizing solution and wash and sterilize all the equipment including the bung, but leaving the corks or Vintops until they are needed. Never boil corks or polythene closures.

Next open the can and pour the concentrate through the larger funnel into the fermenting jar. Previous warming of the can will be helpful as the grape sugar may have crystallized out and become difficult to pour. Add hot, cold or tepid water as instructed. This should produce rather under a gallon of must at a temperature of about 75 °F (24 °C). The 'gallon' fermentation jars will in reality hold rather more, so that a considerable air-space is left above the surface of the must. This will provide both the oxygen that the yeast needs for its initial fermentation and room for the yeast head. If insufficient space is left an amazing quantity of sticky goo will climb out of the fermentation lock and flow down the jar. Play safe at first by standing the jar in a basin.

Stir in whatever quantity of sugar is asked for and the yeast nutrient, acid or any other additives specified, and when they are thoroughly dissolved add the contents of the activated yeast starter bottle. If it is difficult to stir the must properly through the neck of the jar, put the palm of a clean hand over the mouth and shake vigorously.

Next rinse any sterilizer off the bung and fit the fermentation lock to the bung and the bung to the jar, making sure that the two joints are airtight. Half-fill the lock with water and add a little sterilizing fluid. When the bung is later removed for topping up, some of the liquid in the bubbler may be sucked into the jar and if it contains too much sterilizer this may slow up the fermentation. Leave the jar in a warm place, out of draughts, so that the ferment may proceed strongly and quickly.

From here on the various instructions differ widely, but after stated periods more sugar has to be added and the jar has to be topped up with water so that there is no more air-space.

When the fermentation is complete follow the directions for siphoning the wine off the yeast, adding campden tablets and storing in the jar until it is time to bottle it.

Now read the chapter on bottling, wash and sterilize the bottles and Vintops or corks, and bottle your first gallon.

Making Wine from
Grape Juice Concentrates

The two greatest advances in all the history of home wine-making have undoubtedly been the introduction to the amateur market of the concentrated juice of wine grapes, usually known as grape concentrates, and of true wine yeast cultures. Both of these became generally available at reasonable prices early in the 1960s and between them they revolutionized the whole concept of the craft and supplied the impetus for a wave of popularity that within a decade was to transform the hobby of a few enthusiasts into a nationwide cult.

Until the introduction of grape concentrates and wine yeasts all home-made wines were of necessity 'country wines', that is to say wines made almost exclusively by country dwellers from fruit, flowers and vegetables cultivated in their farms or gardens or growing wild in the fields and hedgerows. Though grain, root vegetables and such oddments as tea and ginger were used in the winter, home wine-making was until very recently restricted to certain seasons and to the comparatively small proportion of the community living in rural areas, and even they had almost forgotten the once-traditional skills.

Good though such country wines often were even though they were fermented with wild or baker's yeasts, their successful preparation demanded a considerable amount of luck and more care, work and patience than the average town dweller was prepared to give even if he could obtain the necessary fresh ingredients, especially as the wines themselves did not resemble any of those to which he was accustomed. Grape concentrates made home wine-making a universal hobby by providing wines which are similar, and by no means inferior, to imported wines if fermented with the appropriate wine yeasts, by removing most of the luck, labour and long waiting from the operation, and, most important of all, by being available to everyone, everywhere, all the year round.

At first only red and white grape concentrates were imported and sold by the quart or gallon, often with no indication of the degree of concentration. Very soon, however, importers began to put them up in sufficient quantities to make one, two or more gallons of wine, to state their concentration in degrees Baumé (potential alcohol), and to print instructions for use on the containers. The vignerons of Spain and Cyprus began to realize the potential of the British amateur market as an outlet for their surplus wine grapes and to select and blend concentrates to make not only red and white table wines but also port, sherry, muscatel, madeira and vin rosé types.

Selection

From the start the number of different sizes of containers all sold to make a gallon of wine has been confusing, for they range from one pint (20 fl. oz) through the A2½ can (29·7 fl. oz), the kilo (about the same as the A2½), and the litre (35·2 fl. oz) to one quart (40 fl. oz). Roughly speaking, the greater the volume required to make a gallon the weaker the concentrate, but as the instructions with each stipulate the addition of sufficient sugar to bring the must up to the required gravity they all seem to work out satisfactorily.

When you are selecting the concentrate for your first gallon there is no need to worry about the exact size of the can. Decide what type of wine you prefer and choose the appropriate concentrate and a suitable wine yeast. As with the compounds, make sure that you understand the instructions on the container before you leave the shop. They may well require the addition of nutrient, citric or tartaric acid, and grape tannin. Beware the economically minded distributor who uses the same label, with instructions for making one gallon of wine, on all sizes of container up to a gallon of concentrate, or you will find yourself demonstrating the impossibility of getting a quart into a pint pot.

Equipment and Procedure

These are the same as have already been described in the previous section on wine compounds. The only differences will lie in the possible addition of acid, nutrient and grape tannin as specified in the instructions.

Other uses of Grape Concentrates

Concentrates not only make excellent wines by themselves, used as instructed on the containers; they are also of great value in giving true vinosity to all types of wines. Many recipes for country wines now call for the addition of grape concentrates for this purpose, and it will be found that the presence of the grape juice also produces a quicker and more thorough fermentation, especially when wine yeasts are used. Many experienced wine-makers use a little concentrate with practically all the wines they make. Until their advent, raisins were used for both these purposes but they imparted their own strong, characteristic flavour to the wine, often killing or masking the desired flavour and aroma. This was especially true in the case of flower wines, for the making of which concentrates are ideal. They are also far better than sugar syrup for sweetening over-dry finished wines and for topping up fermentation and storage vessels. In both cases the same type of concentrate as that used for the wine should be employed. For sweetening, small quantities should be mixed with a little of the wine before being added to the bulk, which should then be left for at least twenty-four hours before it is tasted. For topping up dilute the concentrate with four to five times its own volume of boiled water so that it approximates the gravity of the bulk to which it is to be added. Allow it to cool before use.

MAKING COUNTRY WINES

Fruit, Flower, Vegetable and Grain Wines

These are wines made from the produce of the farm, orchard, garden or hedgerow. They were originally known as 'country wines' to distinguish them from those imported from the continent and the term is still used to describe wines based on ingredients other than the grape even though their recipes may include grape concentrate and fresh or dried fruit imported from all parts of the world. Until comparatively recently they were, with mead, cider and perry, the only fermented drinks that could be made legally at home.

The traditional country wine recipe was almost always based upon a single fruit, flower or vegetable, for each had to be used when it was at its peak and compatible crops seldom seemed to coincide on the same farm or in the same garden. As with jam, so with wine: only one kind could be made at a time save when apples, which could be stored, were mixed with plums or blackberries.

Today wine can be made from all manner of blended ingredients with grape concentrate or raisins added to give vinosity, and the home wine-maker has tremendous scope for developing new recipes. It must, however, be remembered that many traditional recipes which are still being reprinted date from those far-off days when we were an agricultural society and each remote village and hamlet was a world of its own, producing all its basic needs and often cut off for a good part of each year even from its market town. In summer and autumn materials from which to make wine abounded in field, garden and hedgerow but storage facilities were almost nil, so that during the winter most wine-makers had only cereals, potatoes and other root vegetables on which to rely. Furthermore, wine of some kind that could be fermented in the warmth of the kitchen was the only alcoholic drink that could be made, for it would have been too cold to brew beer in bulk and the season for mead-making was in late July when the honey crop was gathered. Some of these grain, root and other winter wines can be good after very long maturation, and parsnip wine in particular can be really excellent, but because of the great variety of wine-making materials now readily available all the year round they are not made as much as in former years.

Today fresh, dried and canned fruits and berries form the bases of most country wines, followed by fresh and dried flowers and herbs, a fairly wide variety of root and other vegetables, several types of whole and flaked grains, the leaves and sap of trees and a number of spices, though with the exception of ginger most of these are used as additives to grain and other wines.

Wine from Fresh Fruit

Fruits suitable for wine-making include: apricots, bananas, bullaces, cherries, damsons, figs, grapefruit, lemons, mandarines, nectarines, oranges, peaches, pineapples, plums, sloes and tangerines. Apples and pears are dealt with separately in Section V, Cider and Perry.

Ingredients

As well as ripe, fresh fruit the following are needed:

Sugar

White granulated but preferably as standard syrup (p. 37). The substitution of $1\frac{1}{2}$ lb of a good clover honey for 1 lb of sugar improves many of the sweeter white wines made from fresh or dried fruit. The amount of sugar, if any, to be replaced by honey is very much a matter of personal taste but one half of the total amount is usually sufficient.

Yeast

A starter bottle should always be used, prepared either from an all-purpose wine yeast or from the specific type of yeast most suitable for the fruit used.

Yeast Nutrient

Always use a non-acid, vitaminized yeast nutrient.

Acid

Citric or malic/citric/tartaric formula as directed, or, if the wine is to be bottled, 1 teaspoonful of lactic acid solution per gallon and sufficient of the above to correct the acidity of the must to approximately pH 3·3.

Tannin

This is a necessity for all white and most red wines. Grape tannin powder used as directed guards against flatness and lack of life, faults that are otherwise common in fruit and flower wines. More can be added at any stage and any excess can be removed by using wine finings (not bentonite) or dissolving a little powdered gelatine in the wine.

Pectinaze (pectic enzyme)

Many fruits and vegetables contain pectin, the substance that makes jam set, and this is apt to cause haze in the wine. The addition of a pectic enzyme preparation not only prevents this but also increases juice extraction. All brands carry full instructions for use and one should be used in all wines made from fruit, berries or vegetables.

Vinosity

Only grapes or grape juice can give a wine true vinosity, and these also provide the natural food of the wine yeast. Old recipes therefore included raisins or sultanas and modern ones specify grape concentrate. Raisins can be bought cheaply in small quantities; they may, however, darken white wines and impart their own distinctive flavour if used in quantity, and sultanas are better in these respects. Both must be minced or chopped before use.

Grape concentrate needs no preparation and is more expensive if only a small amount is needed as about 1 kilo (1½ pints approximately) is usually the smallest quantity sold, but the surplus will keep in a well-stoppered bottle.

Bouquet

Nothing enhances the appeal of a wine more than a fragrant bouquet, and the aroma of most fruit wines is much improved by the use of lactic acid and the addition of a very small quantity of fresh or dried elderflowers infused in the must after fermentation has quietened down. They should be contained in a linen, muslin or nylon bag and removed after six days. More can be infused in the finished wine if necessary. Dried rose petals may be used instead and some people prefer a mixture of both.

Quantities for dried elderflowers, which can more easily be infused than the fresh florets, and *either* raisins *or* grape concentrate are given on p. 175. The flowers may be omitted, but if neither concentrate nor raisins are used add an extra ½ lb of sugar (½ pint of syrup) per gallon.

Procedure

Only the grape contains in itself everything necessary to make a perfect wine; all our native soft fruits and berries have either too much acid or too little sugar, or both, so that their juice has first to be diluted to reduce its acidity, after which sugar must be added. It may seem odd therefore that nearly all recipes specify the inclusion of even more acid, but the flavours of most berries and fruits are so strong that it is advisable to dilute their juices more than is necessary to correct their acidity and then to recorrect it before fermentation.

Juicing

If the wine-maker can pick his own fruit or berries he should do so on a sunny day when they are dry. All unsound fruit should be rejected, as bacteria and other spoilage organisms proliferate in wounds caused by birds or insects. Bruised portions of larger fruits should be completely cut out. The fruit should be thoroughly washed under running water and the larger types should then be chopped up and have the stones removed. The fruit is next placed in a polythene fermenting vessel or a large crock (not lead glazed), together with minced or chopped raisins or a suitable grape concentrate if either is to be used. For 1 gallon of wine pour on ½ gallon of boiling water and stir well.

Cover closely and leave until cool to the hand, then add 1 crushed campden tablet, stir well and leave for 24 hours. The softened fruit is next crushed by hand or a flat-bottomed, sterilized bottle filled with water. 1 lb of sugar or 1 pint of standard syrup is then dissolved in or mixed with 1 quart of water and stirred in. The water can be warmed if necessary to bring the temperature of the bulk, now containing about 7 pints of liquid, up to fermentation heat of about 75 °F (24 °C).

Add the acid, yeast nutrient, tannin and pectinaze as directed in the appropriate recipe, stir thoroughly, add the yeast starter bottle and stir again. Keep the must warm and well covered, and stir and crush the fruit daily. The juicing process may be speeded up by the use of rohament P, an enzyme that purées the fruit by digesting the cellulose of which its cell walls are composed. This is especially useful for hard fruit that is difficult to crush. All such preparations display full instructions for use. Wine presses are used for larger quantities.

Pulp Fermentation

The process now begun is known as fermentation on the pulp, that is to say on the juice, pulp and skin of the fruit together with some or all of the additives listed above. The pulp and skin yield both valuable yeast foods and the bouquet, flavour and colour which a pressed juice may lack. As the ferment progresses the alcohol produced will play a major part in extracting these and the results will be much superior to those obtained by the old method of boiling the fruit, which dispelled most of the volatile esters from which come the flavour and bouquet of the wine. The shorter the pulp fermentation the quicker the wine will mature.

Fermentation under Lock

Strain off the must into a fermentation jar through a straining bag or nylon sieve and a polythene funnel and squeeze the pulp lightly. Add either 1 lb sugar or 1 pint syrup or, better, sufficient of either to raise the gravity to G.95 after topping up to 1 gallon (the shoulder of the jar) with water at 75 °F (24 °C). Shake well and check acidity with pH comparison papers. Fit

Nylon strainer

lock, rack after 1 month, and then proceed as instructed in the sections on racking and storage, pp. 57 and 226. Feed the must with the remaining sugar as syrup in small doses as the fermentation dies down, shaking or stirring well each time.

Basic Recipes

Both the sugar and the acid content of fruit may vary by as much as 300 per cent as between a good season and a bad one and personal tastes also differ enormously especially as regards sweetness. It is therefore impossible to give standard recipes that can be followed blindly, and in fact the main function of the recipe now that hydrometers and pH comparison papers are so cheap, so easy to come by and so simple to use is to show how to make an average wine in an average season if no means are available for checking the O.G. and acidity of the must, and to indicate broadly the proportions of fruit, sugar, grape concentrate, acid and other ingredients. A good all-purpose wine yeast can be used in all these recipes if the types suggested are not available. All recipes are for 1 gallon unless otherwise stated.

Apricot

ripe fruit, split and stoned	5 lb
sugar	2 lb

grape concentrate	1 pint
or sultanas	1 lb
acid	2 teaspoons
tannin	¼ teaspoon
sauternes yeast	
yeast nutrient	
pectinaze	

Ferment for 3–4 days on the pulp, occasionally crushing the fruit by hand, then strain into jar under lock.

Banana

Banana wine can be made as Apricot, above, but will need longer maturation before it is drinkable. Fresh or dried elder-flowers (½ oz and ⅛ oz respectively) or the same quantities of rose petals will add bouquet. Bananas are more valuable in giving body to other wines by the addition of 6 oz to 1 lb per gallon or 2 to 5 oz if dried.

Cherry

The fruit should preferably be a mixture of morello and white-heart, though this is not essential.

fruit	6 lb
sugar	2 lb
red or white grape concentrate	1 pint
acid (but see below)	1 teaspoon
tannin	¼ teaspoon
bordeaux or burgundy yeast	
yeast nutrient	
pectinaze	

The teaspoon of acid is approximate: acidity varies so much that the pH of the must should really be checked.

Crush the fruit thoroughly. A pleasant almond flavour may be obtained by cracking a dozen or so cherry-stones and returning the kernels to the must.

Damson

| fruit | 4 lb |

sugar	2½ lb
red grape concentrate	½ pint
acid	1 teaspoon

Other ingredients as for Cherry wine (above), save for the addition of kernels.

Orange

fruit	3 lb
or 9 average-sized oranges	
sugar	2 lb
concentrate	½ pint
acid	1 teaspoon
tannin	¼ teaspoon
A.P. yeast	
yeast nutrient	
pectinaze	

Include some Sevilles with the fruit if possible.

Peel the oranges very thinly and remove all white pith, then ferment on the chopped fruit and the rind for 4 days with the sugar, concentrate, acid, tannin, yeast and nutrient, and pectinaze. Dried rose petals or elderflowers (⅛ oz) give a very pleasant bouquet.

Peach

ripe peaches, stoned and chopped	3–3½ lb
sugar	2 lb
concentrate	½ pint
acid	1 teaspoon
tannin	½ teaspoon

Other ingredients as for Apricot Wine, above.

Plum

ripe fruit	4 lb
sugar	2 lb
red or white concentrate	½ pint

Other ingredients as for Damson wine, above.

Rhubarb

Only the red parts of the stalks of unforced rhubarb picked in May or June should be used. Chop 6 lb finely, pour over it $\frac{1}{2}$ gallon of boiling water, crush the fruit well, and when it is cool stir in 1 oz of precipitated chalk and leave for 48 hours until it has eliminated the rhubarb's oxalic acid. Strain off the juice and re-acidify it to pH 3·3 with 1 teaspoonful lactic and sufficient citric or blended acid. Add 2 lb sugar, 1 pint concentrate, $\frac{1}{4}$ teaspoon tannin, bordeaux yeast, nutrient and pectinaze, and proceed as usual.

Sloe

sloes	3 lb
sugar	$2\frac{1}{2}$ lb
red concentrate	$\frac{1}{2}$ pint
acid	2 teaspoons

Other ingredients as for Damson or Plum wine, above.

Wine from Dried Fruit

Not only is dried fruit to be had all the year round but it is also often more suitable for wine-making than home-grown fresh fruit as most of it is imported from countries that have a great deal more sunshine than we do and it therefore has a higher sugar content. Generally speaking, any fresh fruit recipe can be adapted by using one third the weight of dried fruit, but there are several fruits that can only be bought in the dried form, such as:

Date

compressed (stoned) dates	3 lb
sugar	1 lb
white grape concentrate	1 pint
acid	4 teaspoons
tannin	$\frac{1}{2}$ teaspoon

A.P. yeast and yeast nutrient
pectinaze

Chop the dates finely, pour over ½ gallon of boiling water; when cool add 1 crushed campden tablet. After 24 hours add 1 quart of boiling water, sugar and concentrate, and when cool the acid, tannin, nutrient and yeast starter. Elderflower and rose-petal mixture (⅛ oz) may be added for bouquet. Ferment on the pulp for 5 days, strain into jar and rack when the first ferment has slowed down or after 4 weeks, as there may be a considerable amount of sediment.

Fig

figs (dried)	2 lb
sugar	2 lb
white or sherry-type concentrate	1 pint
acid	3 teaspoons
tannin	½ teaspoon
sherry or madeira yeast; nutrient	
pectinaze	

The procedure is as for Date Wine. Extra body may be given by the addition of 1 lb fresh or 6 oz dried bananas. Figs are an excellent additive to basic ingredients that lack character, especially rosehips, rosehip shells and grains.

Wine from Fresh Berries

All berries should be picked when fully ripe and if possible on a fine, sunny day; they should at all events be completely dry at the time for wet berries never seem to make good wine even if mould does not develop before they can be used. All leaves and stalks should be meticulously stripped and the procedure is then the same as for fresh fruit. The grape is of course the wineberry *par excellence*, but our native bilberry and elderberry make splendid wine and have been employed for centuries (not only in Britain) to 'stretch' the famous wines of commerce.

Basic Recipes

All make 1 gallon unless otherwise stated. Include lactic acid with the acid in all these recipes if possible.

Bilberry

Bilberry, blaeberry, blueberry, wineberry, whinberry, whortle-berry, huckleberry, hurtleberry – no berry ever had so many names as the fruit of the *vaccinium vacillans*, but by any other name the bilberry is still our best native wine-berry.

Bilberry: 1. Table Wine

berries	3 lb
sugar	3 lb
acid	2 teaspoons
burgundy yeast	
yeast nutrient	
pectinaze	

Bilberry: 2. 'Port'

berries	3½ lb
sugar	2½ lb
red grape concentrate, port type if possible	1 pint
bananas	1 lb
or dried bananas	6 oz
or glucose polymer	4 oz
pectozyme	
port yeast	
nutrient	
acid	3 teaspoons

Start with 1½ lb sugar and feed the rest gradually.

Blackberry: 1. Table Wine

very ripe berries	4 lb
sugar	2½ lb
red concentrate	½ pint

acid	2 teaspoons
tannin	$\frac{1}{4}$ teaspoon
A.P. or pommard yeast	
yeast nutrient	
pectinaze	

All berries having deep interstices should be very carefully washed in sulphited water and rinsed. Ferment for 6 days on the pulp.

Blackberry: 2. 'Port'

Use the same ingredients and proportions as Bilberry 'port' but include $\frac{1}{2}$ teaspoon of tannin.

Elderberry

Follow the Bilberry recipes, but the substitution of $1\frac{1}{4}$ lb honey for 1 lb sugar will help to counteract the harshness often caused in young elderberry wine by an excess of tannin. This can be precipitated out by the use of white of egg, gelatine or other protein finings, but the wine is apt to be left flat and insipid, whereas when the excess tannin is matured out over two years or more a splendid wine is produced.

Gooseberry

It seems a pity that luscious ripe gooseberries, sugary as grapes, do not make good wine but so it is; as with raspberries, their strong flavour persists and is less pleasant in wine than in the fresh fruit. One of the best of all country wines is, however, made from green gooseberries, preferably plucked just before they begin to colour and soften.

Gooseberry: 1. Table Wine

green berries	4 lb
sugar	$2\frac{1}{2}$ lb
white grape concentrate	1 pint
acid	2 teaspoons
chablis or hock yeast	

yeast nutrient
pectinaze

Top and tail the gooseberries carefully. Then proceed as usual, but ferment on the pulp for 6 days.

2. Gooseberry Champagne

As above, but use only 1½ lb sugar and follow the procedure in Chapter 17, Sparkling Wines (p. 207).

Grape

Very good wine is now made commercially from British-grown grapes, but their juice, like that of our other native fruits and berries, usually needs the addition of sugar. If large quantities are to be dealt with a press is required (see p. 51) but enough grapes for a gallon or two of wine can be treated much like any other berry. They should be left as long as possible on the vine and picked on a sunny day when they are quite dry. For 1 gallon:

        grapes   10 lb
        sugar   1–2 lb
    or grape concentrate (see below)
        tannin and acid if required
        wine yeast and nutrient

It is not safe to rely on the yeast contained in the bloom on the grapes so they should be washed in sulphited water and rinsed. They should then be placed in the fermentation vessel and crushed, and the free juice poured off into a gallon jar. This will show how much there is and it should be made up to 8 pints at a gravity of 80 to 85 for white wine and 85 to 90 for red by the judicious addition of water and either sugar or red or white grape concentrate. The acidity is corrected to pH 3·3 with tartaric acid or a blend, and since the juice has been diluted add the usual amount of vitaminized nutrient and ½ teaspoon grape tannin to white grape must. Red should not need any tannin.

Return the must to the fermentation vessel and pulp, stir in 2 crushed campden tablets or the equivalent, and leave it closely covered for 24 hours before adding the starter. This should preferably, but not necessarily, have been prepared from ½ pint of the same juice together with 2 teaspoons sugar, a pinch of nutrient and a hock yeast for white wines and bordeaux or burgundy for red. The skins, pulp and pips will form a cap, which must be pressed down several times daily to avoid its exposed part becoming air-tainted.

White wine should be left to ferment on the pulp for only 2 days, after which the must is strained into the gallon jar and the pulp squeezed out in a sterile filter bag or cloth. It is then sparged with a pint or so of warm water (not boiling, or pectin haze may result), once more squeezed out, and the extra juice added to the jar under lock.

Red wine is similarly treated save that it is left to ferment on the pulp for 10 days or until it is sufficiently coloured.

In both cases the wine should be racked at 4 weeks, or earlier if the initial fermentation has died down, and thereafter at monthly intervals with the addition of 1 campden tablet save at the first racking. Storage and bottling is on normal lines but the fermentation temperatures throughout should be lower than for country wines; about 65–70 °F (18–21 °C) to begin with and 60–5 °F (15–18 °C) thereafter.

Mulberry or Loganberry

As Blackberry.

Red Currant

berries	4 lb
sugar	2 lb
A.P. or chablis yeast	
nutrient	
pectinaze	
grape concentrate	1 pint

(use rosé if obtainable; if not use white but this is essentially a rosé wine)

Ferment on the pulp for 5 days. No acid or tannin should be needed but pH should be checked.

Rosehip: 1

hips	4 lb
sugar	2 lb
grape concentrate	1 pint
acid	1 teaspoon
tannin	$\frac{1}{2}$ teaspoon
graves or sauternes yeast	
nutrient	
pectinaze	

When crushing the hips be careful not to crush the white pips especially if a baulk of wood is used, as they are very bitter. Ferment on the pulp for 5 days.

Rosehip: 2

As above, but use only 3 lb hips and add 8 oz chopped dried figs. A madeira yeast goes well with this recipe.

Rowanberry

ripe berries	3 lb
sugar	2 lb
grape concentrate	1 pint
bananas	12 oz
or dried bananas	4 oz
dried elderflower or rose petals	$\frac{1}{8}$ oz
acid	1 teaspoon
A.P. yeast	
nutrient	
pectinaze	

Ferment on the pulp for 4 days.

Wine from Dried Berries

Grape concentrates apart, the home wine-maker's most valuable all-the-year-round stand-bys are undoubtedly dried berries, and although after hundreds of years raisins and sultanas have now been ousted by the concentrates as the sources of vinosity dried bilberries and elderberries are still our favourite indigenous wine-berries despite the fact that they are now all imported and comparatively expensive. It would probably be profitable to set up drying centres here but though there are certainly thousands of children in our villages and even suburbs (for the elder, since time immemorial cultivated and revered as the 'doctor tree' as well as a source of wine, still likes to grow close to man) who would enjoy making some pocket-money by collecting the berries the law* in its wisdom forbids them to do so and adult labour in country districts cannot be spared. During the Second World War country schoolchildren were allowed to collect rosehips, which are a valuable source of vitamin C, and these also are dried and make excellent wine; they are best for most purposes in the form of split shells from which the bitter, white pips have been winnowed. Dried rowanberries are also popular, but the use of hawthornberries is now thought to be inadvisable.

The instructions for fresh berries apply equally to dried ones, but the one-third by weight of dried to fresh fruit formula does not apply to berries, as when dried these have higher concentrations of colour, flavour, fruit sugars and sometimes tannin. All imported dried berries are fumigated but even so the same procedures apply; they should be thoroughly washed in sulphited water, rinsed, have half a gallon of boiling water poured over them and be left to soak, when cool, for 24 hours after a crushed campden tablet has been added, before yeasting. Dried berries vary considerably in quality and it is always best to buy those that are properly sealed in transparent polythene packs and bear the label of a well-known supplier. As they are usually sold in 1-lb or ½-kilo packs the following recipes are based on these quantities. Economy-minded wine-makers have, however, reported unbelievable gallonages of wine from 1 lb of bilberries used and reused as in Recipe 2 and eked out with grape concentrate and raisins.

* Factories Acts and Children's and Young Persons' Acts, as amended.

Dried Bilberries: 1

Makes 3 gallons table wine. No tannin is needed.

berries	1 lb
sugar	6 lb
red grape concentrate	1½ pints
or raisins	3 lb
acid	2 teaspoons
dried elderflowers	¼ oz
A.P. or bordeaux yeast	
yeast nutrient	
pectinaze	

For 1 gallon use one third of the ingredients throughout, but ⅛ oz of dried elderflowers.

Dried Bilberries: 2

(*a*) *1 gallon 'Port'*

berries	1 lb
sugar	2 lb
red or port type grape concentrate	½ pint
or raisins	1 lb
acid	1 teaspoon
elderflowers	⅛ oz
dried bananas, chopped	8 oz
port yeast	
yeast nutrient	
pectinaze	

Again no tannin is used.

Proceed as usual but strain the juice off the crushed berries and bananas 48 hours after full fermentation has begun. More syrup can be added 2 oz at a time when the gravity drops to 05 (or the fermentation has slowed right down and the wine tastes fairly dry) until the wine is as sweet as you want it and fermentation has finally stopped.

(*b*) *1 gallon 'Claret'*

Immediately the first lot of must has been strained off the pulp referment it with ingredients as above. Add more nutrient but no more yeast or pectinaze after making up to 1 gallon with water at 75 °F (24 °C). Stir well and leave to ferment on the pulp for 4 days.

(c) *1 gallon Vin Rosé*

As above but with white grape concentrate; add ½ teaspoon tannin and ferment on the pulp for 5 to 6 days. Bilberries may well provide another gallon of rosé or even more.

Dried Elderberry

Follow the recipe for Bilberry wine, but note the remarks in the recipe for fresh Elderberry wine on excess tannin.

Raisins or Sultanas

Though principally used by home wine-makers as a supplement to give vinosity to wines that would otherwise lack it, raisins and sultanas both make pleasant wine on their own account.

Fruit, chopped or minced	3 lb
Sugar	2 lb
dried bananas, chopped	½ lb
Acid	1 teaspoon
Dried elderflowers *or* rose petals	⅛ oz
A.P. wine yeast and nutrient	
pectinaze	

The procedure is as usual but if a sweet wine is required the must may be fed with more sugar, as under Bilberry wine, and a sauternes or tokay yeast will give better results. A crushed race (medium-sized piece) of ginger or the infusion of ¼ oz of caraway seeds go well with this wine, which makes an excellent, inexpensive base for experiment.

Dried Rosehips and Rosehip Shells

It is usually preferable to use the rosehip shells as the whole dried hips contain pips that may give a slight bite to the wine and it was probably to mask this that the excellent combination of rosehip and fig was first devised. As 1 lb of shells will make 3 gallons of wine, rosehip shells can be treated in the same way as bilberries but ½ teaspoon of tannin per gallon should be added. The first gallon should be a fine, dark after-dinner wine if fed with syrup or sugar in the same way as bilberry 'port', especially if 4 oz of chopped, dried figs are added to the pulp as well as the dried bananas and a madeira yeast is used. A sherry or, if obtainable, a madeira-type grape concentrate should be used. In all the 3-gallon recipes it is economical and quite satisfactory to split a litre or kilo can or sachet of concentrate between the first 2 gallons and to substitute 3 lb chopped raisins or sultanas for the final gallon.

Dried Rowanberries (1 gallon)

berries	1 lb
sugar	2½ lb
white or muscatel grape concentrate	1 pint
chopped dried bananas	½ lb
acid	2 teaspoons
dried elderflowers	⅛ oz
A.P. wine yeast	
nutrient	
pectinaze	

Proceed as with fresh rowanberries. The slight sourness of rowanberries seems to be intensified when they are dried, hence the increased amount of grape concentrate.

Wines from Fresh or Dried Flowers and Herbs

Delicious wine can be made from many sorts of flowers and herbs both fresh and dried, but it should always be remembered that apart from any medicinal virtues they may have these contribute only their fragrance, colour and flavour to the wine and that the yeast therefore has to depend on substances other than flowers and sugar for the nitrogenous salts, acid and vitamins that it needs if the fermentation is to be reasonably quick and thorough and the alcoholic content satisfactory. Additional tannin is also required if the wine, however deliciously scented, is not to taste flat and lifeless. Floral wines should be medium-dry to sweet, full bodied, of good vinosity and fairly high alcoholic content, and if the precious bouquet of the flowers has been carefully preserved the opening of a bottle will bring all summer into a dark, winter's room.

The Base

The success of wines made from fresh or dried flowers depends very largely upon the basic wine designed as a vehicle for their scent, flavour and colour, and the ideal base should be as neutral as possible so that there will be nothing to mask, clash with or distort these.

Flower wines, like fruit wines, should rely upon grape concentrate as the best source of vinosity, but whereas in the fruit wines it is merely an ingredient, in flower wines the concentrate forms the main fermentation base and is also particularly valuable in that it imparts the body which flower wines otherwise lack. The old expedients of adding wheat or other grains to the recipe were never really successful by modern standards, and the wines took many years to mature. The amount of grape concentrate is dictated by the type of wine and ranges from one-half to one of the 1-kilo sachets or cans usually sold to make 1 gallon of grape wine. Apple concentrate carefully blended from a mixture of sweet and sharp fruit also makes a very good base for flower wines; the clean, unobtrusive flavour of the apples goes well with most floral bouquets without masking them, especially if rather more than the normal quantity of blooms is used.

Fresh Flower Wines

Gathering Fresh Flowers

Flowers should be picked on a fine, sunny day when the dew

has quite evaporated and they are at their best, fully opened and warmed through. Avoid bruising the blooms or leaving them long before use, especially in a plastic bag or other airtight container.

Preparation

All stalks and leaves should be discarded and in most cases the green calyces or sheaths should be stripped, as they give the wine a bitter taste. In case the blooms have been fouled by any of the insecticides or other lethal sprays with which we now pollute our countryside the culled blossoms should be thoroughly washed in half a gallon of cold water to which 1 crushed campden tablet has been added and then rinsed in a colander under the cold tap before use.

Making the Wine

First create a vigorously fermenting must from the ingredients suitable for the flowers to be used, as set out below, being careful not to commit the three cardinal errors no matter how many books may tempt you to: these are, first, and worst, to boil the flowers or pour boiling water over them; second, to place them in the must before fermentation begins; and third, to add the pared rinds of oranges and lemons.

Boiling the flowers or dousing them with boiling water will destroy or disperse by evaporation the volatile esters and essential oils that give them their fragrance and flavour. These will similarly be lost in the streaming bubbles of carbon dioxide gas given off by the first, violent ferment if the flowers are already in the must, while the harsh essential oils present in citrus fruit rinds may well mask or distort the delicate floral perfumes which it should be our whole objective to preserve in their full strength and purity.

The starter should be added to the must several days before the flowers are to be gathered so that they can be immersed in it when the initial ferment has died down and it contains sufficient alcohol to leach out their scent, colour and any flavour that they may possess gently and without wastage.

The ideal fermentation vessel for our purpose is a polythene container with a snap-seal lid fitted with rubber grommets to accommodate both a fermentation lock and if necessary a heater/thermostat unit set at 75 °F (24 °C). If the flowers are added loose they will form a floating cap on the must and as only part of this will be in contact with the liquid, extraction will be slowed up and there will be a considerable risk of spoilage, so first put them in a muslin or nylon bag containing a non-metallic weight such as a heavy, sterilized glass or ceramic ashtray.

The flowers should be left submerged for 3 to 5 days during which time the bag may be gently squeezed daily or pressed with a clean wooden or plastic spoon. When maximum extraction seems to be complete the must is transferred to the fermentation jar under lock. The bag should be squeezed only very lightly. The wine should first be racked at about 4 weeks and if the floral bouquet is not strong enough more flowers can be infused in a small muslin bag at any time during the fermentation. When flower wines are racked the end of the outflow tube should be kept under the surface and all splashing avoided.

Recipes for Fresh Flower Wines

It will be seen that comparatively few of our myriad garden and wild flowers are listed below, and that none of the recipes are for blends of different flowers. Comparatively few flowers are both safe and suitable for wine-making and of these a number are of medicinal value only so have been omitted. The remainder range from merely dull to poisonous so that it is important not to depart from the list given here. It should also be remembered that several plants, including for example honeysuckle, have perfectly suitable blossoms but quite toxic berries. The reason that no blends are given is that floral wines should be made from blossoms at the peak of perfection; no two species can be relied upon to reach their best simultaneously. Besides that, most people like to be able to recognize in their wine the scent of the particular flower from which it has been made.

The basic recipes to use are:

(A) All grape concentrate. Use a white grape concentrate with as little character of its own as possible, and certainly not one that has been flavoured or compounded in any way. Make it up as instructed on the sachet or can for a sweet or medium-sweet wine. This usually means adding 12–20 oz of sugar to the gallon.

(B) Use half the kilo sachet or can of concentrate, or ½ litre or 1 pint, and 2 lb of sugar.

(C) If no suitable concentrate is available a gallon of must is made from:

sugar 2½–3 lb
chopped sultanas ½ lb
(Sultanas impart less of their own colour and taste than raisins.)
To each of these add:
Vitaminized yeast nutrient (Vitamins are essential and if vitaminized nutrient cannot be had buy some vitamin B-complex tablets from the chemist and add 2 per gallon, crushed)
citric acid, *or* preferably a malic/tartaric/citric blend, to pH3·3 or 2 level teaspoons
grape tannin ¼ teaspoon (more may be added later)

Base (C) will lack body, so:

(*a*) if you like a honey flavour, substitute honey for some or all of the sugar at the rate of 1¼ lb honey for 1 lb sugar, first raising it to boiling point both to sterilize it and to drive off some of its own scent and taste; or

(*b*) simmer 8 oz dried bananas (or 1½ lb fresh) in about 1 quart water and add the liquor to the must when it has cooled to make up 1 gallon in all; or

(*c*) when stirring in the sugar or standard syrup add 8 oz of glucose polymer. This has little sweetness and only about 10 per cent of fermentables, so no adjustment to the sugar content is necessary.

Use a vigorous starter prepared from a sound white wine yeast. Hock, chablis and champagne are good for the lighter, drier wines, and sauternes, graves or tokay for those intended to be sweeter and more full-bodied. Failing these a good all-purpose wine yeast is usually quite satisfactory.

If apple concentrate is used the (A) recipe would require ⅓ litre (or 1 pint) concentrate and 2 lb sugar; the (B) recipe ¼ litre (or ½ pint) and 2½ lb sugar. To avoid haze add 1 tablespoon pectinaze to all apple concentrate recipes. Other musts are rendered less liable to haze by the addition of half this amount.

Clary (Salvia Superba)
June–July
Clary or salvia is a form of flowering sage once cultivated not only for its beauty but also because it was the accepted specific for good memory and mental health generally and because clary wine was thought to be an aphrodisiac. The flavour and scent are so strong that 1 quart of blooms suffices. Use base (A).

Coltsfoot
March–April
The flowers have been used for centuries for coughs and weak chests and the root makes a kind of herbal tobacco that is also said to be beneficial. The wine is good but all the better for a race (medium-sized piece) of root ginger, crushed. Use base (B), or (A) with honey to soothe a cough.

Cowslip
April–May
Cowslip wine is not only delicious but also a powerful, non-addictive soporific. A wine-glass at bed-time is as good as a sleeping pill and more pleasant to take, and two glasses are twice as good and twice as pleasant. If taken before one lays one's head on a hop pillow this prescription has seldom been known to fail! I was born and brought up as a boy in the most remote part of Worcestershire, a county long famous for its golden cowslip meadows; for centuries the wine had been made in and around Worcester commercially but every country household made their own.

Use 2 quarts with no calyces, stalk or leaves, or three quarts or even 1 gallon if the wine is to be used as a soporific. Use basic recipe (B) with 2½ lb honey or 2 lb sugar.

Dandelion

Most of spring and summer but traditionally from St George's day, 23 April

Dandelion wine, or tea, has long been used as a diuretic. The yellow blossoms make a fine, strong wine and if a few green calyces are left in and the wine is kept for a few years a remarkable whisky flavour emerges. Two quarts are needed. Use base (A).

Elderflower

May–June–July

Rightly called the queen of the flower wines, this has the most delicate fragrance imaginable and was held to purify the blood. The flowers should be in full bloom and of the white variety. The elder was once extensively cultivated, when its blossoms and berries were sold to commercial wine-makers and apothecaries, and there are many different types.

Only 1 pint of blossoms, stripped from the flower heads with fingers or a fork, should be used or the delicate perfume of the wine may suddenly change to rank Old Tom Cat. Use base (B).

Gorse

May–June–July

Said to be slimming, gorse wine is made from the golden blossoms only, and 4 quarts are required to the gallon. Use base (B).

Honeysuckle

June–July

Only 1 quart of the beautifully though strongly scented flowers is required. Make sure that all leaves and green parts are removed, and do not be tempted to try to use the berries later as they are poisonous. Use base (A), with honey.

Marigold

July–August–September

This was one of the most valued heart specifics and makes a pleasant wine. 2 quarts of the petals, gathered when fully out, are sufficient, and no green must be included. Use base (A) or (B).

Oxlip

April–May

It is very many years since I tasted oxlip wine and I have never
seen a recipe for it, but it used to be made in Worcestershire
exactly as cowslip wine. The oxlip is a cross between a cowslip
and a primrose, and in the rare oxlip meadows it grew in
golden-green profusion. The wine as I remember it was a more
fragrant and delicate version of cowslip. Follow the Cowslip
wine recipe.

Pansy

June–July–August

Pansy wine is worth trying as an experiment. It is best to select
one colour only or all yellows or all dark colours. Use a gallon
of petals to a gallon of wine, as the scent is so faint. Use base (B).

Primrose

April–May

The primrose was said to have mildly tonic properties and its
scent is of course deliciously spring-like. It is, however, almost
as elusive as that of the pansy, and 3 to 4 quarts of blossoms
are necessary for a gallon of wine. Use base (B).

Rose Petals

June–July–August

Rose petals make the most delicately scented wine, but they
must be from scented roses just becoming overblown. Use white
or yellow petals for pale golden wine and the deepest red
available for red; a mixture gives a rosé, but this can be darkened with wine colouring later if desired. 2 quarts of really
strongly scented petals or up to 3 quarts of less fragrant ones
are enough for 1 gallon of wine. If the finished wine lacks scent,
a few drops of triple-distilled rosewater from the chemist's may
be added before bottling. Use base (A).

Wallflower

June–July

The wallflower is so strongly scented that only a quart of
blossoms is needed, which should be treated in the same way as
rose petals. Use base (A), with honey or sugar.

Dried Flower Wines

Many dried flowers are sold by herbalists, but most of them are used for therapeutic purposes only and are unsuitable for our purposes.

Home wine-making suppliers usually stock only elderflowers, rose petals, dandelions, cowslips and red clover. All of these make excellent wine and are sold for the purpose in 2-oz packets, each of which is sufficient for 1 gallon. Elderflowers are the exception, needing only 1 oz, to start with at any rate; more may always be infused later in a small bag suspended in the must by a silk or nylon thread held in place by the bung of the gallon jar. All dried flowers should be sold packed in heat-sealed polythene sachets, which not only preserve them perfectly but also allow the purchaser to see what he is getting.

Procedure

This is exactly the same as described for fresh flowers.

1. Prepare a suitable basic ferment (see fresh flowers).
2. Wash and rinse the dried flowers.
3. Immerse them in the must in a muslin or nylon bag when the first, violent fermentation has died down.
4. Rack after four weeks and proceed as usual.

Wine from Herbs, Roots, Etc.

The great majority of herbal wines were originally made not to be drunk for pleasure but in order to preserve and concentrate the therapeutic virtues of the herbs, but those listed below are included simply because they make good wine.

Herbal wines are made by exactly the same process as floral wines, but aromatic herbs are usually much more powerful than flowers and should not therefore be left for too long in the must. It is a simple matter to increase the scent and flavour of the wine by infusion but it is often impracticable to reduce them by dilution if they are too strong. As with flowers, fresh or dried herbs impart only their scent, taste and colour to the wine. For simplicity's sake ginger, caraway seeds, cloves, tea, coffee and so forth are included in this section but vermouths and other herb-based aperitifs will be found in Chapter 24, Fortified Wines, and herbal liqueurs in Chapter 25, Liqueurs.

TABLE 4.

Quantities to make 1 gallon:	Fresh (quarts)	Dried (oz)	Base (as floral wines)
Balm	2	2	A
Lemon Thyme	1	1	B
Mint	1	1	A
Nettles (use young tops only)	2	2	B
Parsley	1	1	B
Sage	3	2	A

Ginger

Crush 2 oz of root ginger to expose the fibres, bring it to the boil in a quart or so of water, simmer in a closed saucepan for 15 minutes and then pour the hot liquor and the root on to the ingredients for base (A) to which have been added the thinly-pared rinds of a lemon and an orange. Citrus peel may be used with strongly flavoured ingredients such as ginger, caraway seeds and cloves as long as no white pith is included and all these may be added to the must when it is compounded and removed when it is transferred to the fermentation jar under lock. Green ginger wine is made in the same way but tinted with green wine colouring.

Though ginger wine is very pleasant and warming and admirable as a component of 'whisky Mac', the main use of the root is to give life and interest to wines that would otherwise lack them. Most herbal, grain and vegetable wines are all the better for a race of ginger.

Caraway Seed

Only dedicated seed-cake addicts can really appreciate wine made from caraway seed alone but the addition of ½ oz of ginger and the pared rinds of an orange and a lemon to base (A) improve it. 1 oz seeds is ample. If they can be cracked (e.g. in a coffee mill) infuse them for 4 or 5 days after the initial ferment is over; if not, treat the uncracked seeds in the same way as ginger. Caraway is an excellent flavouring additive but because some palates react strongly to it a little should be infused in some finished wine so that your own tastes can be gauged before a gallon is embarked upon.

Cloves

Treat these exactly as uncracked caraway seed. Use 1 oz per gallon and base (A).

Tea

1. This is a good stand-by wine with remarkable recuperative powers that needs little or no maturation. Any of the bases given may be used but (B) with 2½ lb honey substituted for the sugar is excellent. Put 4 tablespoons (about 1¼ oz) tea in a warm, dry crock or saucepan, pour on to it ½ gallon of briskly boiling water, cover it closely and leave it to infuse for 5 minutes. Strain the hot tea over the base ingredients to which pared citrus rinds have been added as above, and top up to 1 gallon with the liquor in which ¼ oz ginger and (if liked) ⅛ oz caraway seeds have been simmered for 15 minutes. If any further topping up is needed pour sufficient boiling water on to the tea-leaves, infuse and strain as before. A sherry or madeira yeast is good with tea wine, but any sound all-purpose wine yeast will serve.

2. The above recipe produces a pleasant, warming stock wine from undistinguished tea but if it is desired to retain the delicate fragrance of really good tea the fermentation should be started with only ½ to ¾ gallons of must containing 1 kilo or litre of white grape concentrate and no sugar. The tea should be infused and added when cool after the first ferment has died down. No ginger or other additives are needed and honey may

mask the flavour and aroma of fine tea. The sugar should be fed gradually. When racking, the outflow tube should be kept below the surface and every means described in the general section on flower wines should be employed to retain the bouquet.

Coffee
Use either ½ lb good, freshly ground coffee beans or a heaped tablespoon of the best instant coffee obtainable and proceed as in the second tea wine recipe, save that when the coffee is infused the water should be only just boiling and not at the brisk boil necessary for tea, and the coffee should be well stirred during infusion.

The quantities of ingredients in these wines are dictated almost entirely by personal taste and only average-to-minimum amounts have been given. It is most important to use the best available and not to attempt false economies, as so many recipes still advise, by collecting the small leavings from tea- and coffee-pots instead of using fresh tea or coffee. Such recipes date from three centuries ago, when tea and coffee were expensive luxuries, and have been laboriously reprinted over and over again ever since. Good wine cannot be made from the gallon or so of stale swipes which will result from months of such penurious gleanings.

Peppercorns
Country wine-makers often used to put a few crushed black peppercorns either in the must or in the cask or storage jar, especially when making red wines. They certainly imparted a certain piquancy to wines which were prone to be heavy and dull owing to the use of baker's yeast or wild yeast and what we would consider excessive quantities of ingredients including grain to give body. Peppercorns should not be as necessary in modern wines based on grape concentrate and fermented with wine yeast, but up to 6 to the gallon will often improve any wine that lacks character.

Cereal Wines

Wines made from grain used to be made in quantity in the winter when only cereals and root vegetables were generally available for the purpose but they required long maturation and the addition of spices to relieve their heaviness and impart some zest. The recipes given here are modernized, and the use of grape concentrate and fungal amylase improves them considerably and shortens their maturation time. Barley and rice wines are particularly good. All grains should be carefully washed in several changes of water or in a strainer under the tap before they are used, to get rid of any traces of toxic sprays.

Procedure

This is the same whatever grains or flakes are used, save that flakes are not washed first.

1. Wash grains, not flakes, thoroughly as above.
2. Steep for 12 hours in $\frac{1}{2}$ gallon of water to which 1 crushed campden tablet has been added. Add spices.
3. Strain the unabsorbed liquor off the grain or flakes into a measure, fill up to 1 gallon with water and bring it to the boil.
4. Put all the ingredients for bases (A) or (B) (see p. 191), except for the yeast and vitaminized yeast nutrient, in the fermentation vessel with the steeped grain or flakes, pour the boiling water over them and stir well.
5. At 75 °F (24 °C) stir in the vitaminized yeast nutrient, a starter prepared from any suitable wine yeast and $\frac{1}{2}$ teaspoon fungal amylase, the natural enzyme that changes the starch of the cereal into fermentable sugars.
6. Ferment on the pulp for at least 5 days or until the fermentation has quietened down, stirring daily.
7. Rack first at 4 weeks, discarding any spices that may remain.

Recipes

Barley Wine
> grain   1 lb
> *or* flakes   ½ lb

spices to taste
Use base (B).

Wheat Wine
As barley.

Maize Wine
> kibbled maize (cracked corn)   1½ lb
> *or* flakes   ¾ lb

spices to taste
Use base (B).

Rice Wine: 1
Use 3 lb brown, unpolished rice. This is also called paddy, husked, health and sometimes red rice, and it may be long- or round-grain; it must never be polished rice such as is usually sold for cooking. Use base (B).

Rice Wine: 2
Another method is to steep the rice for 2 weeks in cold water and then boil it gently until the grain and water form a thick, milky fluid which is mixed when hot with base (B), after which the procedure is as above. The most famous rice wine is of course the Japanese *sake*, which owes its surprising strength and speed of fermentation to the use of the symbiotic culture of a yeast and a mould.

Instead of the spices more commonly used in cereal wines dried juniper berries are sometimes used, or gin flavouring if these are unobtainable. If the rice wine is carefully fed with more sugar, a remarkably gin-like drink can be produced. The ultimate refinement is to fortify it with gin or vodka and then to infuse some vermouth herbs in it; this can produce a good (and cheap!) martini.

Flour and Bread Wines
These are for the experimentally minded, but it should be

remembered that powerful drinks somewhere between wine and beer have been made for ages by fermenting rye or wholemeal flour or bread; the Egyptian fellaheen still make their *boozah* by this method. A modernized method is to mix 1 lb of wholemeal (not white) flour with either 1 quart of black treacle or molasses (not golden syrup) or 1 pint of treacle or molasses and ½ pint of white, muscatel or sherry-type grape concentrate. Pour over the mixture 5 pints of boiling water, stir well and when cool add the acid, vitaminized yeast nutrient, wine yeast starter and fungal amylase as usual. The initial fermentation may be very violent and continue for some time, but at least a week should elapse before the liquor is strained off and put under lock. A race of ginger, 4 peppercorns and a pinch of caraway seeds go well in this wine. Rack first at 4 weeks.

Spices

It is traditional to spice cereal wines, and though the need is not so great if they are made by the updated methods given here most people find that the judicious addition of root ginger (a race, or up to ¼ oz), crushed black peppercorns (up to 6), cloves (up to 6) or caraway seeds (up to ¼ oz), or a combination of these to suit personal tastes, cheers them up immensely. Rice wine takes all these flavours particularly well, in addition to juniper berries.

All spices should be added at stage 2 and steeped with the grain. They should have imparted sufficient flavour to the brew by the time it is strained and put under lock; if desired they can be transferred to the fermentation jar (this will entail adding caraway seeds, peppercorns and cloves in a small muslin bag at the start and picking out the ginger), but they should all be discarded at the first racking after 4 weeks.

Wine from Root Vegetables

Like cereal wines, and for the same reasons, these are not as popular as they were in pre-grape-concentrate days, but they can be very good and parsnip wine in particular is well worth the making.

Procedure

1. Scrub the roots very thoroughly under the cold tap to get rid of all the earth, but do not peel.

2. Chop them into medium-sized pieces; if these are too small they will pulp and haze will result.

3. Simmer with spices until tender but not mushy, or the wine will probably be hazy.

4. Only the liquor is used for wine; the vegetables may be eaten. Strain the hot liquor on to base (B) (p. 91) as in the case of cereal wines.

5. When cool add yeast, nutrient and fungal amylase.

6. When the initial ferment has died down, strain the must into a fermentation jar under lock. Discard spices either at this point or when the wine is first racked at 4 weeks.

Recipes

Beetroot Wine

young tender beets	4½
port yeast	
race of ginger	
cloves	4–6

Scrub the beets very carefully to minimize the earthy taste, which may take a year or more to disappear especially if large old beets are used. Make up base (A) with a port-type grape concentrate if available; otherwise an ordinary red one; a port quality should develop as the wine matures, but it will normally fade to a golden colour with age.

Carrot Wine

Use 4½ lb prime carrots, not too old. Other ingredients are as for Beetroot wine, but use A.P. or sherry yeast and white or sherry-type concentrate. Optionally, 4 crushed black pepper-corns. When it has aged this wine should develop a whisky flavour and colour.

Parsnip Wine

Use 5 lb old parsnips, preferably brought in after a hard frost (it doesn't matter if they are a little flabby). Other ingredients as for Beetroot wine, but use base (B) with white concentrate and A.P. wine yeast starter, and a race of ginger.

Parsnips make one of the best of all country wines, but like all root wines they take a year or more to reach their peak even when maturation is speeded up by the use of grape concentrate. As made in the old days, with more roots and no concentrate, parsnip wine was famous for its 'searching' qualities but this modern recipe tames it to the gentlest of laxatives.

Potato Wine

Use 3 lb old potatoes, and base (B). Suggested spices are a race of ginger, and $\frac{1}{4}$ oz caraway seeds or 6 peppercorns or 6 cloves. Simmer gently and make sure that the pieces of potato do not pulp.

Potatoes have for centuries formed the foundation of legend-ary rural recipes for 'jungle juice' and 'tanglefoot'. The latter was made from potatoes, raisins, oranges, lemons and rough cider, and I drank it first in a Warwickshire farmhouse. When I met my host in the local next day he remarked apologetically, 'Ah, 'tes the old scrumpy does it', but it wasn't: our frail state was due to the old spud. The recipe called for 6 lb or more of potatoes per gallon, and these tubers contain fusel oil and other substances that can be unpleasantly toxic at too high a concentration. Regard 3 lb per gallon as the maximum; try 2 lb with base (A) to start with.

Vegetable Wines

Recipes exist for making wine from every sort of kitchen-garden vegetable including cabbages and onions. Those given below are excellent, especially peascod wine (pea-pod if you prefer it), and the procedure is the same for practically all vegetables; quantities are not critical and about 4 lb is usually satisfactory.

Procedure

1. Wash and scrub the vegetable well and (except for beans and very small pea pods) chop it into medium-sized pieces.
2. Simmer in $\frac{1}{2}$–1 gallon of water for 45 minutes or until tender but not pulped, after adding any spices.
3. Pour the hot liquor, the vegetable and spices over the base ingredients.
4. Add yeast starter, nutrient, tannin and 1 tablespoon pectinaze when cool.
5. Ferment on the pulp for a week or until the first ferment has quietened if this takes longer.
6. Strain off all solids including spices and transfer the must to a fermentation jar under lock.
7. Rack at 4 weeks.

Recipes

Broad Bean Wine
4 lb old broad beans, too hard and 'black i' the eye' to cook. No pods. Use base (A). If a starch haze develops, clear it with fungal amylase. A race of ginger but no other spice.

Celery Wine
Use $3\frac{1}{2}$ lb chopped celery, including green parts and root, and base (B), and at most a small race of ginger. This wine has always been held to be good for rheumatism if taken regularly.

Peascod Wine
Use $4\frac{1}{2}$ lb very young, small, tender pods and base (B), a chablis, hock or other white wine yeast and a small race of ginger. A really delicious wine, especially after two years.

Wine from Tree Sap and Leaves

Sap Wine

Though today comparatively few people may have either the opportunity or the inclination to make wine from the sap of trees, quite a lot used to be made in the days when most of the population had to rely on farms, gardens and hedgerows for the basic ingredients for their wines, as the sap starts to flow in late February and early March and is thus one of the earliest of these to become available.

It is a simple matter to tap a tree but unless great care is used it is unfortunately equally easy to kill it. Only birch, and sometimes walnut and sycamore, saps are used, and they should be taken only from mature trees and not later than early March. Select a well-grown tree and bore a hole not more than 1 inch in diameter about 2 feet above the ground and just deep enough to penetrate the bark. A depth of 1 inch is ample; a deeper hole will collect no more sap and may damage the tree. The collection of the sap can be tricky as it is moving upwards and a tube pushed tightly into the hole and right up to the heart-wood may well cut off the supply, while the old method of slashing a V in the bark with its point just below the hole and jamming in a bit of bent tin to act as a spout does the tree no good.

A good way is to bore the hole slanting slightly upwards and to whittle the broad end of the spout cut off an old polythene funnel until it can be fitted really tightly into it but only about ¼ inch deep. The jug or gallon jar should be arranged to support the other end and the whole apparatus should then be covered with a clean cloth to exclude insects and as much air as possible; the cloth in turn should be protected by a rainproof covering. If the sap is running well a gallon may collect within 48 hours; if so remove the spout and on no account fail to plug the hole with a sound cork or wooden bung hammered well in and trimmed level with the bark, or the tree may die.

For 1 gallon:

sap	7 pints
white grape concentrate	½ pint
sugar	2¼ lb
acid	2 teaspoons
tannin	½ teaspoon
A.P. or hock wine yeast starter	
vitaminized yeast nutrient	

Bring the sap, concentrate, sugar and acid to the boil and simmer for 15 minutes. When cool check the gravity and pH and add the tannin, yeast starter and nutrient. Rack after 4 weeks and proceed as usual.

Birch sap certainly makes a pleasant, refreshing wine but I cannot vouch for the others and would be most chary of putting the yield of a walnut tree at risk.

Leaf Wine

The leaves of the oak, vine and walnut may be used for winemaking. Young leaves only are used; old oak leaves in particular are too rich in tannin.

leaves	2½ lb
white grape concentrate	1 pint
sugar	2 lb
acid	2 teaspoons
A.P. wine yeast starter	
vitaminized yeast nutrient	

Wash the leaves well and rinse (see vegetable wines) and remove all traces of stalk. Pour over them ½ gallon of boiling water and when it is cooler add 1 crushed campden tablet and leave closely covered for 24 hours.

Dissolve the grape concentrate, sugar and acid in 1 quart of boiling water; add this and stir well and when cooled to 75 °F (24 °C) stir in the yeast starter and nutrient. Strain after 3 days' fermentation, place under lock, rack after 4 weeks and proceed as usual.

17

SPARKLING WINES

> And her poor but honest parents,
> In the cottage where they live,
> Drink the champagne wine she sends 'em,
> Though they never can forgive.
>   *— Traditional ballad*

Sparkling wines are such fun to drink that even those who habitually store their wine in casks or jars usually summon up enough energy to make the occasional batch, although some people are still deterred by the aura of mystery that surrounds the *méthode champenoise*. It is generally believed that this technique was invented by the very blessed Benedictine monk Dom Pérignon, who was cellarer at the Abbey of Hautvillers from 1668 to his death in 1715, but it would be more accurate to say that through his great skill in blending he first produced a far better champagne wine than had been known before and then made the *méthode*, and champagne as we know it, possible by introducing cork stoppers to the district in place of the oiled hemp that had been used up to that time. His original technique was to bottle the young wine in the winter, when its original fermentation had been temporarily stopped by the cold, and to tie down the corks. In the spring the ferment revived, the new cork stoppers kept in the carbon dioxide and champagne had its bubbles.

Dom Pérignon later discovered how to remove the yeast and leave the wine clear and, despite the scorn of envious contemporaries who described the foaming wine as 'pop' (*saute-bouchon*), lovely, lively champagne was on its way to conquer the tables of the Western world.

The home wine-maker cannot make champagne, but through the use of suitable ingredients including champagne yeast and various modifications of the *méthode champenoise* he is able to produce really excellent sparkling wines with comparative ease.

The Basic Wine

1. A dry, still wine is first made, which may be white, red or rosé.

2. The must may be based on grape concentrate or any other ingredient that will produce a light-bodied, well-flavoured wine. Roots, grain and so forth are not suitable.

3. The maximum O.G. should be 70, equivalent to an alcoholic content of 9 per cent or $1\frac{3}{4}$ lb of sugar (including sugar contributed by grape concentrate or any other ingredient) in each gallon of must. If the O.G. is any higher the alcoholic content of the must may inhibit the secondary fermentation; if much lower the wine may not keep.

4. Champagne yeast should always be used, throughout if possible and certainly at the second stage, as it settles in a hard and compact layer and in other ways is much the best for this particular purpose.

5. The wine should be fermented right out and cleared by racking. It should be fined or filtered only if absolutely necessary, and if so bentonite is the best finer to use as protein finings such as gelatine or isinglass will remove the tannin and with it the zest so necessary to a light, dry wine. More can be added but the result is not quite the same. On no account must the wine be stabilized by the use of sodium metabisulphite or any other chemical or enzymic yeast-inhibitor or the secondary fermentation will not take place.

6. The clear, finished wine is next siphoned into sterilized, unscratched champagne bottles. No other kind will stand the

pressure, and they must be free of chips or scratches or bursts may result.

7. A syrup is made by dissolving sugar in a little of the same wine, which must be gently heated and stirred until solution is complete. A pound of sugar to ½ pint of wine gives 1 pint of

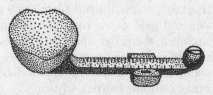

The Mini-Balance operates on the sliding beam principle and dual scales. It weighs accurately from 1/20th to 4·4 oz. or 1 to 1·25 grammes and measures liquid from 4½ fl. oz to 1·25 c.c. (⅛ litre)

syrup or more than enough for 2 dozen bottles as the optimum dose is ⅝ fl. oz per bottle, or 7½ fl. oz per dozen. One of the all-plastic mini-balances that can be washed under the hot tap is ideal for measuring these small quantities. More or less syrup can be made by increasing or decreasing the quantities *pro rata*. This syrup starts the secondary fermentation that provides the head and sparkle just as the priming sugar does in bottled beer, and care must be taken not to add too much or burst bottles may result. The bottle is now well shaken to mix the liquids.

8. Many wine-makers always add a half-teaspoonful of vigorously fermenting champagne yeast starter at this stage, but it should not be necessary to do so unless the wine has been filtered or fined, or the original yeast was of some other type. The bottle is shaken once again.

9. Remembering that the wine will be disgorged and finally recorked at a later stage the professional now checks the level of the wine at about 1 inch from the mouth of the bottle and fits a metal crown cap lined with polythene. If champagne bottles adapted for crown caps can be found this is the best step for the home wine-maker to take whether the bottles are to

be disgorged or not, but at the time of writing British crown caps do not fit continental bottles. Failing these, the hollow, white polythene champagne stoppers are excellent; the wine should be about 2 inches from the mouth, the stopper should need real force to drive it home and it should then be wired down with one of the twisted wire loops supplied for the purpose or a *muselet* (muzzle), a small metal plate shaped to fit over a cork or stopper and held down by a wire harness. Whatever method is employed thereafter the bottles should remain at room temperature for a week or so to encourage the secondary fermentation and then be removed to a cellar or other cool spot so that it may continue more slowly.

Method 1

As bottled beer. Store the bottles right way up in bottle crates or cartons to minimize the effects of a burst, and each week give every bottle a sharp, to-and-fro twist but without shaking it, so that yeast deposit produced by the secondary fermentation does not cling to the sides but drops to form a firm deposit round the punt. This process is known as *remuage* and is continued until there is no more yeast to be precipitated and the wine is brilliantly clear. It may be drinkable at 6 months but will be much better after a year. Chill the wine for not more than two hours before it is to be drunk, remove the cap or stopper carefully while the bottle is held firmly on a table, and pour the wine gently and continuously into glasses (any remainder can be poured into a chilled, screw-top quart beer bottle) until the sediment nears the neck.

Method 2

As Method 1, but store the bottles neck downwards so that the residue is accumulated by *remuage* on the underside of the crown cap or actually inside the hollow stopper. Owing to the shape of the champagne bottles the crate in which they are held should be propped up to begin with so that they are at an angle of nearly 45° and lowered little by little over the months until the bottles are finally inverted. Refrigerate as before, but still upside down, carry the inverted bottle carefully to a large sink or some other place where mess does not matter, hold it in one hand (shielded by a thick glove or piece of cloth just in case), slant it gingerly to about 45° still pointing downwards, with the other hand release the crown cap or stopper and as it flies out with the debris put your thumb firmly over the mouth with the speed of light and either pour as in Method 1 or proceed as in Method 3, below. Some people find it easier to disgorge with both hands and the neck of the bottle under water if the wine is to be drunk at once but the danger of contamination would be too great if it were to be restoppered as in Method 3.

Method 3

As Method 2, but after refrigeration freeze the wine for about 1 inch above the stopper or crown cap by gently placing the inverted bottles in a plastic bucket which contains 4 inches of a freezing mixture consisting of equal parts of crushed ice and salt. Wrap the whole thing in old blankets or towels to insulate it and when the wine in the necks is sufficiently frozen (usually in 30 to 45 minutes) proceed as before. Plastic stoppers may be more difficult to remove as they will be literally frozen stiff but the task as a whole will be much easier and there will be far less foaming. Nearly all the debris should be ejected with the slug of frozen wine but in case any remains in the throat of the bottle clean it out with your little finger and pour half a small glass of wine to complete the job.

The sweetness of the wine is now adjusted if necessary by adding from ½ per cent to as high as 10 per cent by volume of *liqueur d'expédition*, a sugar syrup made as before but with wine to which has been added an equal quantity of very pale brandy to prevent further fermentation. In terms of champagne, *extra sec* will have up to 2 per cent, *sec*, 2½–5 per cent and *demi-sec* and *doux* from 5 to 10 per cent.

The wine is then quickly recorked, this time with crown caps, plastic stoppers or corks, and binned horizontally to mature for at least another year. Sparkling wine should never be chilled to this extent in the ordinary way as it would need months in which to recover.

The wine should leave an inch of air-space below a crown cap or cork and rather less below a hollow stopper, say 1 inch, $2\frac{1}{2}$ inches and just under 2 inches from the mouth respectively. At this stage care must be taken to ensure that the polythene stopper is a really tight fit; it should have to be driven home with a mallet and some form of hollow drift or punch so that the force of the blow is taken on its shoulders. Soaking in warm water helps to make it flexible. Only the best cylindrical wine corks should be used, but stoppers are preferable as neither champagne corks nor the equipment for fitting them are generally available here. A proper champagne cork is some 2 inches long and nearly $1\frac{1}{4}$ inches in diameter and is inserted by two men, the *boucheur* who compresses it to half its original diameter and inserts 1 inch of it into the bottle, and the *ficeleur* who squashes the protruding inch of cork into the familiar mushroom shape and wires it down, usually with a *muselet*.

For wine-makers with large and docile families or amenable friends who wish to do the thing in style the professional team or *chantier* at this final ceremony consists of the *dégorgeur* who extracts the sediment, the *doseur* who adds the *liqueur d'expédition*, the *boucheur* who is always also the *chef de chantier*, the *ficeleur*, and finally a humble, nameless lad who gives each bottle a thorough shaking to ensure that the wine and the added syrup are properly mixed.

Method 4

Dom Pérignon's original technique as already described. Make the wine in August or September and bottle it in December or January or when fermentation has apparently ceased, using the ingredients and taking all the precautions recommended for other methods and proceeding as in Methods 1 or 2. The wine should be pleasantly *pétillant* but not foaming, so that freezing techniques should not be necessary.

Method 5

Light wine can be aerated in an ordinary sparklet soda-water siphon provided that it is chilled first. The siphon should be well shaken for quite a time and then inverted and its handle pressed so that the unabsorbed gas can escape via the central tube which will then project above the surface of the liquid. The sparklet head and the siphon sleeve are then removed and the wine is poured in the ordinary way. It will not be as good as naturally-conditioned wine but is a refreshing drink in hot weather.

Because the wine will probably have been dry to start with, the addition of acid carbon dioxide gas will make it unpleasantly so if ordinary sparklets are used. Importers of 'cheap' light wines in bulk often aerate them with nitrous oxide (laughing gas) which imparts a slight sweetness, and at least one supplier stocks this in sparklet form for amateur use. The quantity of gas in one of these would not incapacitate a mouse.

18

SELECTED RECIPES

As in the section on brewing, these are examples of experimental recipes that have proved themselves worth repeating.

Instant Wine

Various recipes for instant wine have been tried out during the last few years with great success; their secret lies in using malt extract and a vitaminized nutrient to speed the fermentation of canned fruit juices so that the yeast can attenuate all fermentables and bring the gravity down to zero or less in little over a week at a steady temperature of not under 75 °F (24 °C). No taste of malt remains in the wine and some enthusiasts use up to 1 lb of dry malt extract per gallon, but the following recipe is a safe one to start with and has been averaged out from a number which proved successful.

These wines are easy to make and form excellent bases for fruit cups in summer and mulled wine and punch in the winter. Almost any canned or concentrated fruit juice is suitable. The most popular are grapefruit (probably the best), orange, lemon, apple, pear, plum and pineapple, also grape and apple concentrates or bottled semi-concentrates such as Ribena (black-currant) and rosehip syrup. The ingredients and procedure are (for 1 gallon):

sugar	$1\frac{1}{2}$ lb
light dry malt extract	$\frac{1}{2}$ lb
fruit juice	1- to $1\frac{1}{2}$-pint ($\frac{1}{2}$- to $\frac{3}{4}$- litre) can
or grape or apple concentrate	$\frac{1}{2}$ pint
or Ribena or rosehip syrup	1 12-14 oz bottle
A.P. wine yeast as starter	
vitaminized yeast	
nutrient	
tannin	
citric or blended acid	
pectinaze	

To speed fermentation it is best to invert the sugar so first bring this to the boil in $\frac{3}{4}$ pint of water with 1 teaspoonful of citric acid and simmer gently for 20 minutes. Then add another pint of water, the malt extract and the fruit juice or concentrate and simmer for a further 20 minutes both to sterilize the ingredients and to drive off any sulphur dioxide that may have been used as a preservative. It is especially important to boil the malt extract.

Transfer the hot must to the fermentation vessel and add cold water to make up to 1 gallon. When at 75 °F (24 °C) pitch with the yeast as an active starter bottle and stir in the pectinaze and $\frac{1}{8}$ teaspoonful of grape tannin. More acid will probably be unnecessary especially with grapefruit, lemon or apple juice as some has already been added to invert the sugar, but it is always best to test the pH.

Leave the must to ferment in a warm room or with a heater set to 75 °F (24 °C) and stir daily. After 2 to 3 days the probably violent initial ferment should have quietened and the wine must be stirred well and transferred to a fermentation jar under lock. Ten days later fermentation should have ceased and gravity have dropped to zero or below. The wine is now carefully racked and filtered until brilliant. As it will probably need sweetening, ascorbic acid (vitamin C) should be added at the rate of 600 mg (6 Brewitone tablets) per gallon to stabilize it; the smell of campden tablets (sulphur dioxide) would not wear off in time. The wine is left in the cool for a week, sweetened if necessary, chilled if white, and drunk.

Bilberry Plus (5 gallons)

dried bilberries	1 lb
dried bananas	½ lb
red grape concentrate	1 kilo
light dry malt extract	1 lb
sugar as invert syrup	10 lb (5 quarts)
citric/malic/tartaric acid to pH 3·2	(6 teaspoons approx.)
vitaminized yeast nutrient	
A.P. yeast as starter bottle	
dried elderflowers	1 oz
dried rose petals (red)	1½ oz
pectinaze	
(no tannin)	

Day 1. The bananas and malt extract were brought to the boil in 2 gallons of water, simmered for 30 minutes and poured over the washed and sulphited bilberries and the grape concentrate. The invert syrup was stirred in, the must made up to 5 gallons with cold water and the acids, pectinaze, nutrient and starter bottle added and well roused. O.G.100.

Day 6. First violent fermentation over. The dried flowers were immersed in a nylon bag weighted with a heavy glass ashtray, and suspended on a nylon thread.

Day 10. Transferred to carboy; flower bag with weight removed. G.20. 4 pints of invert syrup (4 lb sugar) were added.

Day 38. Racked and returned. Fine flavour and very clear but rather harsh. G.9. In fermentation cupboard (see Glossary) under lock.

Day 100. Racked; G.–5 but still a slight ferment. 3 crushed campden tablets added.

Day 124. 3½ gallons were racked into an oak cask (last contents red cherry wine) and the remainder into 1 gallon jar and 3 bottles. Extraordinarily dry: G.–7, and still a trifle harsh, but very good.

This was left in cask for 6 months and was a splendid wine;

a carbon-dioxide injector was fitted through the bung to prevent air taint and the wine was drunk from the cask, which was later topped up from the gallon jar. The bottles were opened about a year later and were also excellent.

Cherry and Red Grape (3½ gallons)

cherries – mixed morellos and others	6 lb
sugar as invert syrup	4½ lb
red grape concentrate	½ gallon
blended acids	
pectinaze	
tannin	
burgundy yeast	
vitaminized nutrient	

Day 1. The cherries were stripped and left overnight in 1 gallon of water in which 2 campden tablets had been crushed. The starter bottle had been activated early in the morning.

Day 2. 1 gallon of boiling water was added and the must made up to 2½ gallons at 75 °F (24 °C). The cherries were thoroughly crushed by hand and pectinaze, 2 teaspoons acid and ½ teaspoon grape tannin were stirred in, also 2 lb sugar as invert syrup, yeast starter bottle and nutrient. The sulphite had bleached the darker cherries but the colour returned later. G.50.

Day 3. Fermentation had already started and thereafter the fruit was crushed by hand every day and the cherry-stones skimmed off; a dozen were cracked and the kernels were crushed and returned to the must.

Day 9. The must was strained off the fruit. Gravity was zero and the red grape concentrate was added together with 2 lb sugar as invert syrup and about 1 gallon water at fermentation heat to make the must up to just under 3½ gallons. The must was stirred to ensure the presence of sufficient yeast and funnelled into a 3½-gallon oak cask under lock. Temperature (July) 65–70 °F (18–21 °C) in the fermentation cupboard.

Day 10. Fermentation had restarted.

Day 22. Fermentation stopped; wine clear, of a good colour but very dry; G.–5. $\frac{1}{2}$ lb sugar as invert syrup was added and the fermentation restarted immediately.

Day 30. Fermentation had again stopped at G.–5, and the wine was racked and returned to the cask. It was now cloudy and very dry; 1 lb sugar as invert syrup was added and the cask was topped up.

This was at the end of August and save for topping up the lock the wine was left undisturbed until the following February, when the barrel was tapped and it was all drawn off into $\frac{1}{2}$-gallon jars and corked. It was brilliantly clear, dry, strong (approximately 3 lb sugar per gallon or $15\frac{1}{2}$ per cent alcohol) and so good that it was all drunk by the end of April. The object of the experiment was to find out whether the addition of successive amounts of sugar and other fermentables to a must of an initially very low gravity would improve the activity of the yeast over a period, and this was certainly so, for despite the heavy loading on Day 9 energetic fermentation started at all stages directly any more sugar was added and the result was both dry and strong.

Muscatel and Honey (5 gallons)

muscatel concentrate	1 gallon
English clover honey	$3\frac{1}{2}$ lb
sugar as invert syrup	2 lb
acid blend	2 oz
tannin	$\frac{1}{2}$ teaspoon
A.P. yeast as starter bottle	
vitaminized nutrient	
pectinaze	

Day 1. The honey was dissolved in 3 quarts of water over a gentle heat and when cool left overnight with 2 crushed campden tablets stirred in. The starter bottle was made up with a little of the concentrate.

Day 2. 1 gallon of boiling water was poured on to the concentrate and the dilute honey was added. The must was made up to 4 gallons at 75 °F (24 °C) and yeasted after the nutrient, tannin, acid and pectinaze had been stirred in. It was then put straight under lock in a carboy. G.90.

Day 9. Very slow initial fermentation, possibly because the must was under lock from the start; but now speeding up. G.75.

Day 20. Going well. G.48. Added 1 pint invert syrup.

During the next 2 months another 1 pint of syrup was added, the wine was topped up to 5 gallons with water at 75 °F (24 °C) in which 8 oz of honey had been dissolved and was racked at 2 months from yeasting; double the ordinary period but it had been a slow fermentation. It was stored in gallon jars after a final racking 2 months later. It turned out to be a fine, dry wine but took another 6 months to dry right out, and at this stage all jars were racked off the deposit, topped up with the wine and resealed. It continued to improve over the 2 years it lasted but was never bottled.

Test 'Grapple' (5 gallons)

This batch was part of a test series for a new apple concentrate prepared from balanced proportions of sweet and tart apples. Test batches are usually of 5 gallons so that they can be split into reasonably large quantities if any alternative additives or treatments are to be tried. The proportions of concentrates in this recipe may seem unduly small but 1 quart or litre of the apple makes 3 gallons of wine and though 1 kilo or litre of the grape makes only 1 gallon (both of course with added sugar) the latter was included for vinosity only, and it was important that the flavour of the apple should not be masked.

apple concentrate	1½ litres
white grape concentrate	1 litre
sugar as invert syrup	10 lb (5 quarts)
tartaric acid	4 teaspoons
citric acid	4 teaspoons
tannin	1 teaspoon
dried elderflower	½ oz
Hock yeast	
vitaminized nutrient	
pectinaze	5 tablespoons

Day 1. 1 quart of starter was made up with some of each concentrate and 2 'Brewit bomb' starter packs. 1 gallon of hot (not boiling) water was poured over the concentrates in the fermentation bin; when dissolved these were left overnight with 2 crushed campden tablets (first trial of the apple concentrate).

Day 2. Starter fermenting strongly. The must was made up to 4 gallons including 6 pints of the invert syrup, all the additives except elderflowers were stirred in and the must was pitched with the starter. O.G.70.

Day 18. The remaining 4 pints of invert syrup had been added from time to time as the fermentation rate decreased (it was very fast throughout despite being under lock), and the gently fermenting must was now divided into 2 lots of 2½ gallons each and funnelled into two smaller carboys, the only difference being that in one the dried elderflowers were infused in a muslin bag suspended on a nylon thread. As the flowers were dry the bag was weighted with glass marbles.

Day 30. Both batches were racked, returned to the carboys and topped up; the elderflowers removed. G.8. Four weeks later all fermentation had ceased at G.2 in both cases; the wine was racked again and bottled after another 2 months in carboys under lock. G. zero.

Batch A was a very good dry apple wine and batch B, with the elderflower, had a good nose and much resembled a muscatel wine. Both improved in bottle up to a year.

'Red Mex' (5 gallons)

This wine was so called because it was made to try out the addition of a large proportion of strongly-flavoured, exotic Yucatan honey to a prosaic bilberry-elderberry base and is a good example of wine that went wrong but was successfully rescued.

dried bilberries	1 lb
dried elderberries	1 lb
red grape concentrate	½ gallon
Yucatan honey	6 lb
sugar as invert syrup	2 lb

acid blend to pH3·3   (6 teaspoons approx.)
rohament P
bordeaux yeast
vitaminized nutrient
Brewit bomb starter packs
pectinaze

Day 1. Made up 1 quart of starter with 4 tablets of yeast, 2 starter packs and some of the honey and concentrate. Sterilized and rinsed the berries, poured 1 gallon of boiling water over them, added the pectinaze and the rohament P when cool. Dissolved the honey and 2 crushed campden tablets in 1 gallon of hot water.

Day 2. After over 24 hours at room temperature the rohament P had practically puréed the berries. The red concentrate was dissolved in 1 gallon of boiling water, mixed with the honey solution and added. The must was made up to 4 gallons and the acids, nutrient and starter bottled stirred in. Gravity (at 4 gallons) 90.

Day 4. No apparent fermentation: June temperature 70°F (21 °C) approx.

Day 5. Very fast ferment.

Day 9. Strained out the puréed berries using a jelly-bag; a messy business. The must was transferred to a carboy under lock and there seemed to be a slight off-odour.

Day 32. Racked and returned; no off-odour but a slightly acrid flavour. G.01. Added 2 lb sugar as invert syrup.

Day 40. The increased fermentation from the added sugar had slowed down and there was now a strong smell of vinegar. The wine was racked into a sterilized cask with 75 ppm sodium metabisulphite added in case the taint was not acetic and was curable, and 1 pint of fortified rose-petal wine in the hope of restoring its lost nose. A lock was fitted to the cask.

Just over 1 month later – a perfect cure! No taste or smell of either vinegar or sulphite. G.01. The wine was exceptionally good and was drunk young from the cask, but owing to the infection the experiment as such had failed.

Grape and Peach (5 gallons)
This is included as a successful peach-flavoured grape wine
rather than the more usual peach wine with grape concentrate
added for vinosity.

white grape concentrate	3 quarts
peaches, canned	2 lb
sugar as invert syrup	8 lb (8 pints)
mixed acids	6 teaspoons
tannin	2 teaspoons
pectinaze	
Sauternes yeast	
vitaminized nutrient	
starter packs	

Day 1. Concentrate, pulp and 3 pints of invert syrup were
mixed with 2 gallons of boiling water. When cooler 3 crushed
campden tablets were stirred in together with the acid and
tannin. 1 quart of starter was made up from 2 starter packs
and a little of the concentrate.

Day 2. The must was made up to 5 gallons, the pH adjusted
to 3·3 and the gravity to 80 and the starter was added.

Day 5. Vigorous ferment already beginning.

Day 7. The must was strained off the pulp and transferred to a
carboy under lock. G.28. 3 pints of syrup were added.

Day 40. Racked: G. zero, and the must still fermenting. Very
dry, so it was topped up with 1 quart of too-sweet, 3-year-old
peach wine and 1 pint syrup to ensure a good blending
fermentation.

A month later, with gravity just below zero, the wine was
dry, good but opalescent rather than hazy. A methylated spirit
test (see p. 115) showed the presence of pectin, and a good dose
of pectinaze cleared it. It was racked with 50 ppm sulphite
(5 campden tablets) into gallon jars under lock.

Two months later a further deposit had been thrown and
despite sulphiting the fermentation had continued slowly;
G.–6, and wine very dry. Racked, sulphited as before and topped
up with 1 pint of standard syrup. No further fermentation

occurred and the wine was very good; pale gold, clear and dry and with only a faint but pleasant suggestion of peach.

Rowanberry and Apple (2 gallons)

cooking apples	3 lb
sweet apples	3 lb
dried rowanberries	3 oz
white grape concentrate	1 kilo
sugar as invert syrup	5 lb (5 pints)
acid blend	2 teaspoons
hock yeast as starter	
vitaminized nutrient	
dried elderflowers	½ oz
pectinaze	
rohament P	

Day 1. The apples were chopped small and put in the fermentation bucket with just enough cold water to cover them. The dried berries were well washed and simmered for 20 minutes in a quart of water. Berries and hot liquid were then added to the apples with 1 crushed campden tablet and half the acid (this recipe required no tannin), and the must was made up to 1 gallon. The enzymes were stirred in at 75 °F (24 °C) and the starter bottle was prepared.

Day 3. Half (2 pints) of the syrup, the rest of the acid, the nutrient and the starter were stirred in with warm water to make the must up to 2 gallons at fermentation heat, and (December) a heater set to 75 °F (24 °C) was immersed. G.80.

Day 5. Fermentation well away.

Day 9. The must was strained and returned to the bucket. Gravity was zero despite unfermentables. The elderflowers, in a weighted bag, and the remaining 2 pints of syrup were added and the heater left in.

Day 14. The elderflowers were removed and the must was funnelled into 2 gallon jars under lock with a quart over for topping up in a large bottle with a cottonwool plug. Gravity zero; splendid aroma.

Day 34. The must was racked early as there was an unusually heavy deposit of yeast and debris. Oddly, the quart had thrown some 3 inches of lees, was star-bright and pale gold, while the two separate gallons had small lees but while one was clear and deep gold in colour the other was cloudy and pale. These differences must have resulted from the musts having been funnelled, not racked from the fermenter. All were racked into a bucket. Excellent nose, but too dry; G.–5. Stirred in 1 pint of invert syrup and 100 ppm sulphite (4 campden tablets) and returned to 2 gallon jars.

Two months later the wine was brilliant, dark gold and dry but not too dry, with zero gravity. One gallon was lightly sulphited (50 ppm) and bottled and the other sealed in the jar and drunk about 6 months later. It was good, but the bottled wine, at its best after just over a year, was infinitely smoother and better.

Cor! (1 gallon)

This is the only 'jungle juice' to be included. It was made to try out a customer's recipe, and whether or not it justified his claims that it fulfilled practically every function from aphrodisiac to furniture polish it proved to be a better than usual cereal-plus drink and potent enough to justify his name for it.

wheat germ (Bemax)	8 oz
white grape concentrate	1 pint
raisins	1 lb
dried bananas	$\frac{1}{4}$ lb
sugar as invert syrup	$2\frac{1}{2}$ lb
acid, malic/tartaric/citric blend	2 teaspoons
vitaminized nutrient	2 teaspoons (double dose)
pectinaze	
grape tannin	$\frac{1}{8}$ teaspoon
A.P. yeast as starter	

Day 1. The raisins and bananas were chopped and placed in the fermentation bucket with the wheat germ and concentrate, and $\frac{1}{2}$ gallon of boiling water was poured over them. They were well stirred with 1 crushed campden tablet. The starter was put in hand.

Day 2. The must was made up to $1\frac{1}{4}$ gallons including 2 pints of syrup, and the starter, acid, nutrient, tannin and pectinaze were added. The hydrometer read 136, but the must was so thick that this meant little.

Day 3. A fierce fermentation had started and a thick cap had formed, so the must was stirred every few hours (N.B. hottest day of the year: 30 June 1967).

Day 9. The must was strained through a jelly-bag but was still too thick for accurate hydrometer readings. Fermentation had stopped so the remaining ½-pint of syrup was added and the must transferred to a gallon jar under lock and a large topping-up bottle with a cotton-wool plug.

Day 24. The wine was racked from both jar and bottle, leaving a great deal of debris, and returned to one gallon jar under lock.

One month later it was racked again and 1 campden tablet was added, and after 3 more months and 2 more rackings it was fined with Brufina wine finings, but still remained opalescent rather than hazy; very powerful indeed, and without the heavy mustiness that characterizes most grain wines. It needed 6 months in wood but there was not sufficient for a cask. Another ⅛ teaspoonful of grape tannin was added to compensate for the loss by fining and it was left for 6 months in the jar, where it finally cleared.

Though the final gravity was 5° the wine was not unduly sweet, and it was excellent to drink by the small glassful in cold weather or with strong cheese. The estimated alcoholic content was about 17 per cent.

19

BOTTLING AND STORAGE

> O for a draught of vintage! that hath been
> Cooled a long age in the deep-delvèd
> earth . . .
> — John Keats: *Ode to a Nightingale*

Wine should never be bottled until it is completely finished save for maturation. Fermentation, sweetening and blending should all be carried out in the fermentation vessel, and the wine to be bottled should be star-bright and have deposited little or no lees since it was last racked. The last process before bottling should be the addition of either 50 ppm sulphite (1 crushed campden tablet per gallon) or 50 to 100 ppm (between 4 and 8 crushed Brewitone tablets per gallon) of ascorbic acid as a stabilizer and anti-oxidant. Ascorbic acid is simply vitamin C, which can do neither the wine nor the drinker anything but good. It should be added 24 hours before the wine is to be racked and bottled.

Bottles

Wine bottles are of many different colours and shapes, and each is identified with a particular type of wine. White and golden wines are bottled in clear glass to show off their cool brilliance, but red wines are matured in green or brown bottles to protect them from the light that would oxidize them to an uninspiring brown. Some *vins rosés*, such as the excellent Cabernet d'Anjou, are deliberately bottled in clear glass to achieve the colour known as *pelure d'oignon*: the clear, reddish-brown of the outer skin of the onion.

Most home wine-makers reuse their bottles and are satisfied to keep coloured ones for red wines and clear glass for white, but it is pleasing to see different types of wines in the bottles

Bottle brush

traditionally associated with them. Wines similar to Bordeaux should go into square-shouldered, cylindrical bottles each holding one sixth of a gallon (75 centilitres or 26⅔ fluid ounces), dark green for claret and clear for white wine. Burgundy bottles have more sloping shoulders, hold a trifle more and are dark green for red and greenish-white for white wines. Rhine, Moselle and Alsace wines are all in bottles of the well-known tall, thin type and of various colours, and several Italian wines such as Chianti come in the familiar round-bottomed *fiasco* (a *fiasco* is an *empty* flask!) in its cover of woven straw. Champagne bottles are specially made to withstand very considerable pressures; they are dark green and normally hold about one fifth of a gallon. A magnum holds 2 bottles and a Jereboam 2 magnums; the fancy sizes go up to the 20-bottle Nebuchadnezzar but they are usually kept for show and filled up by the wine waiter from ordinary bottles when needed for an occasion. Port and sherry bottles are of various shapes and colours and have flat bottoms, whereas all the others mentioned except the *fiasco* have a distinctive, indented base known as the punt. Litre and ½-litre bottles are usually flat-bottomed and may be either green or clear and the 2-litre Italian bottles have a rudimentary punt. They are perfectly suitable for home-made wines.

Corks and Stoppers

Straight-sided cylinders cut from the bark of the cork oak are the traditional closures for wine bottles, for, though flanged corks are required for show purposes as they are easily removed by hand and tapered corks can be inserted more easily, neither of these form reliable seals for wine that is to be matured for any

Wine closures: standard Imperial straight wine cork, flange cork, polythene stopper and polythene champagne stopper

length of time. The reason that wine bottles are stored on their sides is that the corks must be kept moist, otherwise they will dry out and admit air and the wine will be spoiled. This, and not wine in which a clumsy *sommelier* has left fragments of cork, is properly known as 'corked'.

Flexible red or white polythene stoppers are now extensively used instead of corks by both professionals and home wine-makers. They are easy to sterilize, are inserted by firm hand pressure and are almost infinitely reusable. As they do not have to be kept moist the wine bottles may be stored standing up, so that sediment is deposited in a firm ring round the punt and, unlike that in a binned bottle, is not disturbed when the wine is brought to table. The stopper can be gently eased out by hand and the wine poured clear without being decanted. Another advantage of the polythene stopper is that should newly-bottled wine start to ferment again it will fly out without the bottle bursting or the wine being wasted.

Bottling

Practically all cases of wine becoming spoiled in bottle are due to faulty corks. These are porous and can harbour spoilage organisms and it is therefore most important that they should be clean and sterile when they are inserted.

Soak sufficient corks overnight in a weak sulphite solution; squeeze them in a clean cloth to remove excess solution before they are used. Polythene stoppers should be first washed in warm water, then in the solution, and finally rinsed. Neither corks nor stoppers should ever be boiled or washed with soap or detergent. Boiling ruins both of them by destroying their elasticity so that they will eventually admit air and cause the wine to be spoiled, while soap, and especially detergent, is almost impossible to get rid of and will cause off-tastes.

Bottles should be washed out with hot water, brushed out if they are dirty, sterilized, rinsed and left upside down to drain.

Lever-action hand corker

Again, no detergent should be used. They are then filled to $\frac{3}{4}$ inch away from where the bottom of the cork will be or to 1 inch from the top if hollow polythene stoppers are used. Corks are then inserted by means of either wooden or plastic corking

Wooden or plastic corking gun

guns, through which they are compressed and driven home by blows from a mallet, or the excellent hand-lever type of corker.

They should be flush with the neck of the bottle, and to avoid their being eased out again by the air compressed in the neck a loop of plastic-coated wire attached to some sort of grip or handle should be inserted before the bottle is corked. When it is pulled out the compressed air escapes with it. The same method may be employed with polythene stoppers.

Capsules

If wine is to be matured in bottle for any length of time it is advisable to cover the corks or stoppers and the necks of the bottles with viscose capsules. These are of various colours, which can be used to indicate different types of wines, and are applied wet, after which they shrink as they dry to make a seal which is both airtight and ornamental. Other capsules of lead, foil and plastic can be had but their functions are mainly ornamental as they effect no seal. Capsules should not be applied until the wine is quite stable and not liable to further fermentation.

Jars

Wine that is to be drunk fairly young can be stored satisfactorily in standard gallon or half-gallon jars, clear for white wine and amber, if they can be had, for red. If only clear jars are available brown paper should be taped round them to exclude light. Jars should be closed with good-quality cork bungs, and since they will be standing upright and the bungs will otherwise dry out they should be sealed with melted paraffin or candle wax poured on hot and well rubbed in. Wine will mature more quickly in greater bulk but special wines should be bottled as wine matured in jars never seems to reach quite the same pitch of perfection. The same procedure applies to carboys of all sizes.

Plastic Containers

There are now many types of plastic containers suitable for bulk wine storage, and the 5-gallon semi-rigid cubes, fitted with taps and supported in rigid cartons, are probably the best of these. It is not advisable to attempt to mature wine in plastic over a long period as although the polythene and other containers made for transporting wine, cider and beer impart no taste or odour of their own they can be permeated by strong smells from outside.

Casks

Although red wine matures best in the wood until it is ready to be drunk or bottled the surface area of any barrel of under 9 gallons capacity is too great in proportion to the amount of wine and admits too much air. If a barrel or cask is used follow the directions on p. 141. When the cask is clean and sweet and the wood has swollen, first pour in a quart or so of any sound but rough wine and roll the cask vigorously around so that it reaches all the interior. After a day or so and one or two agitations it will come out flat and lifeless as the oak will have absorbed most of its tannin. Pour it away, and use the cask for at least one fermentation, with a fermentation lock fixed in the bunghole, before it is used for storage. On the whole beginners are well advised to eschew wooden casks and barrels but they provide by far the best method of mellowing a really rough red wine.

Stoneware

Many stoneware jars are suitable for the storage of wine but they are out of favour owing mainly to their weight, the difficulty of cleaning them and the chance that they may be covered with lead glaze, which is very poisonous if it is left long in contact with wine. Salt-glazed earthenware is safe. A rough test is that salt-glaze is hard and lead glaze can be easily scratched, but this is hardly conclusive enough to be safe.

Storage of Wine

Whatever containers are used for long-term storage and maturation they should be kept in the dark and in as cool and even a temperature as possible if they are of glass, plastic or stoneware.

Wine stored in the wood also needs cool but a slight temperature fluctuation that causes the wine to expand by day and contract by night is beneficial as these imperceptible alterations in volume cause the wine to 'breathe' and take in minute quantities of oxygen through the pores of the wood. The great enemy of maturing wine is traffic and other vibration, and every effort should be made to avoid this. Corked bottles should be stored on their sides in bins, and all other containers should stand on wooden planks to insulate them from the chill of a concrete floor.

For some months after it has been bottled wine that has been excellent when drunk from the cask or jar may suffer from 'bottle sickness' and be lifeless and unpalatable, but it will soon recover, and then the still mysterious processes of maturation will steadily improve it. Many home-made wines, especially light table wines, are spoilt by being left too long in bottle; for all save very heavy wines six months to two years should suffice to bring them to their best.

20

BLENDING

The importance of blending ingredients has already been stressed, and the art of blending finished wines is equally important to both the professional and the home wine-maker. Some of the greatest and most enjoyable wines, including champagne, port, sherry and madeira, are blended and there is no doubt that when skilfully carried out this process can make dull wines good and good wines excellent.

The main aim of the professional blender is to ensure consistency of quality, taste, bouquet, colour and strength, whereas that of the home wine-maker is to avoid the necessity of either drinking the dull, harsh or otherwise unsatisfactory wines that must occur from time to time if only through unsuccessful experimentation, or pouring them down the sink.

To make one good wine from two or more indifferent ones may seem difficult but is easier in practice than in theory, for happily the very act of mixing wines seems to diminish their vices and enhance their virtues, provided, that is, that they do not possess similar faults and that none of these is due to any of the infections described in Chapter 23, Ailments of Wine. Both wines must be sound or one will merely infect the other. It is only common sense to blend oversweet with overdry and to mitigate the harshness of a wine that contains too much tannin by blending it with one insipid from the lack of it, and this matching of opposites will usually prove successful.

It is practically useless merely to mix unsatisfactory finished wines; true blending can be achieved only by inducing a new ferment after they have been mixed and allowing this to proceed in the ordinary way. If both wines are finished and stable and the gravity of the mixture shows that it contains insufficient sugar to support fermentation or enough alcohol to inhibit the yeast, or both, the mixture must be diluted with water and sugar and nutrient must be added to it until it will ferment when a vigorous wine yeast starter is introduced. In difficult cases the mixture of wines can be treated as a stuck fermentation and added gradually to the starter bottle as described on p. 245, but simply to mix two different wines very often induces a spontaneous ferment and if one is still working a little extra sugar and nutrient are usually all that are needed.

The wine that results from true blending will probably bear no resemblance to either of its parent wines or to the mixture of them before fermentation, but it will almost certainly be better than either of them. It would be interesting to experiment with *tranchage* (p. 270) as a quicker alternative to the fermentation method, and I shall be interested to hear from anyone who has done so and has kept samples of the two parent wines and the two blends.

21

THE APPRECIATION
OF WINE

> Formal drinking should be slow and
> leisurely, unrestrained drinking should
> be elegant and romantic; ...
> – A Chinese writer quoted by Lin Yutang:
> *The Importance of Living*

There are at least five different ways in which wine can please
the appreciative drinker, and they should lead on in logical
sequence so that the pleasure may be cumulative.

The Eye

Half-fill your glass and hold it to the light. If the wine is cloudy
reject it; if it has fragments of cork floating in it fish them out.
A sound wine will delight the eye with its brilliant clarity and
its colour, from palest greeny-gold to deepest ruby, and the
expert can tell much from the depth of colour that is known
as the 'robe'.

The Nose

Next, the aroma. Swirl the wine gently in the glass to release
its aromatic esters, sniff deeply and know the second of the
joys that wine can give. The bouquets of the classic wines have
been too often described, but those of home-made wines in
which full advantage has been taken of fragrant flowers and
delicately-scented fruits can often run them close.

The Palate

It looks good, it smells good and now comes the crucial test:

will it taste as good as it looks and smells? Taste-buds in different parts of the mouth, tongue and throat register different flavours, and if they are all to be given equal opportunities to do so the wine may seem to have three different tastes: the first, or approach, as the wine is sampled by the front of the mouth and tongue; the second as the wine is warmed in the mouth and rolled round it and up against the palate; and the farewell when it is finally swallowed and reaches the taste areas of the throat after it has been held in the mouth for the space of two or three breaths – through the nose, needless to say.

The Inner Man

The fourth benefaction of good wine is to warm the belly, enhance the appreciation of good food and aid digestion, and its fifth is to calm and cheer the mind.

22

TO SERVE WINE

Fill me my wine in Chrystall; thus, and thus
I see't in's *puris naturalibus*:
Unmixt. I love to have it smirke and shine,
'*Tis sin, I know 'tis sin to throtle wine.*
What mad-man's he, that when it sparkles so,
Will cool his flames, or
quench his fires with snow?
— Robert Herrick: *Hesperides*

So much nonsense used to be written on this subject that the whole technique of wine service is too often dismissed as mere mumbo-jumbo. This is very far from the truth, for the best of wines may be ruined by ignorant handling between the cellar and the table, and although those that we make cannot be on a par with the classic vintages they are often very good and certainly deserve to be presented to the eye, nose and palate at their very best.

Decanting and Opening

The service of wine starts when the bottle is gently removed from its resting-place in the bin or elsewhere.

White wines seldom throw any deposit and may be taken straight to the table or ice-bucket and young red wines may also be taken directly to the dining-room, but even though these wines have little or no deposit to be shaken up they should be treated gently and with respect. No wine is improved by being agitated or banged down on the table.

Red wine that has been maturing for some time in a bin should be decanted as it will have thrown a deposit on the lower side of the bottle. The bottle should be very carefully lifted in order not to disturb the deposit and placed in a decanting basket. This is designed to hold it at a slant just sufficient to prevent the wine from spilling when the cork is drawn by means of a double-lever or wooden-handled double-screw corkscrew. Either of these will remove the cork by steady leverage without disturbing the wine, which should be opened and decanted as near to its storage-place as possible.

The decanting basket should be held in one hand and the decanter in the other with a silver or polythene funnel in its mouth, and they should then be gently inclined towards each other with the neck of the bottle between the eye and a fairly bright light so that pouring can be stopped the moment any clouding or solid deposit appears in the base of the bottle neck.

The decanting basket is essentially a tool of the cellar or pantry and was never intended to appear at table. White and young red wines need neither the basket nor the decanter, and if an old red wine is poured directly from the bottle in the decanting basket into the glasses the constant surging to which it is subjected will disturb even the firmest deposit and ruin the wine. No reputable *sommelier* would dream of pouring wine in this way, and neither should the home wine-maker. Apropos of wine waiters and baskets, it is thought permissible to bring the empty bottle to table in the decanting basket, the label upwards and the cork tucked in by its side, to flank the decanter. This is supposed to show the diner that he has got what he ordered, but one suspects that many an expensively labelled bottle and its authentic cork have made more than one trip alongside a decanter full of a much less distinguished vintage. If the cork is bone-dry the suspicion becomes a certainty!

'*Breathing*'

All red wines should be left to breathe for at least an hour with the cork or stopper out of the bottle or decanter. During this period any traces of sulphite evaporate and the atmospheric oxygen plays an important though still mysterious part in mellowing a good wine and mitigating the harshness of a rough one. The harsher the wine the longer it should breathe but it cannot be left open for more than five or six hours without fear of spoilage.

Service Temperatures

Red wines should be allowed to breathe in the dining-room so that they may become *chambré* – brought to room temperature. If the house is cold they will take no harm from immersion in warm water, but the barbarous practices of holding them under a boiling hot tap or putting them in front of a blazing fire will drive off all the volatile esters and leave the wine flat and spoiled. Red wines should be served at around 50 to 55 °F (10 to 13 °C) and never over 60 °F (15 °C), as should all fortified wines except dry sherry and Sercial, a dry Madeira, which should both be chilled until the glasses mist over on a warm day. Similar home-made wines should be similarly treated.

All light white and rosé wines are improved by cooling but this does not mean freezing until the taste-buds are stunned and the bouquet killed. Many home-made wines have delightful floral bouquets and these should be treated like their nearest counterparts the Rhine wines and Traminers and cooled just enough to be refreshing but not enough to impair their delicate and charming fragrance.

Sparkling wines, whether white or red, should also be chilled, but the secret of enjoyment is to go by the rules to start with and then vary them to suit your own taste. A good wine is a wine you enjoy and a bad wine is one you dislike, and rules are made to be broken. The Portuguese drink iced port as an apéritif and very good it is, and one should have no hesitation in putting lumps of ice into unchilled, light white table wine on a hot day. 'Drink what you like and how you like it' is the best rule of all, but however you drink it your wine will be all the more enjoyable if you know how to bring it to table in the best possible condition.

Wine-Glasses

A wine-glass may well be a thing of beauty, but this is solely because it is perfectly designed to carry out its various functions. It should be of clear, uncut glass to afford the eye a perfect view of the wine it holds, stemmed so that cooled wine will not be warmed by the hand but of thin glass so that red wine that has been insufficiently *chambré* may the better be warmed between the palms, and above all narrowed at the top to concentrate the wine's bouquet. Coloured glasses were used at one time to disguise cloudy wine or 'floaters'. Strange shapes such as the champagne *coupe*, or shallow saucer, and others designed by caterers to make their contents seem greater than they are may be ignored.

The perfect shape for all wine-glasses is the tulip, with foot and stem and a generous bowl narrowed at the mouth, and no glass should ever be much more than half-filled. All wines may be seen at their best and their bouquets may be best appreciated in this type of glass, of which the Burgundy goblet, the sherry copita, the hock glass, the champagne flute and the long-stemmed tulip shape recommended by the Comité Interprofessional du Vin de Champagne and indeed the proper brandy glass (the great *ballon* is a theatrical prop rather than a drinking vessel) are all variants. A medium-sized tulip is the perfect glass-of-all-work, smaller ones are excellent for port, sherry and liqueurs and a big tulip can be used for any and every long drink from wine cup to beer. Glasses from which chilled wine is to be drunk should be cooled in the refrigerator until just before use.

The Wine Cooler

Any crock or bowl in which a bottle can be submerged for half its height or more will serve for a wine cooler or ice bucket in which to cool the wine or keep it cold; if it is ornamental so much the better, as its place is by the dining-table. If the wine is to be cooled rather than kept cool a mixture of ice cubes and water is best as this offers the largest cooling surface to the bottle. Perfectionists may take note that it is theoretically permissible to pour wine from a napkin-wrapped bottle only when it has been in an ice bucket. In such cases the napkin prevents the hand from warming the bottle and drops of water from falling on the table or the diners' clothes; in others it serves no purpose save to hide the label from the diner. Home wine-makers have no need to resort to such subterfuges, and the conscientious host, like the good *sommelier*, should always make sure that the label on the bottle is well displayed. If the wine is to be cooled in the bucket it is perfectly permissible, in fact only common-sense, to invert it for a while to cool the neck, for to pour a cool wine through a mass of warm glass is simply a waste of time and ice. For the same reason a cold bottle should be held by the napkin or the base though a bottle of red wine is best held by the neck.

Labels

A bottle of bright, clear wine looks all the better for an attractive label, or labels if the date is on a separate neck tab. When choosing them it should be remembered that they are supposed to set off the wine and not vice versa; colours should be pleasantly subdued and the label should not be so large that it is difficult to hold the bottle against the light to appreciate the colour and clarity of the wine.

Ready-gummed labels are apt to wrinkle as they dry and to come unstuck after years or even months in bin so it is best to buy ungummed labels and to run a line of one of the many rubber-based adhesives down each edge, with a dab in the middle. After it has been smoothed on from the centre outwards and surplus adhesive rubbed off the label will neither wrinkle nor fall off however long the wine is matured. If ready-gummed labels must be used, it is advisable to add, possibly in the punt, a self-adhesive label just large enough for the cellar-book reference number; this will ensure that the bottle does not end up as one of the dreaded U.A.O.s or Unidentified Alcoholic Objects.

Pairing Wine with Food

Different wines and foods taste differently to different people partly because of the varying degrees of acidity of their digestive fluids, so whatever the pundits may say it is impossible to lay down hard and fast rules about the pairing of wines with dishes, and still less is the problem of what wine to drink with what food to be resolved by reference to any mysterious code of etiquette.

Broadly speaking, most people find that dry or medium-dry white wines, including the home-made versions of champagne on the one hand and light, *vino de pasto* sherry on the other, are excellent with almost any kind of food, that fish spoils the taste of red wine and sweet white wine, and that a too-sweet wine cloys the palate and defeats the appetite if it is served throughout a meal. Doubtless there are many sterling citizens who really enjoy red Burgundy with their grilled sole or sweet Sauternes through the whole of a six-course meal, but they are in a very small minority and the considerate host will bear in mind the tastes of the majority whatever his personal preferences may be.

Red wine goes particularly well with meat dishes and the more highly seasoned the dish or the riper the game the heavier the wine should be. On the other hand young red wine that is too rough to be drunk with most dishes will go well with those cooked in oil in the Spanish tradition, as the richness of the food is mitigated by the roughness of the wine and vice versa. Two rules to which there seem to be no exceptions are that any good, not-too-ferocious cheese will get the best out of any wine and that the surest way of ruining good wine, good food and good friendships is to smoke throughout a meal.

23

AILMENTS OF WINE*

> I counted two and seventy stenches,
> All well defined, and several stinks!
>   – Samuel Taylor Coleridge: *Cologne*

Acetification

Wine unprotected from the air can be turned into vinegar at
any stage by the *acetobacter*, or acetic bacillus. This is airborne
and is sometimes introduced by *drosophila melanogaster*, the
(once) dreaded vinegar fly.

Symptoms

The wine tastes and smells vinegary. The extreme dryness of
wine that has fermented right out is often mistaken for acetification; this vanishes if a little sugar syrup is added but the vinegary
taste will not.

Cure

Normally, none, but if detected soon enough the addition of
50 to 100 ppm of sulphite (1 or 2 campden tablets per gallon)
may halt the process. 24 hours later siphon the wine off its lees
and add a good dose of vitaminized yeast nutrient and vigorously fermenting yeast starter at the rate of ½ pint per gallon.
If a new ferment can be induced the wine may be saved; if not,

---

*See also Hazes, p. 66.

or if the acetification has progressed too far, it can only be poured away or left to become wine vinegar.

Prevention

Sterilize all equipment, sulphite the must and add sulphite to the water in fermentation locks. *Acetobacter* needs air, so cover the must securely at all times, keep containers well topped up after the first, brisk fermentation during which the headroom will be full of carbon dioxide, and make sure that all bungs and corks are sound.

Flowers of Wine

Whitish specks may form on the surface of finished wine and develop into a film over its surface. The cause is a wild yeast called *mycoderma candida* that converts alcohol into carbon dioxide and water – the final stage of the natural cycle of which fermentation is a part.

Cure

If spotted very early when only a few white specks are visible, 100 ppm of sulphite (2 campden tablets per gallon) followed by filtration and re-fermentation as with acetified wine (above) may save the wine, otherwise pour it away and carefully sterilize everything in the winery.

Prevention

As acetification, above.

Stuck Fermentations

By far the commonest ailment of wine is the stuck fermentation, in which the yeast ceases to work before all the sugar in the must has been attenuated although no bacterial infection or other taint is present. Fortunately most cases are curable but prevention is better and simpler.

Symptoms

Fermentation stops while the must is still sweet. The lock ceases to bubble and hydrometer tests show no drop in gravity over a period of days. The gravity may well be between G.10 and G.20 and there are no off-odours or any other detectable signs of infection.

The must still contains sufficient sugar to put it at risk from spoilage organisms and the condition must therefore be tackled at once by discovering its cause and applying a suitable cure.

Causes

The main causes of sticking fermentations are:

1. TOO MUCH SUGAR. If live yeast is exposed to high concentrations of sugar as described on p. 37 it may be killed or its action inhibited by osmotic shock caused by the high-gravity syrup forcing its way through the walls of the yeast cell to mix with the low-gravity fluid that it contains.

Excess of sugar in the must can thus either prevent fermentation altogether or, more usually, cause it to stick when sufficient alcohol has been produced to kill the yeast or render it inactive while the wine is still far too sweet. As the yeast has to struggle against both the alcohol and the excess sugar a comparatively low alcohol content is sufficient to make the ferment stick.

2. TEMPERATURE VARIATIONS. If the must becomes too cold or too hot fermentation can be slowed to stopping-point or the yeast killed. The latter is unlikely but abrupt variations of temperature can also cause a stuck ferment.

3. FAULTY ACIDITY. A fermentation cannot proceed properly if the acidity of the must is higher than pH 3·4 or lower than pH 3·2 and cannot take place at all, or at best only briefly, if it is under pH 3 or over pH 4.

4. LACK OF NUTRIENT. Yeast needs nutrient salts and vitamins, and if these are absent or insufficient the ferment will be reluctant to start and will very soon stick. Flower and herb musts made with sugar only are the most frequent offenders.

5. USE OF DISTILLED WATER. As explained in the chapter on water, trace elements needed by the yeast are eliminated by distillation and the effect will be much as (4) above.

6. RETAINED CARBON DIOXIDE. Very rarely a defective fermentation lock may cause carbon dioxide gas (CO_2) to be dissolved in the must to such an extent that it inhibits the action of the yeast.

7. OVER-SULPHITING. The saturation of the must with sulphur dioxide gas (SO_2) by over-sulphiting will effectively inhibit or kill the fermentation.

Cure

Whatever the cause of a stuck ferment there is always a good chance that the yeast can be reactivated. First rouse the must well, with the lock and bung removed from the fermentation vessel, to oxygenate it, to disperse any excess carbon dioxide or sulphur dioxide and to distribute the yeast. Check and correct the temperature and acidity and note the gravity, then give it a generous dose of either vitaminized nutrient or ordinary nutrient and a crushed vitamin B tablet, rouse it again, replace the lock and leave it in a warm place.

If these measures produce no result after a few days it is clear that the yeast is dead and more than likely that whatever condition destroyed it will also kill any fresh yeast that may be added. The remedy is to make up half pint of vigorous starter from the same type of yeast if possible, to add the stuck must to it little by little and to wait until this mixture is again fermenting briskly before making any further addition. If the must has stuck with too high an alcoholic content the new ferment may refuse to accept it after a time and you will have two stuck ferments instead of one. To prevent this the new ferment should be diluted with tepid water if it shows signs of slowing up. This should reduce the alcohol content to a point at which the yeast can recover its strength; judicious additions of vitaminized nutrient will be necessary as the volume of must is increased by dilution.

If none of these remedies succeed the sticking must have been caused by one of the infections or other ailments already described.

*

Other 'ailments' such as over-acidity, medicinal flavours caused by under-acidity, mustiness through standing too long on the lees, harshness or flatness due to too much or too little tannin and so forth are not really ailments but simply the results of faulty wine-making and are all dealt with elsewhere in the text (see Index).

Given reasonable care, sterile equipment, proper sulphiting of the must, the exclusion of air at all times and the topping up of all vessels, none of these unpleasant things should, or in fact do, occur. In many years of wine-making and testing innumerable samples of concentrates, dried ingredients, yeasts and additives of all kinds my only casualties have been two cases of *mycoderma candida*, both due to the blowing of gallon jar bungs in hot weather when I was away from home. I am incurably vague and unmethodical, but even these defects have been constantly outweighed by lashings of sulphite and keeping everything securely covered at all times. Ailments and their cures must be included in case they occur, but, believe me, they hardly ever do.

Section IV

FORTIFIED
WINES AND
LIQUEURS

24

FORTIFIED WINES

> How goes the time? 'Tis five o'clock.
> Go fetch a pint of port.
>   – Alfred, Lord Tennyson:
>   *Will Waterproof*

A fortified wine is one to which brandy or other spirits have been added at some stage of its manufacture to raise its alcoholic content to 18 per cent or over, but although technically speaking a wine brought to less than 18 per cent by the addition of alcohol is a dessert wine we shall describe all such wines as fortified to save needless complication. Most, if not all, wine-making countries have their own varieties: the best known are port, sherry and madeira, which all owe their development largely to British interests.

Port is made commercially from the grapes of the Douro valley in Portugal, and whether red or white (tawny port is properly red port long aged in cask) the wine is allowed to ferment for a few days only. Before it has achieved an alcoholic content of 10 per cent, brandy is added to raise this to just under 20 per cent and to destroy all or nearly all the yeast enzymes, thus effectively stopping fermentation while the wine is still sweet, heavy and richly redolent of the grape. The wine is then matured in cask, sometimes for many years, and during this stage a very slow fermentation and further fortification may take place. In any case the finished wine will contain 20 per cent alcohol or just over.

Sherry is made from the grapes of the Jerez district of Spain by the *solera* system in which layers of casks of similar sherries are arranged one above the other with the oldest at the bottom. Some years may elapse between the additions of successive layers but no wine is drawn off until three, four or even more are in place. The lowest and oldest casks are then tapped and when not more than 10 per cent of their contents has been taken off they are replenished from the layer above them which in turn is topped up from the third layer. Only the casks of the top layer are replaced when empty, the rest are never removed. This continuous age-blending system ensures that all the sherry drawn off will be mature and of predictable character, though this is finally determined by blending the products of a number of different *soleras* before the wine is bottled.

No amateur could possibly set up such a system, but nevertheless really excellent sherry-type wine can be made at home. Both commercial and home-made sherries are 'plastered' with gypsum, mainly to increase their acidity and thus their resistance to spoilage organisms which might otherwise attack the wine which, unlike any other, has to be exposed to the air during the last stage of its fermentation. This is to allow the formation of the unique sherry *flor*, a whitish skin caused by a secondary yeast, *saccharomyces var. beticus*, and it is this *flor* or 'flower' of the wine which gives sherry its unmistakable character. In Spain all sherry is allowed to ferment right out and not until then is it fortified with local brandy to about 18 per cent of alcohol. At this stage the wine is very dry and pale, and *fino* and *manzanilla* are left thus. Other types, originally developed to suit the taste for sweet wine of long-dead Britons, are sweetened, flavoured and coloured by the addition of special wines and concentrates made from the same grapes: *amontillado* is rather sweeter and usually darker, *amoroso* and *oloroso* are much sweeter, often darker and are used to blend the popular 'cream' sherries, while brown sherry, that bane of Victorian and Edwardian livers, is very dark indeed and far too sweet for modern tastes. After the wine has been adjusted in this way it is matured and often further fortified in cask.

Madeira is a splendid wine but is not now as well known as it deserves, possibly because *bual* and malmsey are a little too sweet for us and the delicious, dry *sercial* is rather hard to come by, though it is the apéritif favoured by many great connoisseurs of wine. Madeira is made in the Portuguese island from which it takes its name and should really spend its early youth in a goat-skin bag, be exposed to great heat and continuous agitation, be fortified and treated much in the same manner as sherry and spend long years in cask. In more leisurely days the casks of madeira were sent round the world as ballast in sailing ships, and if ever some bold soul should seek to reproduce the original conditions by driving some 25,000 miles in hot weather with a cask of home-made 'madeira' in the boot of his car I hope he will let me know the outcome!

Port, sherry and madeira can all be reproduced with considerable success by the home wine-maker, but because of the expense of fortifying port in the traditional manner the brandy is usually added when the fermentation has nearly ceased and the alcoholic content is already high. Whatever means of fortification is employed it is necessary to know how much alcohol to add to the wine, and this otherwise difficult calculation is rendered very simple indeed by what is known as the Pearson Square.

The Pearson Square

A   D

     C

B   E

In this square A, B and C stand for known factors, D and E for those that have to be discovered.

    A = the strength of the spirit to be added.
    B = the strength of the wine.
    C = the required strength of the fortified wine.

D = the proportion of spirit and

E = the proportion of wine to be mixed together.

The use of the square is simplicity itself. First write against A, B and C their strengths *either* as percentage of alcohol *or* in terms of proof, but don't mix them. There is a percentage proof comparison table on pp. 304–5. To find D (proportion of spirit), subtract B from C, and to find E (proportion of wine) subtract C from A.

A (strength of spirit) is usually simple enough, as it is stated on the bottle in terms of proof. It is simpler to calculate in percentage of alcohol as it is then only necessary to remember that Polish spirit at 140 proof has 80 per cent alcohol and most other spirits at around 70 proof have 40 per cent. If the table is not to hand, divide the proof figure by 1·75 to find the percentage of alcohol, or multiply percentage by 1·75 to find proof.

B (strength of wine) should be known; if not guess it; it will probably be 14–16 per cent for these types, and a slight error either way will do little harm.

C (strength of final product): sherry and madeira should contain 16–18 per cent alcohol and port 20 per cent. The addition of any more will unbalance the wine and spoil it.

Example

1. Sherry

A wine of 14 per cent is to be fortified with spirit of 40 per cent to make a sherry of 18 per cent. Scribble a square and write against A 40, against B 14, and against C 18.

$$\text{Then } D = C - B \ (18 - 14) = 4;$$
$$E = A - C \ (40 - 18) = 22.$$

So 4 parts of spirit must be mixed with 22 of wine to produce a sherry of 18 per cent alcohol. 'Parts' may of course be fluid ounces, bottles, gallons or any other measures, provided the same is used for both wine and spirits.

2. Port

Normally this would be treated in much the same way as sherry, but for the sake of the example let us suppose that it is wished to treat port in the traditional way and add brandy at an early stage.

$$A = 40$$
$$B = 7$$
$$C = 20$$
$$\text{Then } D = C - B = 13;$$
$$E = A - C = 20.$$

To every 20 parts of wine have to be added 13 parts of brandy: an expensive matter.

When fortifying 'ports' made from elderberries, blackberries, plums, bilberries and so forth, the addition of brandy sometimes seems to make them lose the luscious fruitiness that is so pleasant a characteristic of these after-dinner wines. Perhaps this is because the brandy is normally added at the end of the fermentation when the fruit sugars have been attenuated and some of the volatile esters and essential oils have been carried off with the carbon dioxide generated by fermentation, but whatever the cause it is usually better to fortify with a neutral alcohol such as vodka, or with Polish spirit which contains 80 per cent alcohol (140 proof).

If Polish spirit is used the Pearson Square shows:

$$A = 80$$
$$B = 15$$
$$C = 20$$
$$\text{So: } D = 5 \; (C - B)$$
$$E = 60 \; (A - C)$$

A little more reasonable!

Procedure

Fortified Wines

If you feel rich enough to make port in the traditional manner go ahead; otherwise treat port, sherry, madeira and other fortified wines all in the same way.

First make a suitable wine from one of the recipes given in Chapters 16 and 18, starting it with not more than 2–2½ lb sugar to the gallon if a fruit recipe is used or about 14 oz with grape concentrate and then feeding with more sugar until the maximum of alcohol consistent with the required degree of sweetness has been obtained. When the wine is clear, finished, racked and ready to bottle decide whether it is good enough to warrant fortification. Very often a good sherry at 16 per cent alcohol or thereabouts will need no further treatment; otherwise fortify with the most suitable spirit in the quantities indicated by the Pearson Square. Port and sherry flavouring essences may be added if necessary after the spirit has been given a week or two to marry with the wine, but they should be the best available and used with discretion.

Wine matures well in wood and finishes best in bottle; spirits mature only in the wood and not at all in bottle; fortified wines mature well in wood and only very slowly in bottle. Maturation in wood is difficult when small quantities of ordinary wines are to be dealt with, but in practice light, dry sherries and madeiras that need no, or very little, fortification can be bottled as soon as the wine is finished and ready or stored in jars or carboys for a more rapid first maturation; other fortified wines should spend a year in the wood if possible. The oxidation due to a small cask (under 9 gallons) having too great a surface area exposed to the air in relation to the bulk of its contents may ruin light table wines but benefits sherry and madeira, which owe much of their distinctive taste to it. The only effect of oxidation upon port seems to be to change the ruby redness of its youth to the tawny hue of age, a coloration which is in fact so prized that it is sometimes produced commercially by the blending of comparatively juvenile red and white ports.

In home wine-making the best of these wines are usually those that have the maximum of natural alcohol and the minimum of fortification. Port yeasts do not seem to withstand a very high concentration of alcohol, possibly because the natural ferment of the wine has always been checked at under 10 per cent, and some of the most realistic and enjoyable home-made ports are therefore fermented with madeira yeast.

Vermouth

There are several kinds of vermouths but the best-known are the white, dry French and the white, sweet Italian types, though the Italian red and dry white are now becoming popular. Vermouth is wine either fermented or flavoured with various herbs, roots and flowers, the chief of which are wormwood and gentian, and fortified to 18–20 per cent alcohol.

Its preparation is simplicity itself both when the various types of ready-formulated herbs are brought and infused and when a liquid essence is used. In all cases full instructions are given on the packet or bottle, and any suitable home-made wine can be used as a base provided that it has not too much character of its own.

The most economical method is to use herbs, and if a really good brand is selected it is possible to make vermouth that will be quite as good as the commercial article. To make one gallon $\frac{1}{3}$ oz is usually sufficient; the herbs should be put in a small linen bag weighted with a glass marble, suspended in the jar of wine by a nylon or silk thread and agitated every day or two until the infusion tastes just right. This may be from 1 to 3 weeks according to the strength and flavour of the wine, but in any case give it a few days longer even though a slight acridity may develop.

The bag is then taken out, the wine is filtered or fined (if the latter, stir in a little grape tannin afterwards), and sufficient vodka or Polish spirit is added to make the strength up to 20 per cent alcohol or just under. Whether fortified or not, the vermouth is then left for at least two months to mature, and it will be found that during this period any harshness or acridity will have vanished. If the vermouth is set aside to mature when it is just right for the palate the flavour may well be too weak after a few months in jar or bottle.

Another method is to make an extract of the herbs and add

this to the wine. They are infused in about 4 fl. oz of vodka or 2 fl. oz of Polish spirit per bottle mixed with enough of the wine to cover them well. After two days at room temperature the rest of the wine is added and after one more day the vermouth is poured off. A better quick extraction of this kind is gained from loose herbs than from a bag and the vermouth will therefore have to be poured off through a quick filter paper or a jelly-bag.

*

Various other herbs and essences are available for making apéritifs and the same methods are used in every case.

25

LIQUEURS

Everyone knows that liqueurs are sweetly seductive alcoholic confections that go well with black coffee after luncheon or dinner (the usual French word for a liqueur is *pousse-café*) and cost a great deal for a very small quantity often served in a cunningly deceptive glass, but not everyone knows how easy they are to make at home at a much more reasonable cost especially if some of their alcoholic content is provided by home-made wine.

There are literally thousands of different liqueurs, but comparatively few have won world-wide recognition and some of those that have done so are closely allied to each other. Liqueurs are broadly grouped as fruit or herbal types, but classification is not easy as many of the basically herbal formulae contain fruit or fruit rind and *vice versa*; the two things that they all have in common are sugar, for all liqueurs and cordials are sweet, and of course alcohol. On the whole the herbal types are sweeter than those wholly or partly made from fruit; they also have a higher alcoholic content, ranging from about 35 per cent (61° proof) to the exceptional 55 per cent (96° proof) of Green Chartreuse as compared to the 25 per cent (about 44° proof) to 35 per cent of fruit liqueurs, some of which are in fact so low in alcohol that they might well be classed as cordials.

Fruit Liqueurs

Liqueurs that can be prepared simply from whole ripe fruit and spirit as described below include apricot, cherry, peach and plum brandies, sloe gin, *crèmes de framboise* (raspberry), *fraise* (strawberry), and *ananas* (pineapple), and as many more as there are suitable fruits. The best known of two groups that are based upon the juice, kernels and pulp of cherries and the rind of oranges respectively, but contain many other ingredients; are kirsch, maraschino and ratafia (cherry), and curaçao, grand marnier, cointreau, mandarine and van der hum (orange).

Herbal Liqueurs

Whereas simple fruit liqueurs and cordials could be made with ease in the kitchen or still-room of any cottage, farm or country house supplied with fresh fruit, home-made brandy, schnapps or other spirit and either honey or sugar, the evolution and preparation of herbal liqueurs were far more complicated. These originated as a result of early efforts to intensify the medicinal properties of herbs by distillation, but the medieval passion for secrecy through tortuosity, and possibly the fact that the monks responsible had little else to do but experiment with different and sometimes most unlikely ingredients and pore over their well-luted alembics, led to the evolution of incredibly complex formulae some of which, like benedictine and chartreuse, number their ingredients by the hundred.

Though the early herbal distillates may have been effective as medicine they probably tasted pretty horrible, but as the monks were the principal apiarists it was only natural for them to add a little honey. It is difficult for us to realize today how precious sweetness was in the pre-sugar era, and it could not have been long before the monkish physician-distillers realized that in this combination of sweetness, alcohol and flavouring they possessed the secret of the greatest luxury of their time. From then on the quest for medicinal efficacy rapidly gave ground to that for delicacy of flavour, and this trend was accentuated immediately the great monastic foundations began to find a rich source of revenue in the sale of the liqueurs for which they rapidly became famous.

The two most famous of these, deservedly known as the King and Queen of liqueurs, are benedictine and chartreuse. Though it has been kept a close secret for over five and a half centuries, the formula of benedictine is supposed to contain over a hundred ingredients and was evolved during the early part of the sixteenth century by one Bernardo Vincelli, a monk of the Benedictine order in the now ruined monastery at Fécamp in Normandy. It has been made commercially for the last century or so, but every bottle still bears the famous 'D.O.M.', standing for *Deo Optimo Maximo* meaning 'to God, the best and the greatest'.

Chartreuse is believed to date from 1602, when the original formula was presented to the Carthusian monastery in Paris by the Marquis d'Estres. Fresh alpine herbs were essential to the formula and partly because these were difficult to obtain in Paris it was handed over in 1735 to the monastery of La Grande Chartreuse near Grenoble. This was burned down during the French revolution, and though the order was much impoverished when the monastery was restored in 1816, by 1883 it had recovered sufficiently to install the latest distillation plant. In 1906 the monks were exiled under the French Religious Associations Act and emigrated with their secret to Tarragona in Spain. In 1910 the British House of Lords decreed that the name 'Chartreuse' could be applied only to the liqueur made by the monks of that order, and today both Green and Yellow Chartreuse are once more made in France as well as Spain. Green Chartreuse is the strongest liqueur on the market, but the almost mythical white Élixir de Chartreuse is reputed to have been even stronger.

The largest group of herbal liqueurs is probably that which relies on aniseed as its basic flavouring and includes anise, anisette, arrack, pernod, pastis, ouzo and the now banned absinthe, though it is doubtful whether all of these are strictly speaking liqueurs and both absinthe and pernod are probably better known for the wormwood from which the former takes its name. Almost every aromatic herb and numberless roots, flowers, seeds, rinds and barks are used in the production of liqueurs among which are *cassis* (black-currant), the hundred or so varieties of green and white *crème de menthe* (mint), *crème de cacao* (chocolate), kümmel (caraway seed), Trappistine (wormwood and mint), tia maria and coffee rum (coffee), *crème de violette*, yvette and parfait amour (violets), and many, many more. There are also liqueurs such as Drambuie (whisky and honey) which fall into neither category. Only the most easily recognizable of their many ingredients are mentioned above.

Procedure

Liqueurs are made commercially by distillation, infusion or the use of essences. We are not concerned with distillation but can use the other two methods with ease and success now that both ready-prepared dried herbs and dozens of essences are sold for the purpose. Infusion simply means the extraction of the flavour, aroma and colour of fruit, herbs or other ingredients by steeping them in alcohol.

Fresh Fruit Liqueurs

Liqueurs are easily prepared from sound, ripe fruit, sugar and spirit. Any fruit may be used but the first method described below is only really successful with bitter fruit such as sloes or morello cherries unless one likes a very sweet liqueur indeed.

Cherry Brandy

Wash and thoroughly prick the ripe fruit and pack it in layers in kilner jars. Use sufficient sugar to cover each layer of fruit and fill its interstices as the jar is packed. If some of the stalks are included they will impart a slightly bitter taste and the delicious 'almondy' flavour of the best cherry brandies is obtained by stoning some of the cherries, cracking the stones and adding the chopped kernels.

METHOD I. Slowly pour in enough brandy to cover the fruit. Seal the jar and leave it for at least 6 months at room temperature, then strain off the cherry brandy and bottle it and eat the cherries.

METHOD 2. Leave the fruit and sugar in the jar for 3 to 4 days. No ferment should occur but slacken the screw top a little just in case. Drain off the syrup (keep it well covered against insects and airborne spoilage organisms) and pour in enough brandy to cover the fruit. After another 3 to 4 days strain off the brandy and mix it with the syrup, adjusting the strength and sweetness if necessary, and bottle. The fruit may be pressed lightly at both strainings. The liqueur will be ready to drink in 6 months if left to itself, but *tranchage* (see the next chapter) may be used at this stage to shorten the maturation period.

Sloe Gin

Follow the same procedure as for cherry brandy above, but use gin (vodka is sometimes preferred), about half as much sugar and no stalks or kernels.

Other Soft Fruits and Berries

Use only sound fruit, and wash berries such as raspberries, blackberries and loganberries with special care. Pineapples, peaches, nectarines, lichees and other imported fruit can be excellent for the purpose: crush, slice or chop them if necessary and use as little sugar as possible if the fruit is sweet, as more can be added later if necessary. Follow the procedure for Cherry Brandy but use only method 2.

Tinned and Bottled Fruit

The first stage of Method 2 has already been carried out for you. Strain off the syrup and proceed as for cherry brandy.

Dried Fruit and Berries

Use about one third the weight of fresh fruit and restore the water content either by soaking until no more water is absorbed or by dissolving the amount of sugar to be used in the water and pouring it over the washed and pricked dried fruit when just off the boil.

Liqueurs from Dried Herbs

The ingredients from which some of the best-known of the herbal liqueurs are made are now being imported dried, already compounded and suitable for infusion. They are not expensive, as only small amounts of the dried herbs are needed in addition to neutral spirits, sugar as wine syrup (see below) and additional wine.

The Spirits

If the true flavour of the herbs, fruit or essence is to be transmitted to the liqueur the spirits used must clearly lack any flavour of their own save when brandy or gin are specified and they should also have as high an alcoholic content as possible especially if they are to be used for herbal infusions. Polish spirit at 140° proof (80 per cent alcohol) is best; if this is not obtainable 80° proof vodka at 46 per cent may be used with success. Unless otherwise stated the times for which herbs are to be infused are based on Polish spirit and the weaker vodka will naturally need almost twice as long to achieve the same degree of extraction.

Wine Syrup

Far too many recipes demand the use of a syrup made from sugar and water. The whole art of making liqueurs is based upon the blending of all the ingredients so that only the desired aroma and flavour can be perceived while those of ancillary components such as raw spirit and sugar no longer exist as separate entities. One of the tastes most difficult to eliminate in this way is that of sugar, whether granulated or as a water syrup; if, however, it is dissolved in home-made wine it will blend much more quickly and thoroughly and as the wine will also contribute alcohol less of the expensive spirit need be used. It is better to make up a quart of standard wine syrup as stock than to produce each small batch separately, since the blending process begins as soon as the syrup is made and the longer it is kept the more of the 'sugar tang' is lost.

To make 1 quart of syrup put 2 lb of granulated sugar in a saucepan, pour over it 1 pint of wine and warm gently, stirring continually until the sugar is dissolved. Never let the temperature of the syrup exceed 158°F (70°C). This should produce almost exactly 1 quart (40 fl. oz) of syrup with an alcoholic content of $7\frac{1}{2}$ per cent.

The Wine

The wine should contain at least 15 per cent alcohol and have no strong flavour of its own. It should preferably be white, since whatever the liqueur it is easier to achieve the right shade by the addition of wine colouring in the final stages of manufacture; a white grape concentrate makes a very suitable wine. Flavouring essences contain the appropriate colouring but though it is often suggested that the wine be fermented with the essence this is not to be recommended as the results are often disappointing and the quantities are difficult to calculate at later stages.

Method

First decide what type of liqueur is to be made and what its alcoholic strength is to be. Refer to the appropriate table to find out how much Polish spirit or vodka will be needed, pour it into a kilner or other wide-mouthed jar, add the quantity of herbs recommended on the packet or in the recipes given here, screw the top on and shake well. Leave the jar in the dark, in a warm place, to infuse for the necessary length of time and shake it daily. At the end of the infusion period strain the contents into the bottle to be used through muslin or nylon to remove the herbs but do not filter, fine or add colouring at this stage.

Next measure out the quantity of wine syrup shown in the tables as equivalent to the weight in ounces of sugar required and the additional amount of wine needed, put them both in a saucepan and warm them gently, stirring the while, until they reach, but on no account exceed, 158 °F (70 °C).

Add the hot syrup to the flavoured spirit in the bottle, using a plastic funnel and taking care to pour the hot liquid directly into the spirit and not down the inside of the glass. When the bottle has been filled almost to the base of the neck put your hand over the mouth and shake the contents vigorously, then continue to fill it so that the least possible air-space is left under the stopper. This will have to be removed several times before the liqueur is finished if *tranchage* is employed so that an easily-extracted and replaced polythene Vintop is best.

Top up with more wine if necessary, stopper the bottle, shake it again, then either put it in the refrigerator and proceed as described in the next chapter. *Tranchage*, or filter (fining is not really to be recommended for small quantities), add colour if necessary (use only wine colours sold for the purpose), re-bottle, and store in a warm, dark place for at least three months and preferably longer.

The packets of dried ingredients should carry instructions for use, but individual tastes in liqueurs differ widely especially as regards the degree of sweetness preferred, and corrections may be made at an early stage, especially if *tranchage* is employed, by adding a little more syrup or spirit or by increasing the body as described below. If the flavour of the liqueur seems too weak it is a simple matter to put a pinch or two of the herbs in a small linen bag and infuse them until the desired strength is attained. For this reason it is necessary to give only the simplest of instructions and quantities correct to the nearest $\frac{1}{4}$ ounce or $\frac{1}{4}$ fluid ounce; the whole process should belong to the kitchen or still-room rather than to the laboratory.

Liqueurs from Flavouring Essences

There are dozens of different flavouring essences on the market and comparatively few herbal formulae so that even though the infusion method may be preferred the use of essences is some-times obligatory. The method is similar to that described above, save that no infusion period or straining is necessary. The minimum recommended amount of essence (more can always be added later) is added to the spirit in the bottle to be used and well shaken, after which the hot wine syrup is added and the process continues as before.

To add extra body

Body, or the apparent weight of the liqueur against the tongue and palate, is of great importance, for however fine its flavour may be a thin liqueur is no liqueur at all. The methods described here should impart plenty of body but this may be increased if desired either by substituting a small proportion of glucose B.P. or honey for sugar or by adding a little glycerine before *tranchage*. The former method is preferable, but in either case the amounts depend on personal taste and can be arrived at only by experiment.

Tables

TABLE 5. SUGAR CONTENT

Sweetness, again, is a matter of taste, but different liqueurs naturally require different proportions of sugar and as these

remain constant whatever the strength of the spirit employed
or the final strength of the liqueur all our tables are based
upon them. The average sugar content of the following
liqueurs is:

	sugar (oz per litre)
Anisette	12
Apricot brandy	4
Benedictine	12
Chartreuse	6
Cherry brandy	8
Crème de menthe	12
Curaçao	10
Kümmel	10
Mandarine	8
Maraschino	12
Peach brandy	4
Plum brandy	4
Sloe gin	4

TABLE 6

The following table shows the amounts of:

Spirit (80° proof vodka) at 46% alcohol
Wine at 15% „
Wine-and-sugar syrup at $7\frac{1}{2}$% „
Sugar
  required to make 1 litre
  (35·2 fl. oz) of
Liqueur at 37% „ (65° proof).

All quantities are based upon the amount of sugar required
per litre of liqueur, taking the minimum at 4 oz and the maximum at 12 oz, and are given correct to the nearest $\frac{1}{4}$ fl. oz.

Sugar oz per litre	Syrup fl. oz at 7½%	Spirit = fl. oz at 46%	Syrup fl. oz at 15%	Totals required Syrup or Wine fl. oz at 15%	Spirit fl. oz at 46%	Top up to 1 litre (35¼ fl.oz) with Wine at 15%
4	5	1¼	6¼	18¼	17	12
5	6¼	1½	7¾	,,	,,	10½
6	7½	1¾	9¼	,,	,,	9
7	8¾	2¼	11	,,	,,	7¼
*8	10	2½	12½	,,	,,	5¾
9	11¼	2¾	14	,,	,,	4¼
10	12½	3	15½	,,	,,	2¾
11	13¾	3⅓	17	,,	,,	1¼
12	15	3¾	18¾	,,	,,	nil
						(½ oz over)

* Example: 1 litre of liqueur requires 8 oz of sugar, the amount contained in 10 fl. oz of 7½ per cent syrup, which needs the addition of 2½ fl. oz of spirit to bring it to 15 per cent. This gives 12½ fl. oz at 15 per cent, so that when another 17 fl. oz of spirit has been added there will be 29½ fl. oz in all, which 5¾ fl. oz of wine at 15 per cent will bring up to 35¼ fl. oz or 1 litre (+ one twentieth oz) at 30 per cent alcohol. This strength requires 18¼ fl. oz of 15 per cent and 17 fl. oz of 46 per cent. In practice the two lots of 2½ and 17 fl. oz of spirit would first be added together to make 19½ fl. oz. The 7½ per cent syrup would be mixed with this and the litre bottle topped up with wine. The topping-up quantities are given as an easy check on the total amounts of ingredients required, but the quantities of wine needed to dissolve the sugar to make a syrup of 7½ per cent alcohol are not listed, as they involve niggling fractions and it is far simpler and better to make up a larger quantity as shown in Table 6 and to add it as required at a temperature of not more than 158°F (70°C).

26

TRANCHAGE

Liquor is quicker.
– Ogden Nash:
Reflection on Ice-breaking

Tranchage means literally a cutting-short, and it is in fact a short-cut to the maturation of liqueurs whereby the time that elapses between making and drinking them can be shortened from the normal minimum of six months and maximum of over two years to a few weeks.

Home-made liqueurs consist basically of spirit, sugar, wine or water and flavour derived from fruit, herbs or essences, and if these are mixed together when cold they are clearly discernable by the taste buds as quite separate entities. This simultaneous assault on the palate by sickly-sweet syrup, raw spirit and unassimilated flavouring is unpleasant, and if the mixture is simply bottled and left to itself it may be a very long time before the ingredients 'marry' to produce a smoothly homogeneous liqueur. *Tranchage* enormously accelerates this process by subjecting the liqueur to alternate heat and refrigeration, a simple speeding-up of a natural process which is extremely effective while in no way sophisticating the formula. This method is widely used commercially for the rapid maturation of liqueurs, fortified wines and even natural wines, and before the purist raises a condemnatory eyebrow let him consider the traditional maturation processes of madeira!

The first step in the *tranchage* takes place when the hot syrup is added to the cold spirit which has already been flavoured by infusion or the addition of essence, after which the mixture is bottled for convenience and protection and refrigerated overnight. It is next heated to 158 °F (70 °C) for 30 minutes and again refrigerated for a minimum of 12 hours, and this process is repeated at least once more. It is essential to check the temperature constantly with a thermometer to ensure that the maximum is not exceeded or the volatile esters to which liqueurs owe their delicate and often highly complex flavours and aromas will evaporate, and since the boiling point of ethyl alcohol is only about 172 °F (78 °C) there may even be a weakening of alcoholic strength from the same cause.

All treatments such as filtration, clarification or the addition of colour must be carried out after the *tranchage* has been concluded, but the liqueur should be tasted during each cycle when it reaches a temperature of 55 °F (13 °C) or rather less so that any additions of essence, syrup or spirit may be made during the process, which will then need only an extra cycle or two to accommodate them rather than complete repetition.

After its last refrigeration period the liqueur should be bottled in such a way that there is as little air-space as possible between the liquid and the cork or polythene stopper and left in the dark and in a warm place. It should be fit to drink in 2 weeks but will in most cases continue to improve with age.

Section V

CIDER AND
PERRY

27

THE HISTORY OF
CIDER AND PERRY

> Stay me with flagons, comfort me
> with apples . . .
> Old Testament: Song of Solomon 2:5

If ripe apples or pears are crushed together with their skins their juice, like that of the grape, will ferment spontaneously, and it contains enough sugar to produce a drink which can be as strong in alcohol as a table wine and like it can be stored and matured for several years or drunk almost as soon as the fermentation has stopped. It is therefore certain that because they can occur naturally the histories of cider and perry probably go back as far as those of wine and mead. The classics are so full of references to apples that it would be wearisome to quote them, and where there were sweet apples there was certainly cider. The word itself is of an antiquity that would seem more respectable if its forebears were not Vulgar Latin *cisera*, Low Latin *sicera* and Low Greek *sikera*, as used in the Septuagint. The Hebrew version was *shekar*, whence came the modern Yiddish *shikker*, meaning drunk. These words meant strong drink and only incidentally cider, but the Old French *cisdre* and the Middle English and Medieval French *cidre* all meant the fermented juice of the apple.

There seems to be no written record of cider-making in England before about 1200, and although the Druids esteemed the apple tree as being the favourite host of the sacred mistletoe there is no evidence that they made cider. Indeed the only apple indigenous to Britain may well have been the crab, whose juice could have contributed acid and tannin to a form of cyser made with honey but would have contained insufficient sugar for cider-making if used by itself.

In his *Vinetum Britannicum, or, a Treatise of Cider*, published in 1675 (the 1678 edition is my favourite bedside book), J. Worlidge, Gent., surely the most dedicated sikerophile in history, argues that the Ancient Britons must have had 'seider' but had no name for it other than wine. Whether this was so or not he certainly helps to confirm the belief shared by most students of the subject that from *Domesday Book* onwards the medieval chroniclers used the Latin *vinetum* impartially for both vineyard and cider orchard.

It is certain, however, that the Romans introduced various types of sweet apples to Britain, and it is likely that they were the first cider apples to be grown here. Cider orchards were under cultivation when the Normans landed, and by Worlidge's time good English cider was more highly esteemed and more costly than imported wine, though he writes that 'it is but of late years that pleasant Fruit, or good *Cider*-Fruit either, have been propagated in most parts of this Country'. Worcestershire, Gloucestershire, Herefordshire and Kent were already famous for their cider, and Worlidge records that a Mr Taylor, a cider-maker, challenged a London vintner and that his cider, made from red-streak apples, 'gained the Victory over the Vintners best *Spanish* or *French Wine*, by variety of Judges'. He also cites Lord Bacon's account of a Morris dance by eight sturdy cider-drinkers whose ages totalled 800 years!

The fact that the best English cider often fetched more, gallon for gallon, than imported wines may have been due in part to the 'secret and concealed mixtures . . . sophistications, adulterations, brewings or compositions' of the vintners of the day as a result of which too-earnest wine-bibbers were known to fall dead in their cups.

Later the increase of arable farming at the expense of cider orchards, the Industrial Revolution and various other factors led to a decline in cider-making and the popularity of the drink. In Worlidge's day the making of cider not only for home consumption but also for sale in the towns and cities was a considerable rural industry, but this trade fell off and it was not until early in the nineteenth century that it was revived. Today cider has more than regained its erstwhile popularity and commercial importance, and good English cider has made fortunes for those shrewd enough to realize the merits and potentialities of our native drink and to merchandize it attractively. Even a generation ago almost the only cider sold in pubs and hotels, and in the public bar at that, was rough draught, but today Old Scrumpy has exchanged his corduroys and spotted bandana for Harris tweeds and a Sulka scarf and is met in all the best places.

Perry is simply cider made from pears. Its history has followed a course similar to that of cider, and its recent commercial success has been equally spectacular.

28

MAKING CIDER AND PERRY

> ... the most excellent liquor this Isle of
> Great Britain affords ...
> — J. Worlidge: preface to 2nd edition,
> *Vinetum Britannicum*, 1678

Real cider is made from a mixture of different types of ripe apples carefully blended to provide the right proportions of sugar, acid and tannin and a characteristic flavour and aroma. The apples are better if they are left to weather and shrink so that their sweetness is concentrated, rather on the same principle that grapes are left to shrivel on the vine for *spätlese* wines. The apples are then crushed in a mill when most of the juice runs free, after which the pulp is pressed to extract the remainder. The juice then ferments spontaneously and often violently through the action of the yeast cells carried on the skins of the apples, and when the fermentation is finished the cider is either racked into barrels or bottled.

Perry is made in much the same way, but, because pears are far more susceptible than apples to oxidation, which darkens the perry, and to spoilage, they are never allowed to weather but are used as soon as they are ripe.

These processes are designed for handling fruit in bulk, and most amateur approximations require a considerable expenditure of time and hard work. It is no light task to crush several hundredweight of apples or pears, and the usual methods employed are either to pound the fruit in a wooden half-cask with a heavy baulk of oak or other non-resinous timber the business end of which has been serrated, or to adapt an old mangle for the job by studding the rollers with hobnails, spacing them about half an inch apart, placing the whole contraption on its side over a half-cask or other suitable vessel, and fitting it with a hopper. In either case the receiving vessel should be pierced at its lowest point with a hole through which the juice can flow free from the pulp into another container. After it has ceased to run the pulp is pressed to extract the remainder.

The must is next put into a fermentation bin, closely covered and allowed to ferment. Any scum should be skimmed off and when the first violent ferment has ceased it can be racked into a suitable container fitted with a fermentation lock. When the ferment has completely stopped the cider or perry can be racked into barrels or jars or bottled in the ordinary way. Owing to their high pectin content cider and perry seldom drop starbright after this kind of natural fermentation but retain a faint 'moonlight' haze, which is attractive, especially in a golden-green perry.

29

MAKING APPLE AND
PEAR WINE

These are also made from the carefully blended juice of apples
or pears but as the recipes will show they are treated with
pectinaze to ensure brilliant clarity, their gravity and acidity
are corrected as with other wines and the musts are first sulphited to kill the natural yeast cells and then fermented with
wine yeast. With the help of vitaminized yeast nutrient strong,
golden, delicious wines of a high alcoholic content can be
produced. A chablis yeast is suitable for a dry apple or pear
wine, a sauternes for a sweeter, heavier one. Light, dry apple
wine fermented with a sherry flor yeast will be excellent even if
the flor does not form, and a very presentable 'dry sherry' if it
does. Apple concentrate, if it is made from the right blend of
apples for wine-making, can also be used for apple wine with
great success – and a great deal less trouble.

The simplest way is to chop the apples (or pears) coarsely
and to purée them with an enzyme such as rohament P. Steam
juicing, while excellent for many fruits, is not advisable for
apples as the juice may be darkened by heat and oxidation,
the wine given a cooked taste and the tendency to pectin haze
greatly increased. Mixed apples should always be used and
should include a good proportion of rough cider apples or

crabs. The weight of fruit can vary from 6 lb to over 20 lb per gallon, but though it is usually true that the more apples are used the better the wine will be it must be remembered that the very large quantities specified in old recipes allowed for inefficient methods of juice extraction.

Save in a particularly good year for apples, and often even then, apple wine was almost always spiced with a race (but not more than $\frac{1}{4}$ oz) of ginger per gallon, a few cloves or black peppercorns, a bit of cinnamon stick, orange or lemon zest, elderflowers, rose petals or any other pleasant flavouring. It was, and is, often mixed with any other fruit that happened to be ripe at the time: blackberry-and-apple wine is delicious. Dried bilberries make a good red apple wine but elderberries should be added very sparingly if at all, especially if a dozen or so pounds of apples have been used to the gallon, as the tannin content will then be too high. 'Apple-and' recipes are fun to experiment with but impossible to list; apple wine will complement almost every flavour.

Procedure (1 gallon)

Wash the apples well, rinse them, and then crush them as described above or chop them coarsely and drop them immediately into sulphited water before they have time to go brown. One campden tablet per gallon is sufficient. Cover the fruit with not more than 6 pints of the water in which sufficient pectinaze and rohament P have been dissolved and leave for 24 hours, after which the apples should be puréed. Add hot water to bring the must to the desired gallonage at fermentation temperature and stir in the sugar (preferably as invert syrup), nutrient and the yeast starter. Check the gravity and pH and adjust if necessary.

A week after fermentation has begun strain off the pulp, put under lock, and proceed as usual. Apple or 'apple-and' wine matures quickly and is usually drinkable at three months but better at six.

Recipes

Basic Apple (1 gallon)

mixed apples	8 to 16 lb
sugar as standard syrup	2 to 3 lb
pectinaze	
rohament P	
acid blend if necessary	
yeast	
A.P. or white wine, as starter	
vitaminized nutrient	

Cyser
Make as Basic Apple Wine above, but substitute ½ pint white grape concentrate for ½ lb sugar.

Spiced Apple Wine
Cyser or Basic Apple Wine spiced or flavoured as described above.

Apple Concentrate Wine
A sound concentrate made from mixed types of apples may be used instead of the fruit at the rate of ⅓ litre or 1 pint per gallon of wine.

Apple Juice
From 2 to 3 pints of canned apple juice per gallon are sufficient, but the amount is not critical and will depend on the size of tin available. Sugar or sugar syrup should be added to G.90/95, and as some juices are sweetened and some are not a hydrometer is almost essential. The pH should be tested and acidity corrected if necessary. Procedure is as with concentrate.

Apple Sherry*
This can be excellent, especially if the flor develops in the dry types.

* See also Section IV, Fortified Wines.

Dry Sherry

mixed apples	4 lb
or apple juice	1½ pints
or diluted apple concentrate	1½ pints
sherry-type grape concentrate (white if this is unavailable)	1 pint
sugar as invert syrup	2 lb
sherry flor yeast as starter	
pectinaze	
rohament P if chopped apples are used	
vitaminized yeast nutrient	
grape tannin	¾ level teaspoon
calcium sulphate (plaster of paris)	1 heaped tablespoon

Mix the grape concentrate with 4 pints of boiling water in the fermentation vessel, and when the mixture is luke-warm add the sulphite, chopped apples and both enzymes; stir well and leave for 24 hours. Add 1 pint of syrup dissolved in sufficient warm water to bring the must to 1 gallon at fermentation heat and about G.90. Check the pH and stir in the vitaminized nutrient, grape tannin and calcium sulphate, and pitch with a vigorous yeast culture.

A high alcoholic strength is necessary so the fermenting must should be gradually fed with the remaining syrup over 10 days to 2 weeks after the fermentation starts, after which any pulp is very carefully strained off and the must put under lock. Any syrup over should be added in small amounts but the gravity should never rise above G.5 if the sherry is to be dry.

When the fermentation has ceased the wine is racked off the lees with great care and placed under a cotton-wool plug, since the flor will form only if in contact with air. The cotton-wool should be lightly flamed with a match or taper when in place to sterilize it. By now the attenuation of the sugars will have reduced the wine to less than one gallon but it must not be topped up, and after it has been put in a cool place it must not be agitated in any way or racked again. With luck the flor will form as a whitish film on the wine and once it has disintegrated and fallen to the bottom the sherry may be bottled. If no flor forms the wine should be stabilized and sweetened if desired with sherry-type grape concentrate dissolved in a little boiling water.

Sweet Sherry
Made as Dry Sherry above, but no flor is needed so any sherry yeast will serve.

Section VI

MEAD

30

HISTORY

And all should cry, Beware! Beware!
His flashing eyes, his floating hair!
Weave a circle round him thrice
And close your eyes with holy dread,
For he on honey-dew hath fed,
And drunk the milk of Paradise.

— Samuel Taylor Coleridge:
Kubla Khan

Mead is the most ancient of all alcoholic drinks, and cave paintings and other archaeological evidence suggest that we were enjoying a primitive version at least twelve thousand years ago. It is basically a fermented solution of honey in water, but over the ages innumerable versions have been devised including hippocras, pyment, cyser, melomel, metheglyn and others flavoured with fruit juices, flowers, herbs or spices. Their composition and production are dealt with in the chapters that follow.

Sugar became generally available in the western world only a little over two hundred years ago. For countless millennia honey was the only sweetener and the honey-bee was naturally revered as the prime source not only of sweetness and mead but also of light, for beeswax candles were the best illuminants. Mead has been woven into the mythologies, fables and religions of most of the races of the world; it was the origin of nectar, the drink of the gods of Olympus, and many honeyed centuries were to pass before the vine stole Bacchus from the bee.

Our only remaining mead ceremony is the honeymoon, a term that harks back to the days when bride and groom drank mead for a month after marriage for its aphrodisiac, philoprogenitive and, fortunately, recuperative powers. The ancient Irish took a tougher line, filling the groom with mead until he could hold no more and then carrying him to his bed and bride. If despite this treatment he managed to do his duty by her the child was guaranteed to be a son.

Unfortunately the history of mead becomes confusing at the era of its greatest popularity. When the Greeks, Romans or ancient Hindus wrote of mead, which they did with great enthusiasm, it was quite clear that they were referring to a fermented drink made from honey, but history's most famous and copious mead drinkers were the Norsemen and Saxons and the picture of their time is not quite so clear. Not only did they drink both mead and ale, but also hop-flavoured mead and ale made with honey, and the Old English *alu* appears to have been used for both.

The word mead can be traced to remote antiquity and through an amazing number of languages. The Greek *methu* gave us mead, 'meths' and amethyst, the gem fabled to cure hangovers, and other sources include the Old Slavic *medu*, Sanskrit *madhu*, Old Prussian *meddo*, Ethiopian *metuq* (mead is still the national drink in Ethiopia), and the Old Irish *mid*. The Old Irish drank almost as much mead as the Vikings and Saxons; possibly the most potent, if not the official, reason for the canonization of St Brigit was her miraculous transformation of a tub of water into mead when the drinks ran out at a royal party, a trick that she may have picked up during her pre-Christian period as Brigantia, goddess of our warlike ancestors the Brigantes, begetters of brigands and brigadiers. The Old English drank *meodu* and the Middle English *mede*, so all through the course of history the traveller with a good ear could identify his favourite drink wherever it was offered.

From the most ancient civilizations down to medieval times priests were the great mead makers, and in Britain the monks were the chief apiarists and carried on this tradition until the dissolution of the monasteries. With the advent of cheap sugar towards the end of the eighteenth century mead and its variants ceased to be the only alternatives to ale and cider for ordinary folk, who could now make country wines from dozens of wholesome and pleasantly flavoured or scented fruits and flowers, to say nothing of root vegetables and grain. For a time mead lost its popularity, partly owing to its very long maturation period compared to that of wine, but of recent years it has come back into favour, to some extent because of the enthusiasm of amateur mead-makers. It is no longer necessary to wait for three years before it can be drunk, and several preformulated mead concentrates are on the market.

31

MAKING MEAD

... I only drinking some Hypocras,
which doth not break my vowe, it
being ... a mixed compound drink,
and not any wine ...
– Samuel Pepys' *Diary*
(29 October 1633)

Varieties of Mead

Mead made in the original and traditional way is simply a fermented solution of honey in water and relies for its appeal mainly on its bouquet, which naturally varies according to the types of blossoms from which the honey has been extracted. Honey is deficient in practically everything save sugar that yeast needs for a proper fermentation and which it normally finds in the juices and skins of fruits and berries, particularly those of the grape, while its lack of tannin tends to inhibit clarification. Up to and for some time after the Middle Ages wine, ale and cider must have been usually murky, sourish and best drunk out of silver, pewter or leathern vessels so that the eye at least was not offended. Mead would have been even murkier owing to the wax, pollen and other insolubles suspended in it but honey had the prime merit of sweetness, and perhaps for this reason mead became the basis for more and odder variants than any other drink. It must always be remembered that until the advent of sugar sweetness was a precious rarity in itself and honey may well have had almost as great an impact as alcohol on the human metabolism.

Modern mead-makers can remedy the natural deficiencies

of honey by the addition of vitaminized yeast nutrient, acids and tannin, but even so mead made in the traditional way from honey alone may take six months to ferment out and over three years in cask and bottle to mature. Before the era of additives and of wine yeasts specially cultured for the purpose it must have been quite impossible to obtain a thorough fermentation from honey, water and wild, baker's or brewer's yeasts, and the result would have been not only murky but also sickly sweet and low in alcohol. Faced with a drink that any modern wine-maker would unhesitatingly pour down the sink it is not surprising that our ancestors experimented by adding many combinations of fruits, berries, herbs and flowers as well as brewing with honey and malted grain. Herbs and flowers could only have mitigated the sickliness of the mead by giving it additional flavours and perfumes, but it must quickly have been realized that the addition of fruits and berries not only varied the taste, bouquet and colour of the brew but also resulted in speedier and more thorough fermentation and a clearer and altogether better drink. All this was of course due to the acids, vitamins, salts and tannin contained in their juices and skins. The malt in ale-mead or mead-ale would also have helped the fermentation and produced a stronger drink, but unless bitter herbs were added these brews would have been sweet and insipid, at least by our standards.

Beside mead itself, the principal honey drinks that can still be made with advantage today are:

(a) *Pyment, Cyser and Melomel*

These are grouped together because although they are usually described as mead made with the addition of grape juice, apple juice and the juices of other fruits respectively it seems equally likely that pyment and cyser were originally wine and cider to which honey had been added in order to boost their alcoholic content or to sweeten them, or both, and that melomels were simply country wines made with honey instead of as now with sugar, since it will be remembered that the juices of nearly all fruits and berries other than grapes, apples and pears have to be diluted and then sweetened before wine can be made from them.

(b) *Hippocras*

This was wine to which honey and spices were added. The honey might be fermented with the wine to strengthen it or added afterwards with the herbs to disguise a poor, sour wine. In neither case was it the origin of Keats's 'the true, the blushful Hippocrene' but took its name indirectly from the Greek physician Hippocrates.

(c) *Metheglyn*

Wales and Cornwall have always been famed for their honey and mead, and metheglyn means medicine in either language. Both the Welsh *meddyglyn* and the Cornish *medheklyn* derive from the Latin *medicus* and the Old English *hlynn* meaning liquor, and the kind of metheglyn made by fermenting or decocting herbs with mead was originally compounded simply as a medicine. The other kind used to be distilled from the fermented cappings and debris of the hives after most of the honey had been extracted. In my young days this variety of 'metheglum' was still to be heard of, at least in Shropshire and the Welsh marches.

(d) *Other Mead Variants*

The scope for experimenting with honey-based drinks is endless, though between them the ancient Greeks, the medieval monks and the Elizabethans seem to have tried out almost every combination. Honey confers its own delicious bouquet on any drinks made from it provided they are even slightly sweet, but attempts to produce dry mead or its variants usually end in failure.

Honey

It is impossible to make a good mead or other honey-based drink out of inferior honey, and while the majority is excellent there are some rubbishy imported blends about. Your specialist supplier will sell you the best type for your purpose, but failing such guidance buy a British blend, light in colour, not too cheap, labelled 'Pure Honey' and with no additional substances listed on the label.

Single-nectar honeys such as heather, rose, acacia, lime, clover and orange-blossom have characteristic and sometimes powerful aromas and flavours and are used for special meads and sometimes for pyments, while the milder blends are better for those pyments, melomels, cysers and metheglyns in which the taste or bouquet of the other ingredients should not be masked or distorted. British honey is supreme for our purposes, especially clover or light blends, but though our dark heather honey may make the best mead of all this will be only after it has been matured for years. When it is blended in small quantities with milder honeys or honey and fruit juices its powerful and persistent bouquet and flavour can help to produce splendid brews and the admixture seems to speed up its reluctant chemistry. New Zealand and Australia send us excellent honey (though the cheaper Australian blends should be avoided as they may contain too much eucalyptus nectar); from Spain and California come orange-blossom and acacia, and the wild honey from Yucatan and Guatemala is also excellent.

If honey is labelled 'pure' this means only that it contains no other substances, not that it is free of the spoilage organisms in which all honey abounds and from which it can easily be freed by sulphiting as described below, so that all good honey may be used with confidence no matter where it comes from. The commercial tendency today is in fact to over-purify honey thus removing pollen and other natural constituents that should contribute to the body, flavour and fragrance of the mead, and the best course of all is to buy your honey from a local apiarist in its natural state, pure, fresh and delicious. Solid honey is just liquid honey that has crystallized and there is no other difference between them.

Procedure

Preparation

Honey owes its flavour and all-important bouquet to the volatile esters and essential oils of the blossoms from whose hearts it has been gathered, and like them it should never be boiled or have boiling water poured on it or this precious fragrance will be lost. In pre-sulphite days the vessels could be sterilized by sulphur fumes but not the must itself, and boiling was the only process available. We can now ignore the old recipes and the modern ones copied from them and use sulphite at the rate of 100 ppm (2 campden tablets per gallon). The must is sulphited after the honey has been dissolved in warm water, any other ingredients have been added and the volume made up. It should then be left closely covered for 24 hours before yeasting. The exception to this rule is that if only the too-powerful heather honey is available it may be 'mildened' by a short simmer after it has been dissolved in water and before anything else has been added.

Fermentation

Proceed as for wine. Pitch with a starter prepared from mead, white wine or general purpose wine yeast and add either a special mead nutrient that may contain the necessary acids, tannin and vitamins or a double dose of vitaminized yeast nutrient and the acids and tannin separately. This is the better course as a dose of special nutrient suitable for mead would contain far too much acid and tannin for, say, a red pyment or melomel, but never on any account omit them if honey is the sole, or main ingredient. The best acid to use for all honey-based brews is a malic/citric/tartaric formula stocked by all good suppliers, but if you have to mix your own use 8 parts malic, 4 parts of tartaric and 2 parts of citric acid for mead and 4 parts each of malic and tartaric and 2 parts of citric for cysers, pyments, melomels and metheglyns. Adjust the acidity to just over pH 3 as with wine or add acids as indicated by the typical recipes given below. Citric acid alone or the juice of 2 lemons per gallon will do at a pinch.

Unfortunately all the honey cannot always be added after the first ebullience of the fermentation is over, and so that the volatile esters are not lost with the escaping carbon dioxide it is best to avoid a violent fermentation by reducing the temperature of the must once it has begun. Move the bucket or fermentation jar to a cool place and feed as much of the honey as possible to the must after the fermentation has steadied.

The must should first be racked only 2 weeks after the fermentation has begun as unless the honey has unfortunately been commercially over-purified there will already be a heavy deposit that will contain wax, pollen and other substances: they will by this time have made their contributions to the aroma, flavour and body of the mead and should now be got rid of. No sulphite should be added either at this racking or at the next, in another 4 weeks' time, but 50 ppm of sulphite (1 campden tablet per gallon) should be stirred in after all subsequent rackings. These should take place every 3 to 4 months as mead takes longer to ferment out than wine and if too much yeast is removed too soon the fermentation may stick. It usually terminates with the mead still slightly sweet and this is as it should be, for mead with a below-zero gravity is not usually a very pleasant drink. Pyments, melomels and cysers should be racked at shorter intervals as they ferment much more quickly than mead.

Mead Recipes (to 1 gallon)
Light Mead

light-coloured, single honey   2½ lb

> *either* *mead nutrient as directed (in which case no additional
>   acid or tannin will be needed)
> *or*   acid blend   4 level teaspoons
> *and*   vitaminized yeast nutrient, double dose
>   tannin $\frac{1}{4}$ teaspoon
>   mead, hock, chablis or A.P. wine yeast as starter

Sweeter Meads

As for Light Mead, but with 3 lb, $3\frac{1}{2}$ lb or for very sweet mead
even 4 lb of honey and a starter made from mead, sauternes,
tokay or madeira yeast.

Pyments

> *either* light, single honey   1 lb
> *and*   white, red, port or madeira
>   grape concentrate   1 kilo, litre or quart
> *or*   honey   2 lb
> *and*   concentrate   1 pint
>   acid blend, in each case   3 teaspoons (check pH)
>   tannin for red concentrate $\frac{1}{4}$ teaspoon
>   for others $\frac{1}{3}$ teaspoon
>   mead yeast or a wine yeast suitable to the type of grape
>   concentrate, as starter

Procedure as under 'Three Pyments' in the chapter of selected
recipes that follows, i.e. ferment the concentrate first and feed
in the honey after the ferment has quietened.

Cyser and 'Cyment' recipes

Either apple juice or apple concentrate may be used for cyser
with light-coloured, single honeys. If white grape concentrate
is added 'cyment' results.

---

  *The mead nutrient label should be checked to ensure that the necessary
acids, including tannic acid, are included in the formula. If not, they must
be added. Owing to the hygroscopic properties of the mixed acids mead
nutrient formulae that contain them are usually sold in liquid form.

Cyser

honey	2 lb
apple juice	½ gallon
or apple concentrate	¾ pint
acid blend	2 teaspoons (check pH)
tannin	¼ teaspoon
vitaminized wine yeast nutrient	
mead, white wine or A.P. yeast starter	
pectinaze	1 tablespoon

Ferment the apple juice or concentrate diluted to ½ gallon first. The nutrient and half the acid should be added. The diluted and previously sulphited honey, the rest of the acid, and the tannin are mixed together and added immediately the first fermentation slackens.

'Cyment'

'Cyment' is the extremely ancient cyser recipe given vinosity by the addition of grape juice or grape concentrate and is usually a much more pleasant drink than cyser and ferments a great deal more quickly. The basic recipe is that given above for cyser but with half the honey replaced by 1 pint of white grape concentrate.

'Cyment' (4 gallons)

This proved a successful cross between a cyser and a pyment, hence its name.

acacia honey	4 lb
apple concentrate	2 pints
white grape concentrate	1 kilo
sugar as invert syrup	4 lb
A.P. yeast starter	
vitaminized yeast nutrient, double dose	
malic/tartaric/citric acid blend to pH 3·3	
tannin	½ teaspoon
pectinaze	

Day 1. All ingredients except the yeast and nutrient were mixed with 2 gallons of boiling water, made up to 4 gallons

H.B.W.M. – 17

and left with 50 ppm sulphite (4 crushed campden tablets) for 24 hours: G.95. Starter put in hand.

Day 2. Yeast and nutrient were added, the must was roused well and put straight under lock in a carboy.

Day 5. G.25. The must was topped up with tepid water sweetened with honey.

Day 35. G. zero. Racked and topped up again.

Day 70. G.0·97 (−3), and the cyment was unpromising; harsh, too dry, cloudy and with a distinct apple tang.

More pectinaze and 100 ppm sulphite were added and the cyment was topped up and left for 6 months, after which it was still very faintly hazy but excellent: dry, with a fine flavour and nose and no tang at all. It was also slightly *pétillant* and both this and the other changes indicated a malo-lactic fermentation.

Three Pyments (1 gallon each)

These were made to test samples of some exceptionally fine honeys and proved so successful that the methods and quantities outlined can be followed with confidence. It will be noted that the flower wine method was used to preserve the remarkable fragrance of these honeys. The progress of the three types, Argentinian clover, Spanish orange blossom and Rumanian acacia, was the same in each case save for minor differences in gravities, which have been averaged.

> honey (for 1 gallon)   1 lb
> white grape concentrate   1 kilo
> grape tannin
> special mead nutrient (this contains the necessary nutrient salts, vitamins and citric, malic, tartaric and tannic acids so that no further addition of acid should be necessary)
> Mead yeast as starter

Day 1. 3 kilos of concentrate were dissolved in 6 quarts of boiling water, and when at fermentation heat the nutrient was added with $\frac{1}{4}$ teaspoonful of tannin and the starter. The must was then put straight into a carboy under lock. The gravity was not taken as the full amount of must had not been made up, but it would have been about G.68 in 3 gallons.

Day 5. The initial ferment had died down and gravity was 49. The honeys had been dissolved in warm water to make 1 quart each and left for 24 hours in 3 sterile Kilner jars with $\frac{1}{2}$ crushed campden tablet each. They were now added to the must in gallon jars, roused well and made up to a gallon each with a little water. Their pH was checked at 3·5.

Day 50. The pyments had been left owing to absence, had dropped to G.o·96 (−4) and were so dry that not much flavour could be discerned. They were racked and 2 Brewitone tablets (200 mg ascorbic acid) were added to each after being ground up in a little of the must. There was some foaming even so. The musts were topped up with boiled water and left to stabilize.

Day 74. Much too dry. 4 oz of honey was dissolved in boiled water and added to each.

Three months later gravity averaged zero and they were racked. Too dry, but as the honey flavour had developed strongly no more was necessary and 4 fl. oz of standard syrup were well roused into each.

Two months after this the pyments were already not only drinkable but quite delicious, with the distinctive flavours of their respective honeys strongly developed. They were still a little sweet and though clear, not quite star-bright. Their strength must have been between 15 and 16 per cent. After a year in bottle they should be exceptionally good. The orange blossom and acacia are pale golden and the clover a darker gold in colour.

Melomels

All melomels are made with honey and fruit juice; the darker kinds are also known as red or black mead and are traditionally made from red- and black-currants respectively. The juice of almost any light-coloured fruit may be used for light melomels, but although some tannin must always be added honey reacts unpleasantly with too much of it and for this reason elderberries and bilberries are not good bases.

The simplest approach to the making of melomels is to treat them as fruit wines made with honey instead of sugar but to dissolve and sulphite the honey and to allow one fifth more honey than sugar by weight: e.g. for 2 lb of sugar allow 2½ lb of honey. Dark or blended honeys may be used, as their flavours are subsidiary to those of the fruit.

Whole or dried fruit or berries should be washed, rinsed, crushed and sulphited. The honey should be dissolved and sulphited as in the mead process and stirred into the pulp 24 hours later.

Additives (including pectinaze), yeasts and procedure are as country wines but the must should first be racked after 3 weeks.

If fruit juice is used it should be sulphited at the same time as the honey and mixed with it after 24 hours.

Light Melomels
Follow the country wine recipe for any fresh or dry light-coloured fruit or berry but substitute:

> *either* 1 lb light honey for 1 pint of grape concentrate
> *and* 1¼ lb honey for 1 lb of sugar
> *or* substitute honey for sugar but leave in the grape concentrate. This will give better vinosity, faster maturation and usually a better drink.

Red and Black Meads
As above but with either light or dark honey and any pleasant red fruit or berry save those mentioned. Almost all honey-based drinks are on the sweet side and seem to preserve the individual flavours of their bases, especially in the case of raspberries. A sweet and fruity melomel is no use as a table wine but will make an excellent after-dinner cordial if suitably matured and fortified. When black-currants are not available a 12-oz bottle of Ribena is enough to make a gallon of good black mead.

Hippocras
Honey, often heather honey, grape juice and spices go to make

the originally medicinal hippocras, so any pyment recipe may be followed and the spices or other flavouring matter infused just as in dried flower wines. The name of the drink derives from Hippocrates who invented this method of infusion; the cloth bag that held the herbs was called the hippocratic sleeve.

Any suitable fresh or dried herbs, spices, peels, flowers, seeds or roots or any combination of them may be used, though most of them will fortunately have little resemblance to Hippocrates' medicinal prescriptions. Among them are cloves, marjoram, sage, thyme, mace, cinnamon, mint, elderflower, clover, dandelion, rose petals, caraway seeds, root ginger, juniper berries and dried and grated orange, tangerine and lemon peel. It is also interesting to experiment with sweet vermouth and other dried herbal formulae.

Metheglyn

This was originally a British version of hippocras without the grape juice, and heather honey was used whenever possible so that its powerful flavour and aroma might somewhat mitigate the acerbity of the medicinal herbs for which it was the vehicle. Metheglyn is made in the same way as hippocras but an additional $1\frac{1}{4}$ lb of heather honey is substituted for every pint of grape concentrate.

Sack Mead

Sack (*seco, sec, siccus*) simply means dry, and means it in many languages. Through some unhappy etymological perversion the term 'Sack Mead' is now sometimes used in contrast with 'Dry Mead' to describe an extremely sweet mead containing some 4 lb of honey per gallon.

ENVOI

Doggerel Latin verse by Canon Walter, chaplain to Henry II and prebendary of St Paul's, attached to his map of the wine districts:

> Mihi est propositum
> In taberna mori;
> Vinum sit oppositum
> Morientis ori,
>
> Ut dicant cum venerint
> Angelorum chori:
> 'Deus sit propitius
> Huic potatori.'

– Author's translation:

> I swear that if it's up to me
> I'll choose an inn for dying,
> And have them bring a cup to me
> As moribund I'm lying,
>
> So that angelic choruses
> May pray: 'O Lord divine,
> Forgive this soul before us, he's
> A man who loved his wine!'

APPENDIXES

Keeping Records

In no hobby is the keeping of records as important or as simple as in home brewing and wine-making. Nothing is more frustrating than to discover that one has made a splendid wine or beer only to find that the gummed label, if any, has fallen off the bottle, that one's memory has failed and that the recipe and method are untraceable. This may seem unlikely, but it happens all the time. Home brewers and wine-makers are apt to be cheerful, optimistic, unmethodical types and the label, if there was one, possibly read: 'as 129 but + 4 oz of (something) and only 5 days on the pulp'. 129, a moderate brew, is in the cellar-book, but that is no help. Never rely on gummed labels or memory.

The answer lies in attaching a stiff, ready-printed log card, duly filled in, to each fermentation vessel by means of one of those strips that are used for closing plastic bags. Better still attach a sturdy transparent plastic luggage label container of a size to take the card, which will then be protected from spilth and can be readily slipped out for periodical entries. After the brew has been bottled the card should be put permanently in a special binder sold for the purpose and each bottle, whatever fancy label it may bear, should carry the reference number of the batch on a small self-adhesive label on the reverse side or in the print.

A cellar-book in which these brief data can be expanded is an excellent thing to have, but the card system is the quickest, easiest to operate and least fallible, and suitable log cards and binders are sold by all good suppliers.

Tables

Tables 1–6 refer to particular processes and are placed in the text at the appropriate places. The following are of more general relevance.

TABLE 7. DEGREES PROOF

The percentage of alcohol by volume in any liquor is multiplied by 1·75 to find its equivalent in degrees proof in the U.K. and by 2 for degrees proof U.S.A., and as we seem to be stuck with this nonsensical system instead of simply stating the percentage figures on the labels of bottles of spirits the table that follows may be of some help.

Alcohol % by volume	Degrees proof U.K.	Degrees proof U.S.A.
2	$3\frac{1}{2}$	4
4	7	8
6	$10\frac{1}{2}$	12
8	14	16
10	$17\frac{1}{2}$	20
12	21	24
14	$24\frac{1}{2}$	28
16	28	32
18	$31\frac{1}{2}$	36
20	35	40
22	$38\frac{1}{2}$	44
24	42	48
26	$45\frac{1}{2}$	52
28	49	56
30	$52\frac{1}{2}$	60
32	56	64
34	$59\frac{1}{2}$	68
36	63	72
38	$66\frac{1}{2}$	76
40	70	80
42	$73\frac{1}{2}$	84
44	77	88

46	80½	92
48	84	96
50	87½	**100**
52	91	104
54	94½	108
56	98	112
57·14	**100**	114·28
58	101½	116
60	105	120
62	108½	124
64	112	128
66	115½	132
68	119	136
70	122½	140
72	126	144
74	129½	148
76	133	152
78	136½	156
80	140	160

Conversely, to convert degrees proof U.K. and U.S.A. to alcohol percentage by volume one divides by 1·75 and 2 respectively.

TABLE 8. EQUIVALENT SOLID MEASURES

British   *Metric*

1 lb = 16 oz = approx. 500 grammes or ½ kilo (more exactly 454 g)
½ lb =   8 oz = approx. 250 g or ¼ kilo (more exactly ¼ kilo − 26 g)
¼ lb =   4 oz = approx. 120 g
         1 oz = approx. 30 g

Metric   *British*

1 kilo = 1000 g = approx. 2 lb (more exactly 2 lb + 3 oz)
½ kilo = 500 g = approx. 1 lb (more exactly 1 lb + 1½ oz)
¼ kilo = 250 g = approx. 9 oz
⅛ kilo = 125 g = approx. 4½ oz
          100 g = approx. 3¼ oz

For most purposes, when using small amounts, the equivalent

of 30 grammes = 1 oz is accurate enough and does away with the necessity to measure half and quarter grammes. The above equivalent measures are rough, but sufficiently accurate for our purposes.

TABLE 9.   LIQUID MEASURES

British

1 gallon	= 4 quarts	= 160 fl oz	
1 quart	= 2 pints	= 40 fl oz	
1 pint	= 4 gills	= 20 fl oz	Note that the British
¼ pint	= 8 tablespoons =	5 fl oz	pint contains 20 fl oz,
	1 tablespoon	= just over ½ fl oz	the American pint
		(more exactly	16 fl oz. The British
		B)	tablespoon is also
	1 dessertspoon	= B fl oz	marginally larger than
	1 teaspoon	= B fl oz	the American, which
			approximates to the
			British dessertspoon.

Metric

1 litre = 10 decilitres = 100 centilitres = 1000 millilitres
        (dl)   (cl)   (ml)

American

1 gallon	= 4 quarts	= 128 fl oz
1 quart	= 2 pints	= 32 fl oz
1 pint	= 2 cups	= 16 fl oz
	1 tablespoon =	⅓ fl oz
	1 teaspoon =	⅛ fl oz

TABLE 10. EQUIVALENT LIQUID MEASURES

British	*Metric*	*American*
5 gallons	22·8 litres	6 gallons
1 gallon	4·56 litres	3 quarts, 8 fl oz
1 quart	11·4 decilitres	1 quart, 8 fl oz (2½ pints)
1 pint	5·7 dl	1¼ pints
½ pint	2·85 dl	10 fl oz (1¼ cups)

1 tablespoon ($\frac{5}{8}$ fl oz)	1·5 cl	$\frac{1}{3}$ fl oz
1 dessertspoon ($\frac{1}{3}$ fl oz)	1 cl	1 tablespoon
1 teaspoon ($\frac{1}{6}$ fl oz)	0·5 cl (5 ml)	$\frac{1}{6}$ fl oz

Metric	*British*	*American*
1 litre	35 fl oz ($1\frac{3}{4}$ pints)	35 fl oz (2 pints + 8 US Tbs)
$\frac{1}{2}$ litre (5 dl)	$17\frac{1}{2}$ fl oz ($\frac{3}{4}$ pint + 4 Tbs)	$17\frac{1}{2}$ fl oz (1 pint + 4 Tbs)
$\frac{1}{4}$ litre (2·5 dl)	$8\frac{3}{4}$ fl oz ($\frac{1}{2}$ pint − 2 Tbs)	$8\frac{1}{2}$ fl oz ($\frac{1}{2}$ pint − 1 Tbs)
1 centilitre (10 ml)	$\frac{1}{3}$ fl oz (1 dessertspoon)	$\frac{1}{3}$ fl oz (1 Tbs)

American	*Metric*	*British*
1 quart (32 fl oz)	9·5 dl	32 fl oz ($1\frac{1}{2}$ pints + 3 Tbs)
1 pint (16 fl oz)	4·7 dl	16 fl oz ($\frac{3}{4}$ pint + 2 Tbs)
1 tbs (less than $\frac{1}{2}$ fl oz)	1·5 cl	less than $\frac{1}{2}$ fl oz

Fahrenheit/Celsius Comparison Scale

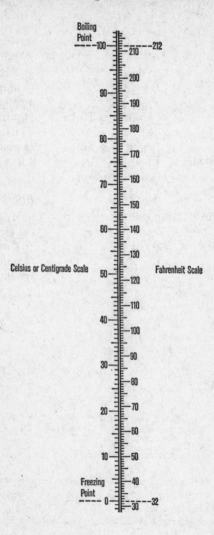

Glossary

b = brewing   w = wine-making

bw *Acetification*. The turning of wine or beer to vinegar through infection by acetobacters.

bw *Acetobacters*. Airborne vinegar bacteria; there are many types.

b *Acrospire*. The embryo leaf-shoot of barley which starts to develop during malting.

bw *Aerobic* — fermentation: the primary fermentation that takes place in the presence of air.
    — bacillus: one that cannot live without oxygen.

bw *Aftertaste* or 'farewell'. The taste that lingers on after the drink has been swallowed.

bw *Air-Lock*. See FERMENTATION LOCK.

bw *Air Taint*. Infection due to air-borne spoilage organisms.

bw *Alcohol*. See ETHYL ALCOHOL.

b *Ale*. Originally unhopped beer.

b *Alegar*. Ale or beer vinegar.

w *All-Purpose Yeast*. A wine yeast usually blended from various cultures to be suitable for most wines; it is often listed as A.P.

bw *Amylase*. An enzyme used to clear starch haze.

bw *Anaerobic* — fermentation: the secondary fermentation under lock from which air is excluded.
    — bacillus: one that can exist without oxygen.

w *Ascorbic Acid*. Vitamin C. Often used to stabilize wine.

bw *Attenuation*. The drop in the gravity of the wort or must during fermentation. The yeast attenuates the fermentable sugars by converting them into alcohol and carbon dioxide.

bw *Autolysis*. Put simply, the process by which dead yeast cells 'go off' through a process of self-destruction and spoil the brew.

bw *B.P.* These initials stand for British Pharmocopoeia and should be looked for on labels of additives, etc., as they ensure a high standard of purity.

bw *Balderdash*. Originally a mixture of mutually incompatible alcoholic liquors.

b *Barley*. The grain from which malt is made.

b *Barm*. Yeast.

w *Baumé*. A scale that indicates in effect the degree of concentration of musts. Grape concentrate is usually about 39 to 40° baumé.

b *Beer*. Originally hopped ale.

w *Beeswing*. Loose sediment in old wine, especially port, in the form of filmy scales.

bw *Bentonite*. A montmorillonite earth used to clarify wine and (on the continent) beer.

w *Bite*. Acridity in wine due to excess tannin.

w *Bottle Sickness*. Most wine becomes flat and unpleasing for some time after it has been bottled and some, especially clarets, suffer recurring bouts. Nobody seems to know why.

w *Bottle Stink*. This emerges when the cork is drawn and soon disperses. It is of infrequent occurrence and partly due to sulphiting.

b *Bottom-Fermenter*. A yeast such as lager yeast that ferments on the bottom instead of forming a yeast cap.

w *Bottoms*. Lees left after wine has been racked.

w *Bouquet*. The aroma of the wine.

b *Brewer's Inch*. The yeasty inch at the bottom of a bottle of home brew. Said to be the reason why brewers have large families and live long.

b *Brewing Salts*. A compound of nutrient salts, vitamins, acids, etc., added to worts to speed and improve fermentation.

b *Brewster*. Feminine of brewer; survives in brewster sessions.

bw *Buffering*. The suppression of the degree of acidity of a liquid in relation to the amount of acid present; e.g. by certain salts.

bw *Bung*. A circular, tapered stopper of wood, cork or (for jars) rubber used to close the neck of a vessel or the bung-hole in the side of a cask or barrel.

b *Burtonizing*. The addition of mineral salts, e.g. gypsum and Epsom salts, to make water resemble that of Burton-on-Trent.

b *Calcium Sulphate*. Gypsum, q.v.

bw *Campden Tablets*. Sodium metabisulphite tablets usually of 7 gr giving 50 ppm sulphur dioxide in one gallon.

w *Capillaire*. A sugar syrup used to make liqueurs, etc. Originally a decoction of maidenhair fern.

w *Capsule*. Any covering for the neck and cork of a bottle.

b *Caramel*. A preparation of sugar syrup darkened by heat and used to colour dark beers.

bw *Carbonization*. The injection into beer or wine of carbon dioxide gas under pressure to make it bubble in imitation of natural conditioning.

b Carlsbergensis. A bottom-fermenting strain of beer yeast.

b *Carragheen* or Irish moss. A preparation of seaweed used to fine beer.

w Casse. A haze due to metallic taint.

bw *Catalyst*. A substance such as an enzyme that causes chemical activity while itself remaining unchanged.

bw *Cellarage*. The proper conduct of a cellar.

w Chambré. At room temperature.

w *Chaptalization*. The addition of sugar to the juice of wine grapes.

bw *Closure*. Anything that closes the orifice of a bottle, cask or other vessel.

bw *Comparison Papers*. See pH.

b *Conditioning*. Causing beer to sparkle and create a head by absorbing its own carbonic acid gas into solution under pressure during maturation.

w *Copita*. The traditional sherry-glass whose sides are straight but converge at the mouth.

b *Copper Break* or hot break. The start of the fining process in beer while the wort is boiling; e.g. by the use of Irish moss.

b *Copper Finings*. See above; Irish moss added during the boil (in the copper).

w *Crust*. The deposit thrown by wine during maturation.

b *Cytase*. An enzyme which breaks down the cellulose walls of the cells of malt and releases the starch that they contain.

w *Decanting*. The art of pouring mature wine from bottle to decanter unsullied by any crust or debris.

w *Dégorgement* or *disgorging*. Removing the sediment from a bottle of sparkling wine.

w *Dessert Wine*. Sweet, often fortified wine to be drunk after a meal.

w Détourbage. Keeping sulphited must cool to allow sediment to clear before yeast is added.

b *Dextrin*. A substance produced from starch by enzymes which helps to give body and character to the brew.

bw *Dextrose*. Glucose.

b *Diastase*. The enzyme that converts starch to sugar.

b *Draught*. Beer drawn from the wood. Obsolete save for home brewers.

bw *Drop Clear*. To clarify spontaneously.

bw *Dry*. Not sweet.

w *Dumb*. Said of a wine that is lifeless, usually from deficiencies of acid or tannin in the must.

bw *Enzymes*. Organic catalysts.

w *Esters*. Products of maturation which are believed to contribute to the bouquet of wine.

w *Ethers*. Volatile aromatic substances formed during maturation that give the wine its bouquet.

bw *Ethyl Alcohol*. The drinkable kind.

bw *F.G.* Final gravity after all fermentation has ceased.

w *Feeding*. Adding fermentable materials to the must at intervals instead of all together at the start.

bw *Fermentation*. The production of ethyl alcohol by the action of yeast on fermentable sugars.

bw *Fermentation Cupboard*. An insulated box or cupboard for fermentation vessels kept at an even temperature by a thermostatically controlled space heater or small electric bulb.

bw *Fermentation Lock* or 'bubbler'. A simple valve that allows fermentation gas to bubble out through water but prevents any air from entering.

bw *Finings*. Any substance mixed with beer or wine in order to clarify them.

w *Floater*. A minute particle of debris floating in wine.

w *Flor* (flower). A skin formed on sherry in the presence of air which gives it its characteristic flavour and aroma.

b *Fobbing*. Frothing, e.g. when beer is bottled.

w Frappé Chilled.

bw *Fret*. To re-ferment in the cask or bottle.

w *Fructose*. Fruit sugar.

bw *Glucose* (grape sugar). A fermentable sugar; dextrose.

bw *Glycerol* (glycerine). A product of fermentation that helps to give smoothness and body.

b *Goddesgoode*. God's gift. An ancient name for yeast.

b *Goods*. Contents of the mash tun; grist and hot liquor.

b *Grains*. Spent goods after they have been sparged.

bw *Grape Sugar*. Glucose.

bw *Gravity*. See SPECIFIC GRAVITY.

b *Grist*. Milled malt.

b *Grits*. Grain, usually maize or rice, 'kibbled' or coarsely broken or ground.

bw *Gypsum*. Calcium sulphate. Used in burtonizing water for brewing and for 'plastering' sherry.

bw *Haze*. Cloudiness of beer or wine.

b *Head*. The foam on beer.

bw *Headroom*. The air-space in a container above the surface of the beer or wine (ullage).

Hippocras. Honey and grape juice fermented with herbs or spices.

b *Hop Bag*. Muslin or other bag in which hops are boiled.

b *Hop Essence* — extract, — oil: Types of hop concentrates.

b *Hops*. Cones or flowers of the hop vine used to flavour and preserve beer.

b *Hot Break*. See COPPER BREAK.

b *Humulon*. A hop resin.

Hydromel. Old word for mead.

bw *Hydrometer*. A scale that measures the specific gravity of the liquid in which it floats.

bw *Hydrometer Test Jar*. A narrow upright container in which the hydrometer is floated.

bw *Hygroscopic*. Absorbing moisture from the air.

bw *Inhibit*. A fermentation is said to be inhibited when the normal action of the yeast is prevented.

b *Injector*. A device for introducing carbon dioxide gas into a pressure keg for beer or wine.

bw *Inversion*. The conversion of ordinary sugar to invert sugar.

bw *Invert Sugar*. See above, and text, p. 35.

bw *Invertase*. An enzyme causing the inversion of sugar.

b *Irish Moss* or carragheen. A seaweed used to fine beer.

bw *Isinglass*. A preparation of the swim-bladders of fish used to fine beer and wine.

w *Juicing*. To extract the juice from fruit, berries or vegetables.

bw *Kieselguhr*. A powdered diatomite clay used in fining.

b *Kiln*. A building in which hops are dried.

b *Krausening*. Addition of a little live yeast or wort from another ferment to beer before it is put in cask or bottle.

w *Lactic Acid*. Used in wine-making to promote maturation.
— bacteria: Spoilage organisms.

bw *Lactose*. 'Milk sugar', normally unfermentable and thus useful to sweeten finished beer and wine.

bw *Lag Phase*. Period during which yeast breeds, before a vigorous fermentation starts.

b *Lager*. Beer brewed and matured at a low temperature with bottom-fermenting yeast; *to lager*, to brew by this process.

bw *Lees*. Sediment.

bw *Laevulose*. Fructose.

b *Liquor*. The brewer's term for water.

bw *Log Phase*. Period of rapidly accelerating yeast growth.

b *Lupulon*. A hop resin.

w *Macerate*. To soften fruit, etc., by steeping and crushing.

w *Maderization*. Commonly used of the darkening of white wine by heat or oxidation (Madeira).

bw *Magnesium Sulphate* (Epsom salts). Used in water treatment.

w *Malic Acid*. An acid used in wine-making.

w *Malo-Lactic Fermentation*. A separate fermentation that changes malic acid to lactic.

b *Malt*. Kilned grain, usually barley, whose starch has been changed to maltose by diastase.

b *Maltase*. An enzyme that changes maltose to fermentable glucose.

b *Maltose*. A compound sugar produced from starch by the action of diastase.

b *Mash Tun*. The vessel in which MASHING takes place.

b *Mashing*. Extraction of the sweet wort from crushed malt by mixing it with hot liquor, holding the mixture at a set temperature for a set time and then SPARGING it with more hot liquor.

bw *Maturation*. The perfection of beer or wine through aging.

Mead. A fermented drink made from honey.

Melomel. Mead flavoured with fruit juices.

Metheglyn. Spiced mead; originally medicinal.

bw *Milk Sugar*. See LACTOSE.

w *Mordant*. Wine that 'bites' through excess tannin or acid or both.

bw *Moulds*. Airborne spoilage organisms.

bw *Mulling*. Heating, but never boiling, spiced ale or wine.

w Muselet. Metal plate and attached wires to hold down a champagne cork.

w *Must*. Grape juice or any other sugary solution prepared for fermentation into wine.

bw *Mustiness*. An off-taste caused by mould in cask or bottle.

bw *Mycoderma*. Literally 'skin yeast', as it forms a surface film. Several species can infect wine or beer; the best-known are *m. candida* and *m. aceti*.

bw *Nose*. Bouquet in the fullest sense; all that may be learned about a drink by smelling it.

bw *Nutrients*. See YEAST NUTRIENTS.

bw *O.G.* Original gravity of wort or must before yeasting.

w Œil De perdrix. Pale *rosé* wine, usually *pétillant*.

w *Œnology*. Science of wine; *oenologist*, from Greek *oinos* = wine.

w *Œnophil*. Lover of wine.

bw *Off-Odours*. Smells that indicate that something has gone wrong.

bw *Off-Tastes*. Tastes, as above

bw *Osmotic Shock*. The often fatal effect of exposing yeast to an excess of sugar (see text, p. 37).

w *Oxidation*. Exposure to air resulting in discoloration of wine and sometimes off-odours and other faults.

bw *pH*. Very broadly, the degree of acidity of a must or wort (see text, esp. p. 39).

bw *p H Comparison Papers*. Slips of treated paper that indicate the pH of a liquid.

w *Pearson Square*. A simple method of calculating (usually) the amounts of spirit and wine or spirit and syrup respectively to mix to make a fortified wine or a liqueur of given strength.

w *Pectic Enzyme* (Pectinaze, Pectolase, etc.). Prevents or clears pectin haze.

w *Pectin*. The substance in fruit that sets jams and jellies but causes hazes in wine.

Perry. Pear cider.

w *Pétillant* also *spritzig, frizzante*. Tingling on the tongue; bubbling but not foaming.

bw *Pipette*. In home brewing and wine-making, a tube designed to hold a hydrometer so that it may be read without disturbing the beer or wine.

bw *Pitching*. Adding yeast.

w *Plastering*. Adding gypsum (plaster of paris) to a sherry must.

w *Pousse*. Lactic bacillus infection that makes wine sour and gassy.

w *Press*. A mechanical device for expressing the juice from fruit: e.g. grapes (wine press) and apples (cider press).

b *Pressure Vessel*. A container in which beer can be stored under pressure from carbon dioxide supplied by secondary fermentation or an injector.

w *Prickle*. Tongue-tingling effect of dissolved carbon dioxide even when no bubbles are visible in the wine.

bw *Primary Fermentation*. See LAG PHASE.

bw *Priming*. Addition of sugar or syrup to finished beer or wine to produce a second fermentation in pressure vessel or bottle.

bw *Proof*. A quaint method of expressing the alcohol content of spirituous liquors.

bw *Protein Finings*. Finings made from animal proteins, e.g. isinglass and gelatine.

w *Pulp*. The skins, flesh and juice of fruit, berries or vegetables to be used for wine.

w *Pulp Fermentation*. Fermentation on the pulp to extract the colour, flavour, etc., from the skins and flesh.

w *Punt*. The indentation in the base of a wine bottle.

Pyment. Mead made with grape juice – or wine made with honey.

Race. (of ginger) a piece of root ginger; lit. a root.

bw *Racking*. Siphoning beer or wine off its lees.

w *Robe*. The quality of a wine's colour which helps an expert to assess its age.

w *Ropiness*. Oiliness caused by lactic bacteria.

w Rosé. Pink.

bw *Rouse*. To shake or stir briskly.

bw Saccharomyces or 'sugar fungi'. Generic term for wine and beer yeasts.

w *St Vincent*. The patron saint of wine-makers.

bw *Secondary Fermentation*. Sometimes confused with the lag phase (q.v.) but properly a fermentation in cask or bottle.

bw *Shive*. A shallow bung often with a central hole for the spile.

bw *Siphon*. Tube whereby wort or must is drawn off the lees by gravity (see RACKING).

bw *Sodium Metabisulphite*. See CAMPDEN TABLETS and SULPHITING.

b *Sparging*. Spraying hot water on to the goods in the mash tun to extract wort.

bw *Specific Gravity*. The weight of wort or must as compared with that of the same volume of water at a given temperature and pressure.

bw *Spile*. A tapered peg fitting the central hole in a shive or bung.

bw *Spoilage Organism*. Any mould, bacterium, yeast or other organism that can infect beer or wine.

w Spritzig. See PÉTILLANT.

w *Stabilize*. To treat finished wine so as to guard against further fermentation.

bw *Standard Syrup*. 2 lb sugar in 1 pint water = 1 quart of standard syrup.

bw *Star-Bright*. The highest degree of brilliance in beer or wine.

bw *Starter; Starter-Bottle*. A vigorous culture of active yeast used to start the fermentation of wort or must.

bw *Sterilizing Fluid*. A preparation of sodium metabisulphite and acid in water.

bw *Stillage or Stillion*. A cask stand.

b *Stout*. Dark beer.

bw *Stuck Fermentation*. One that stops before it ought.

bw *Substrate*. Broadly, the substance on which an enzyme acts.

w *Succinic Acid* is produced naturally during fermentation and has a beneficial effect on the bouquet and vinosity of matured wine. It was first extracted from amber.

bw *Sucrase*. The enzyme that converts sucrose to glucose and fructose.

bw *Sucrose*. Ordinary cane sugar; domestic granulated.

bw *Sulphiting*. The addition of sodium metabisulphite to wort or must to sterilize them; also to wine during and after fermentation.

b *Sweet Wort*. Unhopped wort.

bw *Tannin*. An astringent substance from the skins, pips and stalks of grapes that gives zest and finish to wine. As tannic acid it is necessary in beer.

w *Tartaric Acid*. The chief grape acid and an aid to maturation.

w Tastevin. A wine-taster's silver cup.

bw *Titration*. A method of determining the total acid content of e.g. beer or wine.

b *Top-Fermenter*. A yeast that ferments on the surface of the wort.

bw *Tolerance*. The capacity of yeast for resisting alcohol.

w Tourne. A non-gassy form of POUSSE. q.v.

bw *Trace Element*. A micro-nutrient; a metallic or other substance whose presence in very minute quantities is necessary to support fermentation.

Tranchage. Accelerating the maturation of liqueurs by heating and cooling them alternately.

bw *Ullage*. See HEADROOM.

bw *U-Tube*. Used on the intake end of a siphon tube to avoid sucking up the lees when racking.

w Valenche. A tube used to remove samples of wine from jars or casks. A wine-thief.

w Vendange. Grape harvest; vintage.

w Vigneron. A vine- or wine-grower.

bw *Vinegar*. See ACETIFICATION, ACETOBACTERS.

bw *Vinegar Fly*. or fruit fly (*Drosophila melanogaster*). A source of acetic infection much dreaded in pre sulphite and fermentation-lock days.

w *Vinometer*. An unsatisfactory instrument intended to measure the alcoholic strength of wine.

w *Vinosity*. The true 'wininess' that only the grape can impart.

w *Vintage*. See VENDANGE.

w *Vintage Year*. A *good* vintage year.

b *Water Treatments*. See BURTONIZING; but there are also treatments for softening water.

w *Weeper*. A bottle in which the wine has oozed through or past the cork.

w *Wine-Thief*. See VALENCHE.

b *Wort*. Malt-based solution prepared for fermentation into beer.

bw *Yeast*. See SACCHAROMYCES.

bw *Yeast Nutrients*. Mineral salts, vitamins and trace elements needed by the yeast for an optimum fermentation.

w *Zest*. The essential oils in e.g. orange and lemon peel.

bw *Zymase*. Broadly, the group of yeast enzymes that cause fermentation.

INDEXES

Section I: General

Section II: Home Brewing

Rowanberries, 126–8
  dried, 126
Rye, 121

Saaz, *see* Hops
Saddle of mutton, 145
Salt, 103, 130
Scots, 78
Sealing rings, 135
Sediment, yeast, 94, 133
Semi-rigid containers, 140
Shives, 141
Sieve, nylon, 90, 122
Siphon, siphoning, *94*, 102, 133–42
    passim
  pump, 94
  tube, 94
Soap, 140, 141
Soda, 110
Smoothness, 110
Sparging, 111, 116–23 *passim*, 129–31
Spilth, 135
Spoilage organisms, 82
Stabilizing, 122
'Star-bright', 108
Starch, 85, 114, 117–23 *passim*
  haze, *67*, 119, 120
  test for, *115*
Starter bottle (yeast), 96, 98, 102, 104
Steam cleaning, 141
Sterilization, 97–8, 122, 135, 142, 146–7
Sterilizing fluid, 97, 98–110 *passim*
Stillage, 141
'Stinkers', 141
Stirrers, 93, *102*
Stock bottle (sterilizer), 97
Stockists, 91
Stoneware, 142
Stoppers, screw, 95, 102, *135*
  polythene, 95, 102
Storage, 104, *137*
Stout, 86, 91, 96, 103, 107–11 *passim*
  Russian, 106
Straining, strainers, 103, 119, 131
Strawberries, 145
Sugar, 81, 88, 91, 95, *96–133 passim*
  Barbados, 96
  brown, 96
  Demerara, 96

granulated (household), 96
lactose, 147
maltose, 116
milk, *see* Lactose
pieces, 96
priming, *133*, 148
syrup, invert, 133
  standard, 133
Sugar tang, 111
Sulphite, sulphiting, 140–42, 146
Sumerians, 77
Sweet wort, 116
Syrup, invert and standard, *see* Sugar

Tankards, 144–6
Taps, 141, 142
Tap barrel, 140
Tap hole, 141
Tap water, 118
Taxation, 79, 82–3
Temperature, 104, 147
  air, 119–20
  fermentation, 98
  mashing, 115, 116, *117–18*, 122
  serving, 144–5
  storage, 106, 123, 141
Tests: iodine (starch), 115
  malt, 114
Thermometer, 81, *94*, 102, 103
Tigris, 77
Tissues, kitchen, 97
Topping up, 147
Torrified grains, 120, 121

Under-hopping, 100, 105
U-tube, 94, 102, 133, 135

Vented caps, 140
Villeins, 78
Vinegar, 148
Vitamins, 97
Volatile esters, 103
Water, 78, 80, *96*, *118*
  treatment, 90, 97
Welsh ale, 79
Wheat, 78
  flour, 121
  malted, 121
  syrup, 120, 121

Section III: Wine-making

Section IV: Fortified wines and Liqueurs.
Cider and Perry. Mead.

Tables